Q Model

The Coaching System for Universal Agility, Team Alignment, and Strategic Implementation

By Paul Gossen

Special thanks to:

    Chris Polvi for extensive rewriting, text revisions and editing.

    Marilyn Atkinson for all her support

    The Q Model China team and community

Publication:	Revised June 1 2020	Text Version: 6.5.1
		Layout Version: 2.6.6
Published by:	qDrive Institute Inc.	
Contact:	Paul Gossen	
Telephone:	+1 604 872-4300	
Email:	info@QModel.com	
Web Site:	www.Enterprise-Transformation.com	

ISBN: 978-0-9783755-2-2

Library of Congress Control Number: 2019903311

Q Model / The Coaching System for Universal Agility, Team Alignment, and Strategic Implementation / Paul Gossen

1. Business. 2. Leadership. 3. Business Transformation. 4. Coaching. 5. Agile. 6. Organizational Change Management. 7. Project Management

I. Paul Gossen II. Q Model - Coaching Agile Transformation

Q Model
The Coaching System for Universal Agility, Team Alignment, and Strategic Implementation

Table of Contents:

The Q Model

3 Questions:

Approach the Q Model as three simple questions or conversational stages:

    1 - Trust: What is the current state?

    2 - Vision: What is the desired state?

    3 - Action: What is the next committed action?

3 Stages:

Q Model conversations move around a triangle with three objectives:

1 - Current State:	Drive trust and relationships
2 - Desired State:	Drive performance and solutions
3 - Committed Action:	Drive business results

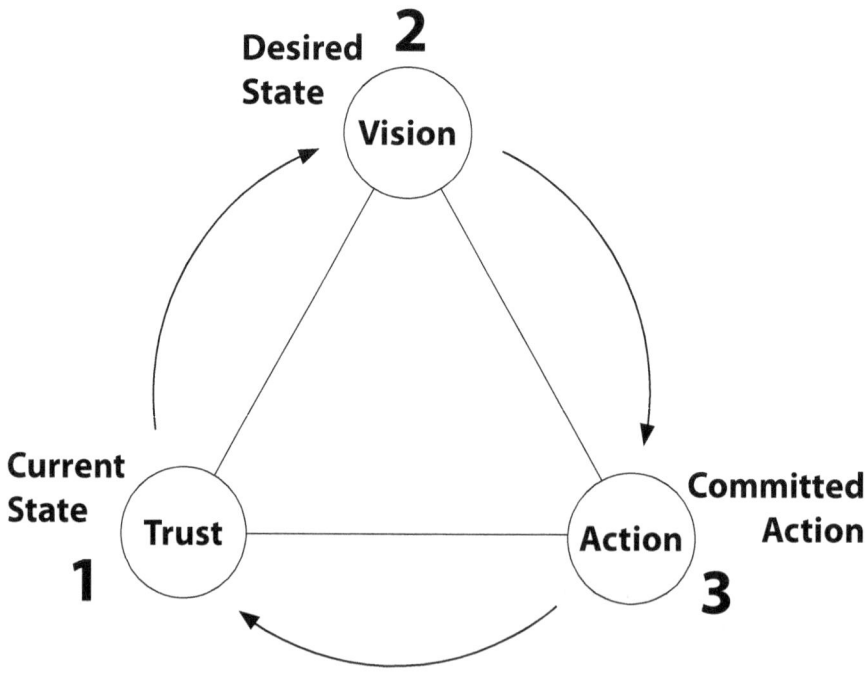

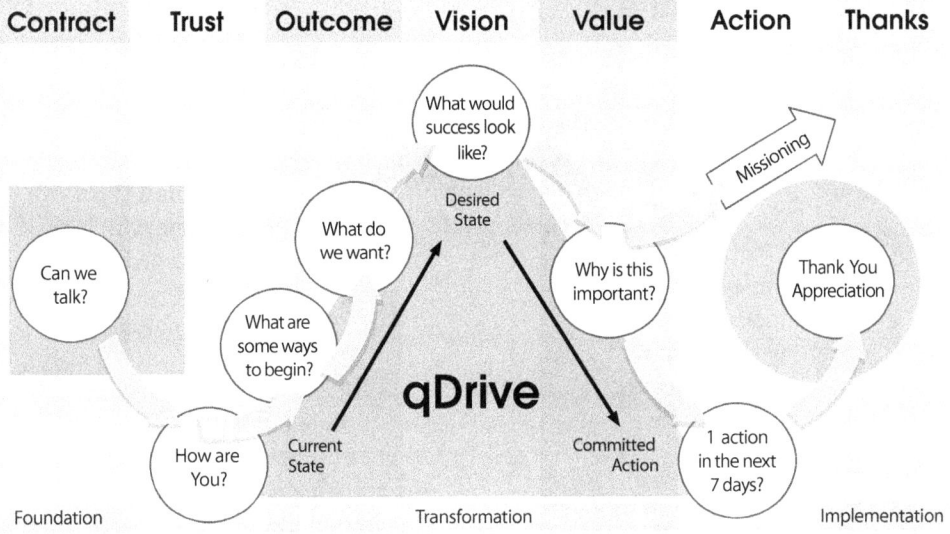

Contract | Trust | Outcome | Vision | Value | Action | Thanks

(Diagram labels: Can we talk? | What do we want? | What are some ways to begin? | What would success look like? | Desired State | Why is this important? | Missioning | Thank You Appreciation | How are You? | Current State | qDrive | Committed Action | 1 action in the next 7 days? | Foundation | Transformation | Implementation)

Nine qDrive Questions:

1 - Can I ask a question?
2 - What is the challenge?
3 - How is the project going?
4 - What are some ways to begin?
5 - What do we want?
6 - What would success look like?
7 - Why is this important?
8 - What is our mission?
9 - 1 Action in the next 7 days?

Key Tools:

Contract, agreement, permission
Focus on the hard part
Current state, listening, trust
Questions, brainstorm
Clear outcomes, goals, measurements
Vision, a picture of success
Value, engagement, motivation
Passion, big picture, contribution
One key action, in 7 days
Finish with appreciation

The qDrive States:

Tool	State	Key Questions
1 - Contract	Agreement	Can we talk?
2 - Current State	Trust	How is your project?
3 - Questions	Open	Some ways to begin?
4 - Outcome	Clear	What do we want?
5 - Desired State	Vision	What does success look like?
6 - Value	Motivation	Why is this important?
7 - Missioning	High Energy	Who else benefits?
8 - Action	Commitment	What can we do in the next 7 days
9 - Thanks	Appreciation	Thank you for being... (value word)

The Q Model Rules:

Rule 1:
The Golden Rule:
Trust comes from an open dialogue about the current state

Rule 11:
The people with their hands on a problem are the best people to solve it

Rule 2:
You cannot accurately identify the current state unless you face the challenge

Rule 10:
To get to simplicity you must first pass through complexity

Rule 3:
Dealing with whatever is blocking the project is the real project

Rule 9:
We live in an age of accelerating change. Complexity is the new normal

Rule 4:
The ultimate measurement of the future success of an enterprise is the speed at which strategic change happens

Rule 8:
Don't try to fix the company or the people, just focus on speed. Accelerating strategic implementation speed fixes everything else

Rule 5:
Unless you have a clear plan to transform your entire industry, you don't really have a strategy

Rule 7:
When everyone fully aligns on the strategy, expressing that strategy in day-to-day actions becomes natural and automatic

Rule 6:
Cascading a strategy is the opposite of owning a strategy

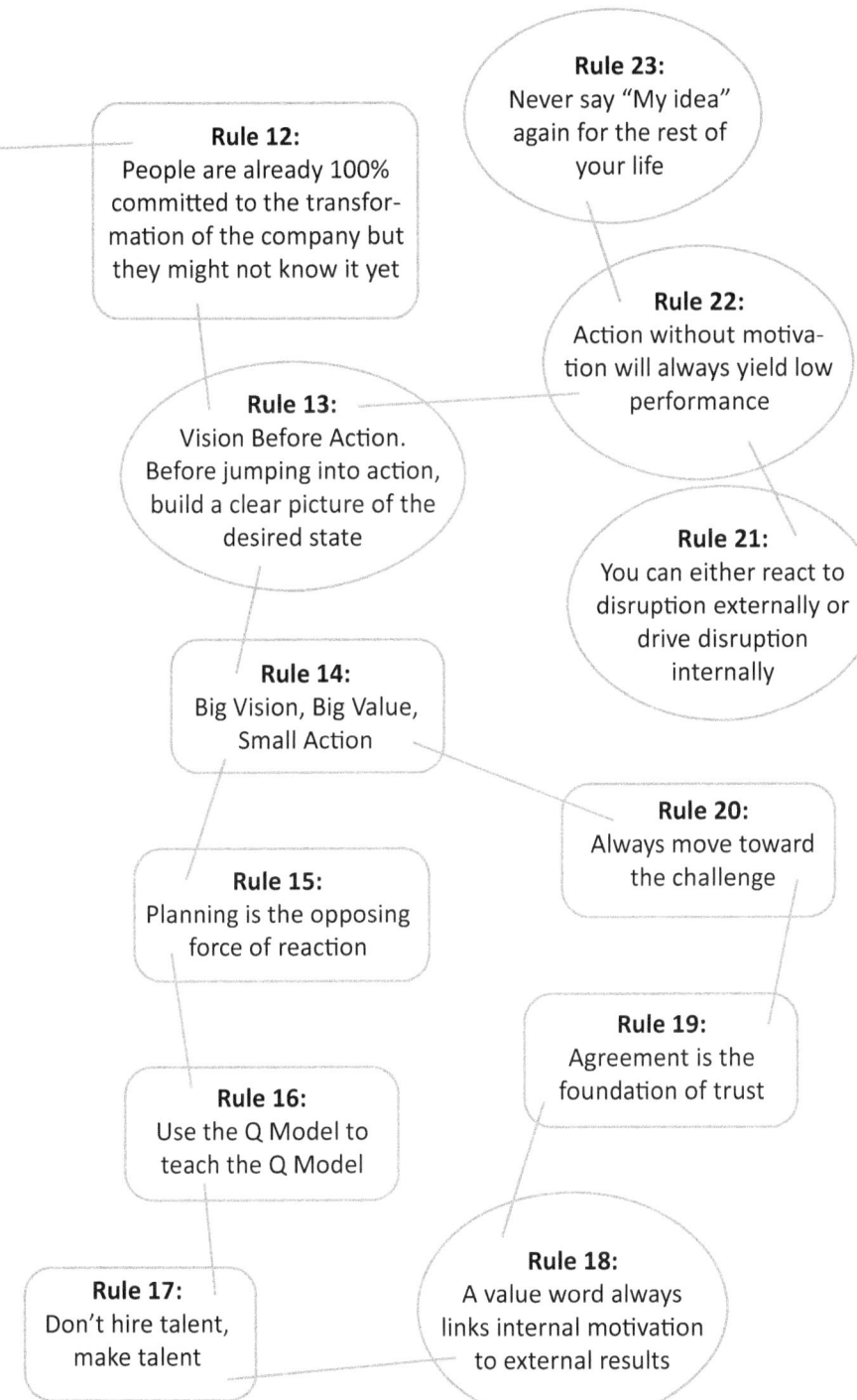

Rule 23:
Never say "My idea" again for the rest of your life

Rule 12:
People are already 100% committed to the transformation of the company but they might not know it yet

Rule 22:
Action without motivation will always yield low performance

Rule 13:
Vision Before Action. Before jumping into action, build a clear picture of the desired state

Rule 21:
You can either react to disruption externally or drive disruption internally

Rule 14:
Big Vision, Big Value, Small Action

Rule 20:
Always move toward the challenge

Rule 15:
Planning is the opposing force of reaction

Rule 19:
Agreement is the foundation of trust

Rule 16:
Use the Q Model to teach the Q Model

Rule 18:
A value word always links internal motivation to external results

Rule 17:
Don't hire talent, make talent

Four Core Values of Universal Agility:

1. Individuals and Interactions *Over* **A Fixed Plan or Process:** This first core value stands the test of time and remains unchanged. Essentially it states that *we the people*—who are doing the work and have our hands on the challenges—are empowered to discuss, engage, and collaborate. Furthermore, our breakthrough interactions are more important than blindly sticking with a flawed plan, procedure, process, or set of tools.

2. Working Solutions *Over* **Hierarchy and Authority:** Here we are boldly expanding from software development into a Universal Agile context. We suggest that in the world of accelerating complexity, *working solutions* are the ultimate currency. We do not wish to overthrow all hierarchy and authority, but simply state that they will always be *less important* than a working solution to a challenging problem.

3. Customer Collaboration *Over* **a Fixed Product Mindset:** We must attack the idea of a fixed product mindset and can expand this to include any fixed process, strategy, or service. We are really attacking the fixed mindset itself, and we have to state that *people won't know what they want until they see it.* This is the idea that innovative solutions *emerge* naturally when a committed team faces a challenge.

4. Responding to Change Over Following a Plan: This is not saying that every plan must be discarded or that we reject the very *idea* of planning. This is about knowing when the plan is no longer working and putting an iterative process in place to synchronize the plan with the reality of the current state regularly.

Alignment is Everything:

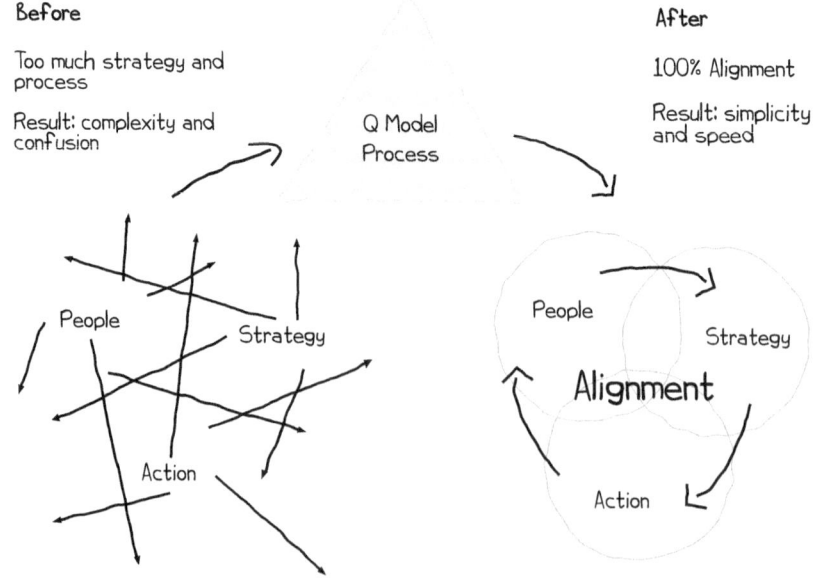

Before

Too much strategy and process

Result: complexity and confusion

Q Model Process

After

100% Alignment

Result: simplicity and speed

People

Strategy

Action

People

Strategy

Alignment

Action

Twelve Principles of Universal Agility:

1 – Agile Planning: We agree that any plan can change and all plans must be open for periodic reassessment. We agree that high-quality planning requires open dialogue with a team of stakeholders.

2 – Customer's Point of View: We agree that stepping out of the corporate point of view and being able to take the customer's perspective is a core principle of Universal Agility.

3 - Sprint and Iterate: We agree to go fast, as long as work is conducted in short team-directed iterative cycles that have a measurable end state.

4 – Collaboration & Alignment: We agree that open discussion, team collaboration, and alignment between key people and stakeholders is the foundation for high-quality work.

5 - Support, trust, and motivate: We agree that supporting each other, building trust, and developing a strong structure of motivation is the foundation for great results.

6 - Face-to-Face Interactions: We agree that text-only communication destroys collaboration and that authentic communication requires face-to-face interactions or voice-based dialogue with key people and stakeholders

7 – Team Solutions to Measure Progress: We agree that dealing with non-linear complexity requires team-developed solutions to challenges and that these solutions are the basic measurement of progress.

8 – Realistic speed: We agree that *speed* will always balance against *reality*, and that going fast requires pushing back on unrealistic deadlines, stopping work to deal with challenges, and investing time to develop a smooth and repeatable process.

9 – Quality and design: We agree that everyone owns quality and design and is responsible for dealing with problems, technical details, constant improvement, and sustainable changes.

10 – Simple: We agree that simple solutions and systems are worth the effort required to work through all the challenging requirements, constraints, and complexity that come with doing hard things.

11 - Self-directed teams: We agree to fundamentally respect the principle of self-directed teams, where motivated team members have decision-making power, take ownership, communicate regularly, and share ideas that deliver quality results.

12 - Regular reflection and improvement: We agree to regularly engage in team dialogue to reflect and improve our process, skills, and effectiveness.

Why Agile Innovation?

Foreword by Marilyn Atkinson

In many companies, innovation is an elusive quality that is either present or not. Coming from the Solution Focused Coaching world, we see innovation as a process that can be trained and managed. What can a manager, team coach, or agile coach do to build innovation? We need to support people to build solutions and develop flexible thinking habits. This takes a special kind of mastery, one that you can discover as you explore. Leaders can begin by aiming for the elusive elixir of *team spirit*. Start to ask: "How can we design an environment that consistently generates innovation?"

Team Spirit: Strong managers, team coaches, and Agile evangelists know their job is to develop *team spirit*. They support the structure and principles of innovation and provide specific tools to enhance the creativity and strategic thinking of individuals, teams, and organizations. This is not an idealistic goal. Effective projects and solutions need to be practical and operational. They must align with a corporation's aims, yet seed innovative thinking as well. We challenge you to learn how to unleash this team spirit.

The Vision Function: All this requires a very specific kind of professional mastery. We need to know how to initiate the quality of *visionary* thinking. We must assist people to develop a team's *vision function* as a part of every single meeting. The right brain hemisphere manages this vision function and this is by far the most integrative function of the human brain. By stimulating right brain processes, we also create synergy and holistic thinking.

Why Agile Leadership? Over the past few years, I have become more and more inspired by the Agile movement. In many ways, the Agile evangelists of today remind me of my community in the 1980s, as we were developing NLP. Inspired by our mission, we were building new models faster than we could test and validate our results, never caring about how we were viewed by the mainstream. Fast-forward 30 years and many of these early models have *become* the mainstream of positive psychology.

What can Coaching Bring to Agile? Managers and talented staff need freedom to perform well, and many corporate leaders now understand the limitations of *command and control* leadership. Coaching and Agile are both about creating high-performance teams that excel in complex environments. In Agile, people talk about *Servant Leadership*. However, in the coaching world, we simply say *Coaching Culture*. Coaching has a rich 30-year lineage that can deeply enhance the world of Agile.

Coaching Style Communication: Solution-Focused Coaching is really about communication. Just like Paul Gossen's earlier work, *The 17 Questions that Transform Business*, the Q Model is full of Solution Focused *question sets*. These allow anyone to step into the shoes of a master coach.

When I first looked at the Q Model, I asked myself, "Does the world need another coaching model?" Frankly, I was skeptical. But as I explored the Q Model, I began to notice the principles of Milton Erickson embedded throughout the Q Model and saw how elegantly the system fit into the world of Solution-Focused Coaching.

The Q Model focuses the entire coaching process into the three tiny points of **Trust, Vision,** and **Action,** and this reduction resets the entire frame of reference for corporate coaching. People who have never heard of coaching can approach these three points with ease, and they also allow experienced coaches to approach their practice with a beginner's mind.

Why simple? As coaches, we all enjoy going deeply into breakthrough models of transformation. Some of these ideas can get complex, and this can be a barrier for people who are just discovering coaching. Try to remember that most people on Earth have never even had the thought, "I could have a breakthrough in my life." What people like most about the Q Model is its simplicity: it is an easy way to introduce a coaching communication style to non-coaches. In today's workplace of information overload, people need to start with a simple model to begin their practice of coaching.

Business Transformation: Bringing breakthrough technologies into the business workplace is critical, but the discussion of business transformation and digital transformation has become commonplace to the point where many of us have become jaded due to overexposure. We can use the Q Model to approach things anew, and I encourage you to use the Q Model to communicate the value of corporate coaching in a simple yet revolutionary way.

Transformation ROI: Sometimes a passion for technology gets in the way of clearly presenting the ROI of these practical tools, and most coaches and Agile evangelists have done a poor job of selling the benefits of transformation to business leaders. More coaches need to meet business people in their model of the world, inspiring leaders and managers to take on the mindset and use the tools to achieve business results.

Missioning the World Game: I encourage you to play a big game of transformation. Keep expanding your stakeholders to include everyone on Earth. Keep scaling out time and success. Keep asking, "Who else benefits from our success?" Here is a good question for scaling up to the world game:

If the Earth were a company, how would we transform that company?

If you are in a company, play a game to transform your industry. If you want more, ask "How will your company's success help every person on Earth?" This is the *world game*, and we are all playing it.

Marilyn Atkinson

Chapter 1 - Speed - The Q Mindset

- Strategic Transformation Speed

Pan Fei had a problem. Every quarter his gross revenue was increasing but his net margins were decreasing. This loss of margin was accelerating, and he could see that in a few quarters his company would be operating in the red. The cliff was rapidly approaching. Pan Fei was a rising star at Blue Focus, China's largest advertising company. He had just been appointed the CEO of Domob, which had been acquired by Blue Focus about a year earlier. Domob was the centerpiece of the digital strategy for Blue Focus, so the success of this business unit was critical.

Mobile Ad Platform: Domob was founded as a mobile advertising bidding company, focusing on mobile game companies that needed a high volume of new users to drive in-app purchase revenue. They developed an exchange platform to connect buyers and sellers of mobile ads, and from 2012 onwards the company went through a period of extreme growth, building up to about 400 employees by 2015 when Domob was acquired by Blue Focus for $325 million US. Blue Focus runs a similar business model to WPP, the world's largest advertising consortium, where growth is primarily driven by acquisition.

At the beginning of 2016 Domob margins began to slide, as copycat competitors duplicated the business model and launched competing mobile ad exchange platforms. The company revenue kept increasing, but facing a red ocean of competition the margins became paper-thin. Although they had deep pockets and could offer better payment terms than their competitors, increasingly the company was competing by financing its customers' advertising budgets, which was an unsustainable practice.

Pan Fei needed to find a blue ocean strategy for high-margin revenue with a defensible barrier to competition. He had already run a McKinsey Consulting program, which had little impact, and was searching for a fresh approach. He was working with Alice Wang, who ran talent for the entire consortium. Alice and I had worked together before and we had a high level of trust. In the fall of 2016, Alice made a strong recommendation for a company-wide Enterprise Transformation program based on the Q Model.

> "We already hired McKinsey Consulting. They presented their report and nothing much happened. That was *why* we ran the Q Model program."
> **- Alice Wang, VP of Talent, BlueFocus**

The Challenge: Domob faced many of the same challenges as other high-growth technology companies in China: changing market conditions, intense competition, and internal pressures to produce KPIs and revenue targets. The Q Model team met with Pan Fei and the executive leaders to get a clear picture of the current state of the company and discuss the goals and challenges for 2017.

Strategic Breakthrough Set-up: The program kick-off was a two-day executive strategic implementation retreat for the 14 members of the leadership team and a few additional technical leaders. We worked with the CEO and GM to select four initial company breakthrough project areas, the initial goals being to define some breakthrough strategies and warm-up the executives to the Q Model process. We selected the four top projects and began to negotiate what a real breakthrough might look like, then we selected the most influential leaders and technical experts to be part of each team.

Strategic Implementation Retreat: We introduced the basic idea of the Q Model and gave some general instructions on how to ask the questions. For the next two days, we spent all of our time working on the four breakthrough projects. Each team was working within one quadrant of how to design a company breakthrough; we introduced many Q Model tools, which each team would immediately use to refine their strategic breakthrough and every few hours each team would have to present their progress to the entire group. The CEO and GM made firm agreements not to *tell* their ideas or give negative feedback, and we had an external team of four Q Model experts who ran around keeping each group on track. At the end of the two days, we had developed a core group of seven champions who each made a strong promise to deliver breakthrough results in their project.

Strategic Confusion: A small group of executives were still skeptical or confused by the idea of a company breakthrough, although the CEO remained a strong supporter. We began working one-on-one with some of the executives to support them in their operational goals, and over the next three months the leaders began to face the challenge of strategic confusion. There were many conflicting strategies, overlapping priorities, and problems nested within other problems, so we adopted a model of monthly on-site Q Model strategic sessions. This created a monthly cycle of strategic planning, followed by an operational implementation with a 30-day review of progress. The management team began to schedule their working meetings just before each monthly on-site, so they could review progress and select the best project focus for the next strategic session.

Projects Scale Up: The four original breakthrough projects began to split up into many smaller projects focused on dealing with narrow challenges, and at one point, we counted 17 active breakthrough projects in the company. The group of seven internal Q Model champions continued to push for results, setting up multi-silo teams to focus on the issues requiring collaboration between departments and reporting their progress back to the CEO and an internal program coordinator.

It is important to note the application of the Q Model process for these project groups. At first, we facilitated the strategic sessions using the exact Q Model process as outlined, conducting many whiteboarding sessions to lay out all of the issues and co-create solutions visually, so each team could see their strategic implementation map. At the same time, we also gave them some simple training in the basic Q Model process. Many of them quickly modeled us and began to use the Q Model approach throughout their working teams.

The qTeam and whiteboarding process became standard practices and the champions quickly understood that building a strong team identity for each breakthrough project was critical. The leaders were under extreme pressure to produce results. The teams needed the strength to face these challenges.

Intelligent Marketing: In the third month we achieved a key traction point. The entire management team aligned around two words: Intelligent Marketing. They broadly defined this as anything that could add value to marketing activities through technology, automation, analytics, optimization, customization, or a unique process. Intelligent Marketing became the rallying cry for the entire enterprise transformation process, and the 17 projects turned back into one big project.

The executives aligned on a single goal: to become the leading Intelligent Marketing (IM) company in China. To achieve this they needed to develop the most comprehensive Intelligent Marketing platform in the country, and this triggered many new challenges. The company had invested years of development into a mobile advertising platform that was no longer fully aligned with this new goal. Over the years, the company had developed many *programmatic* ad buying projects that used elements of an Intelligent Marketing approach. They had some existing paying customers for these customized high-value projects, and while they accounted for less than 10% of total revenue they had much higher margins. However, integrating and scaling up these high-value projects required a fresh approach.

No Bonus Pay: A key challenge was that the old business model was still generating most of the revenue. All of the business measurements and incentives still correlated with the old model; the incentive plan, their KPI system, and the annual bonus were all linked to it. With this new approach, the executives were at risk of losing their year-end bonus, which amounted to up to 40% of their annual pay. I recall one strategic session where this issue came to light. I asked the 14 executives if they would be willing to give up their annual bonus to make this new system work, and 11 out of the 14 executives said yes. In effect, they were declaring that they would be willing to lose 40% of their pay to make the company transformation happen. The CEO later negotiated to realign the incentives, but this moment demonstrated the state of 100% commitment in the team.

Automate Talent: Through 2017 the core group of champions persevered, and during a series of Q Model sessions one multi-silo team developed a powerful approach: finding key staff who had unique talents that could drive high margin projects. This core group began modeling these talents, turning these skills into a business process, testing and retesting the process, and finally automating it into software and integrating it into the platform. One example of this was ad optimization — by modeling a small group of talented mobile ad optimization experts they began to scale that expertise across the entire business platform.

KA Growth Model: The second big breakthrough came in the fourth month when the core team began to profile a target group of high-margin and high-profile key account (KA) clients; customizing their intelligent marketing services to provide high-value projects became the KA growth model.

Mobike: A good KA Growth example was Mobike, the bike-sharing service which at that time had 30 million shared bikes across several major Chinese cities. A *unicorn*

with a valuation of around $3 billion US, Mobike is the kind of high-profile account that every advertising agency dreams of winning. Offering Mobike a free pilot for a customized system to attract new users, Domob developed a new user acquisition system for the bike-sharing app, and once the system was working they refined it to achieve a low user acquisition cost. When Mobike reviewed the numbers, they naturally began to scale up the project's advertising budget, turning the Mobike pilot project into a real corporate account. This raised Domob's profile in the industry, further opening new doors for other similar Intelligent Marketing plus Key Account projects. This was a validation of the new IM+KA growth model and the beginning of a new virtuous cycle.

Transition: It was a challenge to shift resources to this new Intelligent Marketing and KA Growth business model. Resources were scarce, it was difficult to prioritize high-potential projects with low initial revenue over large stable business units with declining margins, and the CEO had to get board approval and calm investors. Ultimately, the stakeholders began to recognize that the company's future was in this new business model.

At the end of six months, the entire management team was focused on a single company metric: the number of IM+KA potential projects in the pipeline. At the end of eight months, the number of IM+KA projects had climbed from one to eight. The company still faced many challenges, but the momentum of the enterprise transformation was now firmly established.

For many business leaders, executing a complete strategic transformation of a tech company in eight months might seem impossible. Many companies start these kinds of projects, but few finish them. Every element in this company transformation project was based on the Q Model, and the transformation of Domob is a clear illustration of the power of the Q Model mindset.

- The Mindset of Q:

A unified theory of business transformation, we will present the Q Model as a manifesto of enterprise agility. However, first, we will reduce our big company transformation ideas into bite-sized pieces that are easy to use.

The Q Model is a simple approach to having powerful conversations that drive breakthrough business results. It is a system that naturally scales, so you can use the Q Model to transform the results of *people, teams, projects,* and *companies.*

The Q Model is highly integrated, with each and every element interwoven into the whole. Q began in 2005 as a coaching culture leadership system, and over the years many new elements were blended in. More than anything, the Q Model is a map for transformation, where everything fits together.

The Q Model is also a do-it-yourself system, and thousands of busy managers have used it to achieve a breakthrough in their projects and teams; if they can do it, so can you. But before you begin, start by exploring the Q Mindset.

Now we are 3: With the Q Model we are always working with *strategy, process,* and *people* at the same time:

Strategy: You want to produce some result, so you introduce a new strategy
Process: This new strategy won't do much unless you have a process to get there
People: None of this will be effective unless you also shift the mindset of the team and the leaders to be fully aligned with both the new strategy and process

Refine & Align: When you ask good Q Model questions, people, process, and strategy all start to shift at once, and with Q conversations these elements move forward in unison.

Projects Everywhere: We loosely use the term *project* to refer to almost everything. The Q Model runs on projects. As we proceed, we will define strategic breakthrough projects, run by multidisciplinary teams, as the ultimate rocket fuel for company transformation.

3 Questions: The Q Model begins with three simple questions that have been battle-tested in the transformation of hundreds of companies:

1 - What is the current state of our project? Where are we at right now?
2 - What is the desired state of our project? Where do we want to go?
3 - What is the next action? What is the first step?

3 Results: Here are the intended results of the same three questions above:

1 - Trust: Awareness of current state builds high-trust relationships and teams
2 - Vision: Drives solutions, strategic engagement, and ownership
3 - Action: Supports people to focus on the key action and implementation

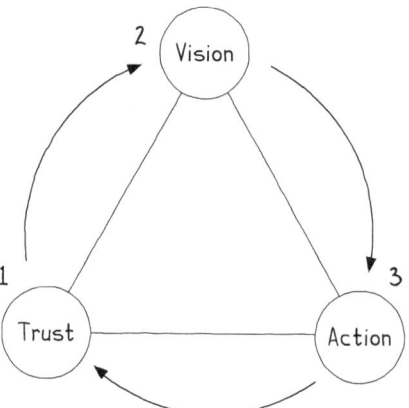

The Q Mindset may sound like a bunch of *too good to be true* marketing slogans. How can three questions produce all these results? It is useful to be skeptical, but at the same time go forth in your exploration of the system. The Q Model is simple yet profound: each question unlocks a domain of business transformation with a few simple questions, and the first step is to be curious and keep exploring the mindset.

More Q Mindset Basics:

Low Performance is Normal: Most companies operate from a low-performance leadership model. 89.7% of managers will say yes without thinking, pretend to be happy, and work their hardest at looking busy.[1-1] This low-performance leadership model will not transform your business results. You need a fresh approach.

Alignment is Everything: Most leaders want high-performance *people* and high-performance *results*, but performance is always preceded by alignment. As you delve further into the Q Model, you will discover that what most people call alignment is *not* alignment. With the Q Model, we are presenting a system for bringing people, teams, and projects into a *high-alignment* state. As you achieve this you naturally get results faster.

Questions are Transformational: The ultimate Trojan Horse, a good question bypasses all defenses and triggers new thinking. To process a question, the listener has to refocus their attention as they reflect on the new ideas, and these tiny, transformational questions can build momentum and shift the entire point of view of a skeptical executive. More than anything, the Q Model is a system for asking great questions.

Ask Leadership Model: The Q Model is a system of powerful questions and structured conversations. We also call it an *Ask Leadership* model because anyone in a team can trigger a breakthrough by asking great questions. And unlike most complex leadership models, the Q Model is easy to implement and immediately relevant. This approach is ideal for strategic *push back* — you can ask your boss Q Model questions to refine and align the strategy.

More than Process: Some people might approach the Q Model as a pure process methodology, like Agile. These Agile methods often produce great results in small teams, but when you start to scale up Agile beyond the team you can end up isolating yourselves from the rest of the company. In a process-only mindset, you look solely at the "how" of achieving the goal. This misses the "why" of motivation, which is the heart of the Q Model.

The Q Conversational Model: The Q Model is a series of structured breakthrough conversations. Mastering this conversational model is the foundation for driving transformational business results.

Who is Q for?

Q is for busy managers who want simple tools they can use right away to solve real business problems and get important projects moving faster.

Q is for company leaders who want a breakthrough in business results. Q is for executives who want to accelerate their company into a continuous state of transformation.

Q is for HR managers and organizational change professionals who want to step into mastery with down-to-earth questions and conversations that drive real business results.

Why does Q Work?

Q produces fast results. Leaders use Q to quickly solve challenging issues.

Q is easy to use and immediately effective. Busy managers can use the questions and tools right away.

Q is immediately accessible. You don't have to stop your work to use it.

Q builds viral momentum. The more you use the Q, the stronger the Q gets.

Why is Q unique?

Q is a high-alignment road-map. The Q Model accelerates people, teams, and projects.

Q is transformational. Each Q tool and question creates tiny shifts. All the shifts combine into a larger transformation.

How has Q been tested and proven? The Q Model has been refined in tens of thousands of breakthrough conversations. It has been battle-tested by thousands of managers over the past 15 years, transforming hundreds of start-up teams and dozens of Fortune 500 companies. The Q Model is built on a legacy of 40 years of cutting-edge cognitive research and development that began in 1980.

How does Q help companies? The Q Model is the DNA of business transformation. Business breakthrough tools and ideas are woven into the structure of the Q Model. Every company wants more high-margin revenue growth. Every company wants to accelerate strategic implementation. Every company wants an effective transformation. Just as the mantra "Toyota Quality" is about empowering front-line managers to own quality, the Q model allows middle managers to engage in continuous enterprise transformation as a normal part of their everyday work.

Q is easy to understand: We all love simple, and Q is so simple you don't have to understand it to do it — just do the Q.

- Q Transformation:

Everything is not Transformation: The word *transformation* has become so commonplace in the corporate world that it is now almost meaningless. Managers complain about *too much transformation*, which is a common scenario where every change initiative is labeled as a transformation. Consulting companies use this word to sell the latest quick fix proposal that will inevitably die in implementation.

What is Q Model Transformation? Real transformation is about addressing the core of a company. A Q Model transformation generates a rapid shift in strategy, technology, process, leadership, and people all at once. Accepts no substitutes.

Many companies begin with a strategic transformation that zeros in on some kind of high potential revenue opportunity. A good example of this would be the Intelligent Marketing project we developed with the BlueFocus executive team.

Strategic Transformation often links to the concept of a *Blue Ocean*,[1-2] a Lean Start-up term referring to the development of a high-growth market opportunity that includes some barrier to competition. This must be built on a company's strengths or some competitive advantage and might include digital transformation since the internet is often the best path to a blue ocean product or market. However, it is also important to remember the leaders and managers who must do the work. As they build this company breakthrough, leaders gain a new level of focus and enthusiasm, and this leads to a new level of confidence and commitment. The Q Model will also drive this mindset transformation, and all of it can be packaged into a single project.

Need 4 Speed: What turns change into transformation is the speed of the results. Every company is already trying to change or adapt, but the pace is too slow. A transformation is when you shift many things at once and rapidly make it all work.

Digital Transformation is Not Enough: Today most companies realize that they must have a digital strategy or some internet-based business model to remain competitive. Armies of digital transformation experts are approaching every large company and asking, "What is your digital transformation strategy?" This leads to a *catch up to the competitors'* mindset that focuses on technology and misses the point of what real company transformation is all about.

Technology is not enough. Along with internet strategy, it is only part of the equation. An army of competitors is working hard to eat your lunch, and creating the best digital transformation strategy on its own will not save your market share.

There are five main kinds of company transformation:

1 - Strategic Transformation: Working through the maze of competing opportunities to find the ideal business strategy or business model is the core challenge of every business leader today. The Q Model will drive the strategic ownership and team alignment required to make this happen.

2 - Technology Transformation: Integrating the next level of technology requires clear thinking from talented technical people. Developing an effective go-to-market digital strategy is complex, and while the Q Model will not tell you how to do this, it will give your top technical people the tools needed to drive the best solution through to successful deployment.

3 - Process Transformation: Every new strategy or technology integration also triggers the need for a clear process to integrate all the changes. Most leaders underestimate the amount of process development required to integrate a transformation. One reason that Agile has become popular is that it offers a process-driven model for dealing with complex issues.

4 - Leadership Transformation: No human is born a great leader. Leadership is the ability to take people somewhere new, and it is forged by continuously facing new business challenges. It is a quality many people can possess, and it is not owned by CEOs or executives — you can transform leadership at every level of a company because the Q Model is a system for *making* leaders.

5 - People Transformation: All humans freeze in the face of a sudden and new challenge. But some people take days or weeks to recover and formulate a solution, while others take only a few moments — the latter is an example of a Q Model *champion*. The more you use the Q Model, the more you create Q Model champions who then spread out and shift the mindset and culture of the company. We call this effect *people transformation*, which is a key metric of success in all of our Q Model corporate projects.

One ring to rule them all: When all five of these areas are integrated, you deliver a higher-order transformation that governs all other change initiatives. A true transformation delivers a high-alignment state for everyone involved. This transformation goes beyond strategy, technology, or implementation and takes place at the higher level of *vision and identity,* and drives all the lower-level implementation activities required to integrate the change.

Continuous: Q is a continuous transformation system. Business transformation is not a one-time event, and the accelerating rate of competition never stops. The Q Model embeds business transformation into every conversation; once a core group of Q Model champions gets established, they use the Q Model constantly. This builds a culture of continuous company transformation where the Q Model disappears and becomes simply *how we work.*

Internal Disruption: It should be noted that company transformation programs are disruptive. New growth initiatives require people to radically rethink their business assumptions, taking time and resources away from existing job functions, and reducing the focus on existing revenue resources. This is why we begin a company transformation with small *breakthrough projects.* You can think of a breakthrough project as a container that isolates disruption from the rest of the company.

Q is both top-down and middle-out. Executives rarely have the information and insights needed to address the real issues that are blocking the implementation of their key strategic projects. Engaging people to confront the challenge is key to achieving traction. Conversely, senior leadership support is essential in every company transformation. Executive sponsors have a critical role to play in designing a company transformation and ideally the process can begin formally from the top down and organically from the middle out. However, you must achieve some traction at both the top and middle to scale up a breakthrough project.

Q is a Fully Integrated Transformation Model: The Q Model is self-reinforcing. Each element supports every other element and each iteration cycle increases the engagement. A company transformation process contains core elements that must work together and be balanced — if you remove five spokes from a bicycle wheel, the wheel will warp and twist as you ride it. If you remove ten spokes, you will not be able to ride the bike at all. Everything needs to work together to deliver an integrated system.

Master the Q: Mastering the Q Model and conversational system is the foundation for driving transformational business results. The Q Model is a fully integrated company transformation system, where each element is indispensable and must work in unison.

- Q is Speed:

10x Speed: Companies decline and fail because they cannot change fast enough. Remember, a new generation of faster companies is always coming to destroy your competitive advantage. Q is the ultimate system for increasing the speed of your projects, team, and company in order to stay ahead.

Life is Going Faster: We live in the age of accelerating change, complexity, and competition. Producing breakthroughs in the face of challenges is not just about having the best strategy, it takes courage to meet the challenge. Q is the system for building that courage.

Go Fast or Die: Every organization must shift to meet changing market conditions and accelerating competition. The ability to rapidly change strategic focus, core capabilities, and culture is the most critical predictor of survival for every 21st-century enterprise. Most leaders and companies will change, but the change will be too slow, and many will stagnate or disappear. The critical element for business success is speed.

Agile at Scale: A start-up will always have more agility and speed than a big enterprise, and speed will transform any enterprise into a start-up. This is not just a catchy marketing phrase — breakthrough projects and teams with an entrepreneurial mindset are the core of the Q Model.

Business as Usual is Slow: Most people are stuck in business as usual, and leaders will agree that changing the direction of a company is slow: leaders are slow to adapt to new strategic demands, and managers are slow to implement new business processes. The Q Model provides a formula for corporate speed, and shifting out of the slow mindset is the first step to changing company direction.

You Need Business Results: You cannot wait for another long and slow strategic project or business change initiative that never seems to get going. People resist change: you can tell them what to do but they don't seem to listen. In the end, bottom-line numbers are the only thing that matters and you need to quickly achieve change, which is measured with numbers, action, and results. There is no other way.

Alignment is the Key to Speed: Being right or smart is useless if no one will agree with you. The Q Model is a team alignment system, and getting your team to be fully aligned on a single strategic breakthrough plan will naturally accelerate performance and business results. Getting an executive team to fully align is one of the most valuable outcomes of the Q Model.

Strategic Breakthrough On-Demand: In the age of accelerating competition, you must adapt to the next strategy the moment it comes along, driving strategic leadership and high alignment continuously. On-demand breakthrough is a key function of the Q Model.

Why Q is fast: Conversations are the actual environment in which breakthrough results take place. If you can increase the efficiency of the critical conversations that drive company success, the rate of all other change operations will accelerate.

- Strategic Implementation:

One Metric - Strategic Implementation Speed: Companies that accelerate their strategic deployment speed will dominate. Companies that get stuck in the slow lane of strategic change will disappear. Most leaders now understand that accelerating change is the new normal. However, they still struggle to adapt.

> **Rule 4:** The ultimate measurement of the future success of an enterprise is the *speed* at which strategic change happens

92% are not Strategic: In 2015, PwC conducted a study of 6,000 senior executives, asking them a series of open-ended questions to determine their leadership preferences. In analyzing the results, they found that only 8% of the executives functioned as strategic leaders who possessed the mindset required for leading transformation.[1-3]

Don't Change, Transform: Most leaders start with an ambitious strategic vision but get stalled repeatedly in the implementation of their initiatives. This happens because what passes as strategy is often little more than an incremental change or short-term holding pattern. Most managers stop asking for more and get stuck in short-term reaction mode.

> **Rule 5:** Unless you have a clear plan to transform your
> entire industry, you don't really have a strategy

Implementation Speed: Accelerating the speed of strategic implementation changes everything. If you really knew that you could scale up your business quickly, you would naturally want to transform and dominate your entire industry. If you knew with 100% certainty that your innovative product or process would be an industry game-changer, you would naturally commit and accelerate investment.

Strategic Drill Down: Many leaders in large organizations know where they need to go. However, when the time comes to implement the big picture strategy, the process seems to freeze. Translating the big picture strategy into concrete projects and measurable results is a key challenge. This process — embedded in the Q Model — is the essence of strategic implementation.

Strategic Project Integration: The Q Model runs on key strategic breakthrough projects that get implemented by multi-silo teams. The system is designed to scale, but start with a small exploration of what might be possible. When you are ready, move to a real company project. Once you have reliable results, run a company-wide transformation program. Carefully selecting, defining, and developing breakthrough projects is the key to high-impact results.

Strategic Ownership: Unless managers and leaders can *get their hands on* the development and implementation of the plan, they will not be able to own the new initiative fully. When we say *"get their hands on,"* we mean getting senior leaders involved in lower-level discussions with key technical experts and implementation managers so that everyone can get on the same page and collectively own the strategic implementation.

> **Rule 6:** Cascading a strategy is the opposite of owning a strategy

Doing this kind of work requires the energy and problem-solving focus of a small and committed multi-silo team. Ideally, these teams run on engagement, collaboration, and visual thinking. Leveraging the power of the Q Model, the team can work through the implementation details until they can fully see the strategy as their own.

Strategic Alignment: Most leaders will say they are fully aligned with the new company strategy. But in reality, they face confusion and complexity when they move into the implementation phase. Rule 7 (below) is what strategic alignment looks like. If you don't see this, you don't have strategic alignment.

Rule 7: When everyone fully aligns on the strategy, expressing
that strategy in day-to-day actions is natural and automatic

Strategic Implementation Drives Everything Else: Many companies want better leadership, engagement, talent, and retention. They may also want an Agile culture or a coaching culture. However, all these issues disappear when an organization succeeds in accelerating strategic implementation. The Q Model embeds leadership, engagement, talent, retention, coaching, and Agile into the enterprise transformation project. But most people don't need to understand all of that — they simply need to see that the strategic implementation is moving with increased velocity.

Rule 8: Don't try to fix the company or the people, just focus on speed.
Accelerating strategic implementation *speed* fixes everything else

- Accelerating Complexity:

We live in the age of accelerating complexity: As competition becomes global, the speed of innovation increases.

Rule 9: Accelerating complexity is the new normal.
We live in the age of accelerating complexity

Life is going faster and growing more complex. The speed of competition is accelerating, along with complexity, market risk, and volatility. How will you and your company rise to face this challenge?

The World has Changed: Have you noticed that the world has changed? We used to have a floor of predictability and certainty. We now have dynamic systems that far exceed our capacity for understanding. Think about markets, globalization, and interdependency. We live in a world of far less certainty, and each economic overreaction has more unintended consequences.

VUCA: This acronym was first used in 1987 as a military term to highlight the growing *Volatility, Uncertainty, Complexity,* and *Ambiguity* of modern leadership. Today leaders and companies continue struggling to adapt to the reality of the VUCA world.[1-4] Most people perceive VUCA as an external force. Volatility and uncertainty seem to be happening out in the world and be outside our span of control. The Q Model is a system for pushing back and dealing with the reality of VUCA.

Red Ocean: The great thing about working in China is that I get to see the speed of the red ocean. Contrary to a blue ocean of growth without competition, a red ocean sees increasing competition with reducing margins. In China, as soon as one company comes up with a hot product or business model, ten other companies copy them within a year. If you work outside of China, get ready — the red ocean of competition is upon your shore.

For many companies, this accelerating global competitive cycle can push strategic thinking into a narrowing band of near-term reaction. The Q Model is a system to take back control of your long-term strategic success.

- Simple = Mastery:

Simple Equals Mastery: To be powerful in the face of the accelerating rate of change, you must deal with the complexity of business and life:

Rule 10: To get to simplicity, you must first pass through complexity

The team must pass through the complex cloud of strategic confusion to achieve simplicity, and the most efficient path through this cloud is revealed by focused questions and open dialogue.

> "If you can't explain it to a 6-year-old, you don't really understand it yourself." **- Albert Einstein**[1-5]

If you look at an Apple product or the Google search page, you will see an intuitive user interface. The design seems so simple that a child could have made it. But the path to simple goes through complexity. Here is the process map:

Simple - Complex - Simple

You cannot see complexity from within, and it is easy to become lost in great ideas. You must churn through these ideas, stepping outside your point of view to see your product through the eyes of your end-users. You must be able to see the core features as an interlinked system, cutting away everything until you find a single lean idea, an idea that encompasses everything into one simple thing. While the concept of simplicity is the essence of outstanding product design, it is even more critical in developing an effective business strategy.

> "Simplicity is the ultimate sophistication." **- Leonardo da Vinci**[1-6]

Intelligence Lives in Paradox: If you want to get to simplicity you must pass through complexity, but getting to simple takes brainpower. IQ is overrated — just pretend that there are no smart people, that intelligence is simply the skill of being able to hold many ideas in your mind at once, and that the real challenge is to work with two ideas that seem to be in opposition. Anyone can expand their capacity to hold many conflicting views in their mind at once, and it is even better if a team can do this, harnessing their combined brainpower. The ability to deal with conflicting or paradoxical viewpoints is the fastest path through the cloud of confusion that every strategic breakthrough team must face.

Is Q too simple? At first, it may seem that the Q Model is mind-numbingly simple — do we think that business leaders are stupid? Why not tell us all the secrets behind the system upfront? It is not that we don't think you are a smart person. The issue is that overly complex models are hard to use. Once you have experienced using the system to solve problems it will all start to make sense. Here are a few of the design secrets that govern the Q Model.

6 Simple Q Learning Principles: Consider that each element of the Q Model uses the following six embedded learning principles:

1 - Sticky: The goal is to make the ideas and tools stick in the mind — simple is sticky. We live in the age of information overload, and the brain discards information that does not have an immediate application. The Q Model questions, ideas, and tools are designed to stick in the mind, and using the system to work on your most important projects makes the process all the more sticky. Everything interlinks to self-reinforce skill adoption, and this fully integrated approach is the key to delivering high-impact results in your day-to-day work — with a minimum of practice.

2 - Learn by Doing: The Q Model is a *learn by doing* system.[1-7] If you try to understand everything, you won't get anything. Instead, start by using it, beginning with the three basic questions and a test subject, someone who has a project or business challenge. Just try out the system, and keep going if you hit a challenge.

3 - Baby Steps = Mastery: The Q Model is a mastery system. The paradox of mastery is that it starts with baby steps. *Beginner's Mind* is the strong force, one of the four fundamental forces in nature. If you bring a beginner's mind and take the baby steps, you will get results, and the Q Model will begin to make sense. If you continue you will produce more results, and you'll want to go faster. Keep going — mastery is calling.

4 - Insight Driven: Each time you go deeper into the tools, ideas, and philosophy of the system, you will gain insight into mastery. However, you must use the tools to produce results. If you only ever study the ideas, you may become *smart* but you will also become *weak*. The longer you wait before practicing your first few Q Model conversations, the more theoretical ideas become. Theory without practice is useless. If you use the tools, you will have your own insights into the Q Model, and insight is the true path to mastery. If you stay on this path and use the tools every day, you will begin your journey towards mastery.

5 - Deep: Once you explore the model you will discover that there is a vivid, intricate philosophical system behind each idea that interconnects everything in a holographic pattern. In a hologram, each fragment of an image contains the entire image. Holographic *learning* is an old idea from the 70s, in which all learning elements are self-reinforcing. As you use one part of the system, all other parts get stronger. If you keep exploring, you will become a Q Model *geek* or *power user.*

6 – Just do Q: Finally, you have to use the tools and ideas every day, or there is no point. The Q Model tools are straightforward and easy to use, so there is no excuse not to use them. Implementation is the key to success, and we will reduce all the tools and ideas into one small action that you can do daily.

- The Science of Q:

Is Leadership a Science? Most leadership theorists look to data-driven or evidence-based research when building their theories of management or leadership. But this is a slow process, as it takes a lot of research data to build a useful empirical model that can be statistically proven.

Economics is called the *dismal* science because economists are endlessly looking for the perfect Newtonian formula to explain everything. They never find it, and the same can be said about leadership, since many in the field of leadership can plead guilty to 'stretching the link' by jamming some data-driven research into an existing model or theory. But before we dismiss the entire idea of evidence-based leadership, let's go back to the foundation of science.

The Scientific Method: Science is a method of asking questions. These questions challenge prevailing assumptions about how the world works, or in the case of the Q Model, how management and leadership works. The scientific method reflects four core stages:

Observation: Directly observe the physical world and collect data
Synthesis: Look for patterns in the observational data that can fit into a model
Hypothesis: Build an abstraction of the model and test cause-effect relationships
Predictions: Use the model to make predictions and begin the cycle again with more detailed observational testing.

The scientific method is an ongoing process for asking questions and testing observational data against evolving models that can be validated through prediction.

Refine the Model: Just like the scientific method, the Q Model is a system for asking questions and observing results. But with the Q Model we are not trying to prove truths nor predict human behavior. Rather, we are using the scientific method to refine a series of questions, models, and tools that enhance business results. Your job is to use these tools and refine them based on your own observational experience. Over the past 15 years, thousands of managers have used this ongoing process of *question, test, observe,* and *refine* to develop the Q Model.

Since people tend to validate the models they are presented with, it is true in a sense that this approach demonstrates an implicit bias. But we balance this by asking some people to take a skeptic role. And while we do not test against a control group, our goal is not to demonstrate that the Q Model is the truth, but to refine a working solution that quickly resolves the day-to-day challenges that managers and leaders face. The ultimate measurement of success is always a system that works to solve problems and deliver business results.

Is the Q Model true? Contrary to popular belief, scientific theories can always be challenged. The Q Model is a *working approach* and should not be considered to be a proven model. As we proceed, we will cite some solid supporting research that has been generally accepted through peer review, but we will also use some non-scientific language that you will not commonly see in neuroscience and behavioral research publications. For example, when we refer to *visioning* in Chapter 12 we are referencing the visual rehearsal function of the cerebral cortex. There is a significant body of research in this realm, but if you read through the literature you will not find the word *visioning* used in the Q Model way.

The Brain versus The Mind: It is critical to make a distinction between the *brain* and the *mind* while we discuss what can be proven empirically. The brain versus mind debate goes back at least as far as Aristotle and Plato, and it seems evident that while the brain is the physical organ that occupies the inside of your head, your mind is defined as your own internal experience of being you.

From a scientific point of view, the brain is anything that can be measured externally by a scientist, and the study of the brain is the domain of neuroscience. Meanwhile, your mind is fundamentally defined by your own subjective experience of being yourself, and the study of it has been traditionally the domain of cognitive psychology. Cognitive psychologists could ask questions about your thought processes, but traditionally they have had difficulty in proving objective truths.

Neuro-Everything: For decades the two disciplines of neuroscience and cognitive psychology were dramatically separated, but since the advent of fMRI scanning in the late '90s the two disciplines have begun to merge. Since researchers can now see areas of brain activity or blood flow in subjects lighting up in real-time in response to the questions they ask, a craze of *neuro-everything* has pop psychologists eager to call almost anything brain science. Consequently, a healthy dose of scientific skepticism is useful in approaching this subject.

What is Mind? We must be honest and state that science knows very little about human consciousness. Scientists can measure levels of subjective self-awareness in animals and humans, but this does not reveal the underlying process that is actually occurring. While understanding the human mind is traditionally a domain limited to psychologists and philosophers, in a business context we can still make use of our subjective experience when asking questions and observing results with the Q Model.

The Subjective: The Q Model fundamentally takes place in the domain of subjective experience. Your point of view is essential to the Q Model because most of the Q approach is *experiential* in nature. The Q Model is a system for getting the best results out of the human mind in a business context, and we will work with concepts like *trust, vision,* and *motivation.* These elements are inherently subjective, so to use the Q Model you will have to examine your own experience and be curious about the experiences of other people. The observational feedback process in the Q Model mirrors the direct observational approach of the scientific method, but for it to work effectively, you must first become comfortable with approaching your work as a subjective thought experiment.

Chapter 2 - The Q Model
- The Q Model Triangle

The Q Model - Level 1:

The "Q" in Q Model stands for *question*, or a *question-based model* of transformational leadership. We will explore the Q Model in stages, and layer by layer the tools will become more powerful. Later, we will introduce *qDrive*, a more advanced conversational system with additional high-impact tools. Further on, we will explore the *qTeam system*, a potent set of tools for energizing teams and projects. At this stage, we will start with the three most powerful elements; trust, vision, and action.

At the first level, the Q Model is dead easy: ask the following three questions at any meeting or project discussion and you will get immediate results.

3 Questions:

1 - **What is the** *current state?*
2 - **What is the** *desired state?*
3 - **What is the** *next action?*

3 Corners: Q Model conversations move around a triangle with three key objectives:

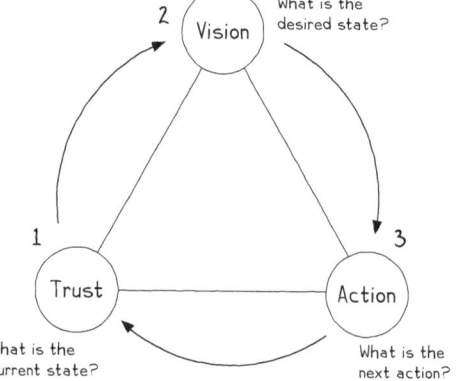

1 - **Current State:**
Drive trust and relationship
2 - **Desired State:** Drive solutions, vision, and alignment
3 - **Committed Action**: Drive implementation and business results

1 - What is the current state? If you don't know where you are, you won't be able to get where you want to go. To begin the entire Q Model process, you must start by being curious about the current state of a problem or project.

2 - What is the desired state? Managers often assume that everyone knows the goal, but usually it is discussed in broad strokes, with a fuzzy outcome. To make progress, you must define the desired state in a narrow and specific way. In Agile this is known as the *definition of done*, but in regular business parlance you might call it a measurable end state.

3 - What is the next key action? Humans try to do many things at once and end up doing nothing. Because there will always be more things to do than can be done in the available time, identifying and aligning on the next most important action or result is critical. Fitting that action into the next seven days or the next iteration cycle makes the action *doable*.

At level 1, the Q Model is a straightforward and practical business tool that managers can use every day. If you practice asking the three questions you will start generating results.

The Q Model - Level 2:

At level 2, we focus on the result of asking the three questions, and we start to view those questions as three domains of exploration:

1 - Trust
How to build trust in your team
How to analyze the current state of a project
How to have an open dialogue about the challenges

2 - Vision
How to ask compelling questions
How to get new ideas and find solutions
How to build a clear picture of the desired goal

3 - Action
How to focus the team on the critical action
How to stay 100% committed to this result
How to keep project implementation on track

The three questions link to these three domains of transformation:

1 – Trust: Trust is the foundation of high performance. A multifaceted domain, we need to have a basic level of trust in ourselves, our team, our project, and our strategy to perform well. To acquire this trust, we need to ask basic questions about the current state of affairs in an open and non-judgmental way:

Rule 1: The Golden Rule. Trust comes from an open dialogue about the current state

The ability to have an open dialogue about the current state of a project or business challenge is the foundation of trust. Trust comes from addressing the "elephant in the room" — if you cannot have an open conversation about the current state, you will default to a lower level of trust, alignment, and performance.

What is the challenge? By focusing on your biggest challenges and tackling the hard parts first, many small issues will be resolved at the same time.

Rule 2: You cannot accurately identify the current state unless you face the challenge

The more you use the Q Model to build solutions to challenging issues, the more trust you will have in your capabilities. Turning to face the challenge is a skill you learn through practice and experience.

2 – Vision: Vision is very simple. It is the ability to *see* where you want to go. The core vision question is *What would success look like?* To build a high alignment state, you must not only plan for success, but imagine it as well.

The desired state of a project can scale to many levels. You can scale up to a big goal or down to a near-term result or next iteration cycle; it all depends on what part of a project you are focusing on in your current conversation. In general, a team will not be able to engage and take action effectively unless they can see the desired state at many levels.

Vision Increases Performance: You can increase performance by up to 30% by visualizing the desired outcome in your mind's eye.[2-1] This has been demonstrated in sports psychology and is equally applicable to written plans and visual models of process breakthroughs. If you and your team have a clear picture of where you want to go, you will dramatically increase performance.

A Plan is Not a Vision: Vision is a high-alignment state that can be activated by a clear picture. At some point in the planning process the visioning system may turn on, and the team may get a small boost of energy. However, a plan does not necessarily contain a vision — you will not automatically turn your team into high performers with another *low-energy* project planning meeting.

3 – Action: To produce results we must take action. Everyone knows this, however most actions do not produce breakthrough results. In the Q Model, action refers to a highly-focused state of 100% commitment. While action is important, it is the committed state behind the action that makes all the difference.

> What is the most important action to get this going?
> What is the first step to start that action in the next seven days?
> What can we *actually* complete in our next sprint?

100% Commitment: In the Q Model we take a very pessimistic or *postmodern*[2-2] view of productivity. We assume that every team already has too many things to do, so they need to be 100% committed to the key action steps. However, you cannot *make* someone be 100% committed and even that person may not *know* if they are actually 100% committed; teams must develop towards a state of 100% commitment in stages. The team commits to one iteration, does the work, assesses their results, and then recommits. In this fashion, they move one step closer to a team state of 100% commitment.

Action Makes the Vision Real: Committed action is not just about getting your team to do things. It is about taking the first step to turn the current state into the desired state by transforming your vision *into* reality. When you perform the action, the vision gets a little stronger, and this moves the team one step closer to a state of high alignment.

Implementation: Building a project plan is *easy*, but keeping the project on track is *hard*. You must be able to see what you are trying to do, and by building a visual map of the implementation process, you and your team can see the implementation process visually. Only then can you and everyone make a solid commitment.

Strategy Without Implementation = Zero: Success lives in the tiny details of implementation. In the traditional model, the executives *set* the strategy and assume the middle managers will *implement* it. This is how projects get stuck.

Accountability: The number one way to ensure a project's success is to regularly check in with your team to track progress and assess challenges. Assume the project will not go as planned and schedule these check-in conversations in advance. This is the structure of accountability. Building this check-in process into your day-to-day activities is one of the core elements of Agile. You can do this in a very formal way with an Agile debrief or in a very casual *manager as coach* style.

- How to Approach Q?

Q is a system to drive business results. Forget about leadership theory or management models — just think of a place where you really need business results and reflect on how you could use the Q Model in that specific context.

A Universal Tool: The Q Model is a Swiss Army knife for leaders and managers. It has lots of simple tools that are right there when you need them, and although you can apply the Q Model everywhere, it is very useful to imagine *one* specific area where you can use it.

A Specific Context: Try this one. Imagine you are a busy manager. You have a critical project, and you have just discovered that it's stuck or way behind schedule. How will you get your team and your project back on track?

Think of some area of your work where this scenario could apply, and turn getting the project *back on track* into a sub-project. Keep this sub-project in your mind as you proceed and test the Q Model against your real work context, and ask yourself how you can use Q to get your project back on track.

Everything is a Breakthrough Project. The Q Model runs on projects, specifically breakthrough projects where a small amount of effort can produce a big impact. These projects are the fuel of the Q Model, and since a company is nothing more than a *hierarchy* of potential projects, any goal can be turned into a breakthrough project. These are projects where a *small* amount of effort could quickly have a *big* impact.

Projects Get Stuck. Projects have a default state, which is *behind schedule* and *over budget*. Most people laugh when I make this statement but it is funny only because it has some truth.

> **Rule 3:** Dealing with whatever is *blocking* the project is the real project

The Q Model is the simplest way to get projects moving, and getting the project moving again is the most immediate business result of the Q Model.

Compare Q to What you Already Know:

At the Question Level: Working with questions, the Q Model is often compared to SWOT analysis or SMART goals. With SWOT analysis, you ask questions to explore Strengths, Weakness, Opportunities, and Threats. With SMART, you ask questions to make a goal even more Specific, Measurable, Achievable, Realistic, and Timed.

Both SWOT and SMART are simple *frameworks of questions*, and the Q Model is also a framework of questions. The beauty of both SWOT and SMART is that they can be applied to many kinds of projects, challenges, or business situations.

However, unlike SWOT or SMART, embedded in the Q Model are sets of questions that are fundamentally *transformational* in nature. For this reason, the Q Model questions are much more expansive than either of these frameworks.

Is Q Model Coaching? Working in a one-on-one conversation, the Q Model is often compared to professional coaching. While the Q Model was developed from coaching and is a coaching system, it is more universal than coaching. Coaching is about asking questions and listening from a place of non-judgment to create a shift, while the Q Model is more focused on business results and is presented entirely in a business context. Coaching also tends to be more focused on personal reflection or leadership development. Conversely, the Q model is more focused on problem-solving and strategic implementation.

Coaching usually takes place with a set format, which is often a one-on-one 30–60-minute conversation. In contrast, the Q Model can scale up from single questions to casual chit-chat, formal conversations, team collaboration, breakthrough projects, and all the way up to the transformation of an entire company. You could say that the Q Model is a high-performance style of coaching focused on business results. Many experienced professional coaches study the Q Model to step out of the world of complex coaching systems and get back to the basics of simple business coaching.

At the Team Level: Working with a team, the Q Model could be compared to *Scrum*, an Agile framework for self-managing project teams. Scrum was developed in the '90s by software developers who were tired of managers giving them conflicting priorities and unrealistic goals. To deal with the reality of these technical challenges, Scrum teams hold daily stand-up meetings where everyone estimates resources (story-points) for a work increment, checks in on their collective progress, and promises to accomplish one small goal. As Agile has taken over the world, Scrum is now considered to be a framework that sits within Agile. Likewise, the Q Model can be considered an Agile framework, and it is another way to implement an Agile transformation. We also include some *Scrum Artifacts* in a very general way, but we have refined them into a *universal agility* context.

Baked-in Transformation: The Q Model is transformational. Every question and idea has been carefully designed to generate a tiny shift or breakthrough, and by putting the questions and ideas into practice in real conversations, these small shifts add up quickly. When you conduct a series of Q Model conversations, a person, team, or project moves quickly into a higher state of alignment.

You do not need to understand the design of the Q Model to use it. As an Agile coach or team member, you simply need to ask the questions that will move a person, team, or project toward the next breakthrough result.

Q is Easy: Although the Q Model has many intricate parts and tools at the most fundamental level you can boil it down to the three questions introduced in Chapter One. Gradually, as you ask the questions and explore the answers, extraordinary things will emerge. The Q Model needs a strong foundation of trust, and as the process builds momentum you will feel a kind of *passion* pulling you, a passion that will pass quickly from person to person in your team and transform into engagement and results.

Anyone can do this. It is a basic skill, and the more you use it the better you will become at it. Whether you're the leader of a team, a member of the team, an Agile coach, or an outsider coming to support a team, you can introduce a Q conversation at any stage of a project. Of course, there are more challenging parts, such as selecting the right project focus and dealing with projects that are stuck or out of alignment. But the process itself has been reduced to the simplest of elements.

- Where to use Q:

The universal nature of the Q Model presents a challenge. The idea that you can use this tool everywhere may seem *too good* to be true. Likewise, it can be hard to approach the Q Model and take the first steps when it seems like you can use it *everywhere* to fix *everything*. Avoid this trap by focusing on specific areas where you can use the tools to achieve small results.

Here are some general areas where the Q Model can be very effective:

Finding Solutions: If you don't know where to begin, start with problem-solving first. The Q Model is a highly effective problem-solving toolkit. Think of the real business challenges you are facing and take on the task of finding a solution. Look for the difficult issues as the Q Model is ideal for dealing with complexity, and the Chapter 10 *Open Questions* and Chapter 13 *Whiteboarding* tools are especially useful for problem-solving.

1-on-1: If you wish to develop your Q Model capacity, start by having small breakthrough conversations with a few trusted associates. One-on-one conversations are easier than team conversations, so this is one of the best ways to get started. As a leader or manager, think about where you want to build a few *high-alignment* relationships and work with the people you already trust most.

Career Breakthrough: Having a career-focused breakthrough conversation is the fastest way to turn average staff into high-performance team members, and the Q Model is an ideal format for having these discussions. As a leader or manager, supporting your team members on their individual path towards career achievement is the fastest way to earn their trust.

Meetings: Turn every meeting into a Q Model conversation. The basic three questions of the Q Model provide an elegant structure for most meetings. Almost everyone in the business world will complain about the time wasted in unproductive meetings. Stop complaining and use the Q Model to own the result. Jump to the *Result Contracting* section in Chapter 7 for more on this topic.

Teams: Much of the Q Model system is dedicated to small team conversations because this is where you and your team will get the most results. The Q Model team approach interlinks with many Agile, team coaching, and facilitative leadership principles. We will cover this topic in great detail in Chapter 14.

Projects: Projects are the primary *thing* that we are *working on* in the Q Model, and any business goal or result can become a Q Model project. For now, start by writing down three important projects, goals, or results and keep them in mind as you study the Q Model. If you don't apply the Q Model to a real project, all the tools and ideas will simply turn into another *useless* leadership theory. We will discuss the merits of Q Model breakthrough projects in great detail in Chapter 9.

Agile: The Q Model is an ideal conversational structure for Agile coaching and Agile team conversations. If you are part of an Agile team that has a stand-up meeting every day, use the check-in meeting structure. Likewise, if you have an Agile project review meeting at the end of every two weeks, you can follow the basic Q Model structure: 1- Current state, 2 - Desired state, and 3 - Committed action in the next 14 days.

Agile at Scale: The Q Model is effective for developing Agile project implementation, high-alignment teams, and a higher level of corporate culture. While some have scaled up the Q Model into a complete enterprise transformation system, this is a big leap for most beginners, so it is best to start with one project and one team.

Company: While scaling up to a company-level breakthrough is the ultimate goal, it is also quite challenging so starting small with a team project is the ideal way to begin. The easiest company to transform is a startup in which the entrepreneurs have a clear vision for success. As you scale up to larger and more mature companies, the complexity of the process increases dramatically; enterprise-scale transformation programs require careful planning and execution. The toughest challenges at the enterprise-scale are executive buy-in, strategic alignment, and initial traction.

Products, Customer, and Sales: Many leaders have used the Q Model to develop breakthrough products, Q Model conversations are very effective with customers, and using the Q Model for sales can transform the entire sales process. However, each of these areas require several modifications to the standard Q Model approach and we will come back to them later.

Make Strategic Projects Go Faster: With the Q Model, you turn company strategy into a set of projects, focusing on the implementation of the strategy. You find out what is blocking the implementation, then you design sub-projects to unblock it. You teach your team to repeat this process without you.

- Use the Q Model to identify the company's core challenges. Find out what is blocking growth.

- Use the Q Model to assist the team in developing in-house solutions. Develop a champion team that can function as elite internal consultants.

- Use the Q Model to get everyone into open dialogue. Build cross-functional co-operation and multi-silo communication.

- Use the Q Model to align different levels and different departments. Build a common strategy, goal, and mission. Become one team with one dream.

- Use the Q Model at the technical level. Ask tough technical questions to drive technical solutions.

Question: Can I use the Q Model on myself?

Attempting to have a conversation with yourself is a bit like *cutting your own hair* — it's certainly possible, but generally impractical. The general answer is *NO*, you can't have a Q Model conversation by yourself. It is a bad idea and runs counter to the aim of the process. When faced with a challenge, most people will isolate themselves and try to find a solution. This is a bad idea that violates the Q Model principle of carefully selecting a trusted associate and having an open dialogue about your challenge.

There are some exceptions and some Q Model evangelists have success writing down the three Q Model questions and reflecting on their answers in a journal, while other people use the Q Model questions to analyze their project challenges. But it is almost always more effective to have a Q Model conversation out loud, with another person.

The Elementary Particles of Q:

Questions: Questions are the most *elementary particles* for transforming business results, and you can ask your team Q Model questions at any time of the day. Master the art of asking transformational questions.

Conversations: Business transformation always begins in a conversation and mastery of the Q conversation system is the skill of generating a business breakthrough *on-demand*. Remember, the ultimate goal is to deliver high-impact business results with minimal amounts of time and energy.

Casual: Many managers prefer to use the Q Model in a very relaxed way, and you can certainly have a useful Q conversation in two minutes. Use your intuition to ask the questions that seem most relevant to the situation, and don't worry about following every step exactly. Because the questions use ordinary business language, you will quickly forget that you are even using the Q Model and it will simply become your default communication style.

Management by Walking Around: A natural extension of the casual approach is management by walking around. Conduct a series of short check-in conversations that can turn into regular Q Model conversations if needed. Some managers physically walk around at a set time each day so that their behavior becomes an expected pattern, while others publicly set an open-door *time-block* and invite people to come to them. In either case, the Q Model is an ideal tool for having these conversations.

Formal: Permit yourself to follow the Q Model exactly and you may be pleasantly surprised. It may seem awkward at first, but the questions will still work, and over time you can tailor them to your own voice, to the point where it becomes your unique communication style.

Get Real: The point of the Q Model is to focus the conversation on the most challenging issues you and your team are facing. By using the Q Model in a down-to-earth manner, key challenges will be identified and you and your team will naturally become focused on solutions.

Use it: Theory alone will never deliver mastery. To understand the Q Model you must apply the questions and skills in a real business environment to tackle tough business challenges. Try this business context:

Imagine...

You are a business leader in a high-growth company.
You work with executives, managers, and project leaders.
You have to meet your *short-term* KPIs and *long-term* business goals.
You have a bunch of strategies and projects to grow the company.

The Challenge:

You have constant challenges, technical problems, and emergencies.
There always seems to be a lack of time, made worse by conflicting priorities.
There seems to be a lot of people challenges and communication issues.
There seems to be a lot of technical challenges, which slow down critical projects.
Sometimes the team doesn't seem to be fully committed or engaged.
Team members complain and don't seem to agree on essential plans.
There are always challenges with suppliers, customers, and stakeholders.

You Need Results:

You need results, so you tell everyone to focus on short-term KPIs.
You often ignore all the *long-term* issues that keep bothering you.

- How to Begin?

Pick a Project: Start with one of your current projects or a key goal. If you can, add a small stretch to the end result to turn it into a breakthrough project.

Start small: The big company transformation can come later. It is best to begin within your immediate sphere of influence, building a small team with the people you most trust. Pick a minor issue and turn 'getting the solution' into your first project, using Q to produce immediate results for you and your team.

More external, less internal: Too much internal focus can trigger criticism, defensiveness, and blame. Focus instead on building great products and providing unique and helpful services, always being on the lookout for external growth opportunities as you discover new ways of adding value to the customer experience.

Build your breakthrough team: Since high-performance attracts high-performance, you can begin with a carefully-crafted tiny team and quickly scale it up into a larger breakthrough team of highly committed people.

Focus on breakthrough projects: Don't try to fix all the other stuff; focus on where you want to go rather than what is wrong. Develop a plan, create a small set of breakthrough projects, and get things moving.

Go Fast: Don't do slow. Use Q and go fast. Pick a project and start using Q today. But don't wait for your boss — authority alone does not create leadership. Anyone on the team can transform the team and the project and create a breakthrough in his or her team's business results. Company change is often perceived as a slow and difficult process, but with the right questions, even an enterprise-scale transformation can be fast.

Learn by Doing: Everyone likes things that work quickly, and you can introduce the Q Model to your team and have them working on projects in only a few hours. Go back and forth between focusing on the project and the analysis of the process, keeping your team working, and giving them a few weeks to practice. Upon assessing their performance, you may discover that their skill level exceeds the "experts" who have years of formal study; mastery is automatic if you repeatedly learn by doing.

- Think Tech:

Q is a Tech Thinking Style:

Traditional executives ran most companies when I began my career, most of them using an MBA-style of communication and decision-making. They would have a tech department where a small group of geeky people kept a few databases and back-end servers running, but it was always a very ragtag and sometimes even an unofficial department in a company. Somehow, over the past 30 years, almost every company has become primarily a tech company at some stage of digital transformation — the techies now run the show, and scientific, engineering, and technical leaders dislike fuzzy leadership theories and MBA or marketing jargon. Instead, they need a clear process that uses simple and effective management tools and systems.

Myth: Technical leaders are bad at communication: Here is my experience of working with hundreds of technical leaders over the past 40 years:

- Technical leaders tend to be very good at process thinking
- They enjoy details and but can also scale up ideas
- They often like systems and think systemically
- They enjoy visual models and are usually great at whiteboarding
- Technical leaders can have a big advantage but they need a system
- The Q Model is an ideal tech-thinking system
- Anyone can learn to think like a techie, and technical thinking is a desired skill.

More on the Tech Thinking style: Here are some common elements we observe when working with highly technical groups:

Specific: They like down-to-earth ideas that are specific and detailed
Process: They prefer procedural thinking and need a process map.
Mismatch: They can react negatively to fuzzy leadership theory, MBA jargon, or an overly aggressive marketing style of communication.
Data-Driven: They prefer models based on empirical research and data-driven numbers.
Empirical: They look at things scientifically, and thus it is essential to be honest about what can and cannot be proven.
Skeptical: Since they don't believe what cannot be proven, it is important to honor the skeptic as a critical part of the scientific method.

How to turn technical staff into strong managers in 90 days: Contrary to popular belief, technical staff, engineers, and scientists can become strong managers and effective communicators. Technical people like tools that work, and they need a logical and scientific model for how to solve problems and lead teams. Over the years the Q Model has helped thousands of technical people become influential leaders.

Q Engages Technical Leaders: When complexity increases the level of engagement must also increase, but technical leaders need to understand a challenge before they can engage with it. Asking someone to do something is not enough — by asking the right Q Model questions, a vibrant technical leader can engage anyone in a challenge.

Chapter 3 - Ask Leadership

Key Ask Ideas:

Fake Alignment Destroys Trust: By default, leaders say they are aligned with each other, but true alignment can only be achieved by facing the challenge and developing an effective strategy to which you and your team can commit.

Low Performance is Normal: 89.7% of managers will say "yes" without thinking, and most companies operate from this kind of low-performance leadership model, which forces team members to look busy and pretend to be happy. [1-1]

Stability versus Growth: Individuals in an organization will naturally focus on either stability or growth, and these forces can work in opposition or harmony.

Short-Term versus Long-Term: In every organization, there will be those who focus on short-term results and those who focus on long-term strategy. While a strategic transformation is something you build for the long-term, the cycle of deadlines, interruptions, and emergencies entrenches short-term reactions, to the point where short-term thinking is the prevailing trend in most organizations.

Directive Leadership: There is a right way to do things, and it is important to "tell" people the correct solution. The complexity of operations increases over time, and a company is continuously developing rules, processes, and systems to contend with these complexities. But eventually, all this red tape becomes the barrier to speed, and leaders will find they have a limited capacity for generating strategic transformation.

- Low-Performance Leadership:

Before we can address high-performance we have to deal with the reality of low performance. Most companies fundamentally operate from a low-performance leadership model and this approach is entrenched into the actions, behaviors, and mindset of most staff.

In 2002, HBR completed a 10-year study of 10,000 managers, entitled "Beware the Busy Manager." They found that 89.7% of managers squander their time in all sorts of ineffective activities, rushing between tasks, and putting out fires. This means that a mere 10.3% of managers spend their time in a committed, purposeful, and reflective manner.[1-1]

More Low Performance: Most companies operate from a low-performance leadership model, and if we extrapolate the HBR Study we could say 90% of managers operate from this low-performance mindset.

3 Rules of Low Performance: Most companies are stuck in the cycle of low-performance leadership, and work habits are insufficient for the increasing complexity, competition, and rate of change. Without the skills to transcend this challenging and confusing minefield, the modern corporate worker can only survive by adhering to the *3 Rules of Low Performance*, a quick corporate survival guide:

Rule 1 - Say YES: Always immediately say YES when your boss or supervisor asks you to deliver an impossible project or KPI. Don't bother to think through the details of the time or resource requirements, and don't worry if it is entirely impossible to deliver — just say YES right away and make a big promise without a second thought.

Say Yes: An unrealistic promise without a plan or solution often triggers a freeze. In the Q Model, dealing with brain freeze is part of the project challenge cycle.

Rule 2 - Smile: Everyone will expect you to be "happy" all the time, so you must always remember to be a *team player*, the secret codeword for someone always smiling, saying "yes," and pretending to be happy on the outside. Remember the big promise you made with rule 1? Well congratulations, you now have an impossible project deadline and you know you will fail and die. On the inside, you are panicking and ready to quit, but on the outside, you must pretend to be a happy professional. We call this "fake "happy," and the funny thing is that everybody knows that everyone else is unhappy but we all keep pretending.

Fake Happy: Most companies operate within a culture of fake happiness and fake alignment, and the former is the most effective way to maintain a low level of trust. Many people prefer this, as they don't have to get messy with real emotions and authentic communication.

Rule 3 – Look Busy: Even though you have no idea how to deliver on your impossible project or KPI and you are really just killing time, you must always look like you are very busy. Make sure to get scheduled into every possible back-to-back meeting so that people will see you rushing between them. This way, since companies have no idea who actually produces results when it comes time to fire a bunch of people in a "restructuring," they will keep the busy-looking ones like you and fire everyone else. There's no escaping it — if you want to survive you must look busy.

Look Busy: Projects move slowly, but teams and their leaders always seem to be engaged in action. This is because people hide negative issues as they scramble for solutions.

JOB = Low Performance: Once upon a time you hated your boss and wanted to quit your job. But you said to yourself, "I need the money, so I guess I will stick around for a little while longer and see how it goes." You didn't want to work too hard so you decided to stay just above the line below which they would fire you. Almost everyone in the modern working world can relate to this story, and the essence of it is contained within the acronym J.O.B, which stands for "just above."

J.O.B. – The Low-Performance Formula: You Trade Your Time for Money

Everyone has some element of J.O.B. in their career, and no matter how mission-driven you are there will always be a point in the natural cycle between engagement and disengagement that governs every career where you consider giving up. But since many companies have a culture based on gossip and complaint resulting from the J.O.B. mindset, the natural cycle can become stuck, freezing many employees in a permanent state of disengagement.

- Scarcity Based Leadership:

Scarcity Based Leadership: Just as a lack of time and money governs most human behavior, managing a budget requires scarcity thinking. While every company needs stability, stability on its own will never generate a breakthrough in business results.

> "The biggest risk is not taking any risk." **- Mark Zuckerberg**

Conserve your battery: We conduct business in a low-performance world where time, money, and talent always seem to be scarce. It is like when your smartphone battery is running low and you switch to energy-saving mode to conserve the juice — even when we recharge our batteries and find the resources we need, we often forget to turn off our low-performance mode and continue to do business with a mindset of scarcity.

Scarcity of Money: Money is easy to see. Almost all humans operate from a shortage of money. We all want more money and never have enough of it; have you heard about the worldwide "shortage" of money? Every day it gets worse and it is running out! It is amazing how many people connect with the last statement because it aligns with the way we see the world — we all agree that money is valuable and we never have enough of it, and this agreement keeps us stuck in a scarcity mindset.

Humans Create Money by Agreement: In case you are curious, the world is most certainly not running out of money. Since the 2008 banking crisis, the global financial system has been awash in excess liquidity. If you were the head of the US Federal Reserve, how would you relate to money? In this role, you could create unlimited amounts of money by pressing a button, and if you created too much new money, triggering inflation, the value of all money would go down. Ultimately, money is a common agreement for how we exchange value. But seeing money as an agreement is very intangible; it is much easier to want to buy a new car or house and realize you don't have enough money. Once again, by default, you are stuck in the scarcity of money mindset.

Scarcity of Time: Most of us operate as if we are perpetually running out of time, rushing around being "busy" and doing "stuff," but very little of the stuff we do creates much value. If you ask people how they are doing, they proudly say they are "busy," as if busy was a good thing rather than something they should be embarrassed to admit; what if you said it like this instead: "My ability to produce results is so poor that I spend all my time doing things that produce little value, so I don't have any time to talk right now. Bye." People will fight very hard to justify and maintain their state of "busyness."

> "Busy is the new stupid." **- Bill Gates**

Behind Schedule and Over Budget: In most companies, the default project state is "behind schedule and over budget." Consequently, if a project is on track it creates an imbalance, and the project will need to get back to its default state of being behind schedule and over budget. This default state is the result of a time scarcity mindset, where it is assumed that if leaders and their teams do not look suitably busy there must be something wrong. The Q Model is a system for asking tough questions that will push against the dominant force of busyness. Expect resistance.

100x: What if you could flip your relationship with time?
Person A needs **ten units** of energy to produce **one unit** of results.
Person B needs **one unit** of energy to produce **ten units** of results.
Can you see that person B has *100 times* the power of person A?

100x Results: This math formula might seem impossible, but you can easily produce 100x the results of most other people. It is not about working harder or working longer hours — consider the difference in mindset and results between a junior manager and a high-end venture capitalist. There are many ways to leverage your time or get other people to do the heavy lifting, and the entire Q Model process will train you to do this. Still, most people will not do this because they are too busy "doing busy" to acquire the skills needed to achieve breakthrough results. You can naturally acquire these skills as you work with the Q Model mindset.

This approach can be applied to talent and solutions as well; the scarcity mindset makes teams unable to see solutions, managers unable to see talent, and this keeps the organization perpetually in the dark. By using the Q Model questions you can shine a light on the scarcity mindset to find the hidden solutions and talent that are already in your team.

Getting the Money from the Future: Debt is a bad way to get money from the future. Companies exist to create value, but some companies are better at creating value than others. While you may have no budget for the moment, it is not unreasonable to say that if you do the hard work of executing a company transformation you will have the money you need soon. In MBA language this is called expansion planning, but the Q Model approach — called *Visioning* — is much more effective than traditional planning.

Value is Created: The very idea of a breakthrough in results or a company transformation takes place inside a frame of abundance, so we need to develop the skills needed to operate within it. Individuals create value, and companies are clusters of individuals that band together to produce more value collectively than they could do so by themselves. To give you the time and space needed to make the result happen, build a solid breakthrough strategy and a realistic implementation process that takes the future value you create and invests it back into the present.

- Reactive leadership:

Reactive Leadership: Problems will come to you if you wait around for them. Notice your reactive habits and that you have no time to generate a breakthrough in business results because you are too busy doing "stuff"; reactive leadership alone will never deliver a strategic breakthrough. Ask proactive Q Model questions to actively seek out problems before they reveal themselves out of the blue.

2617: We live in the age of distraction and your phone is a weapon of *mass distraction* — we touch our phones 2617 times per day.[3-1] What percentage of your smartphone usage is actually producing results? How do your smartphone habits negatively impact your ability to deliver results?

From Wikipedia: Mutually Assured *Distraction*, (MAD), is a doctrine of military strategy and national security policy in which a full-scale use of high-yield weapons of mass *distraction* (your smartphone, email, and social media) by two opposing sides (your need for distraction vs. your desire for results) completely annihilates the focus of both the attacker and the defender. Everyone in the MAD world of social media agrees to inundate each other with "important" communication, ensuring that everyone has an unlimited source of distraction.[3-2]

Busy = Low Performance: Go back to the HBR Study, where Harvard conducted a ten-year, evidence-based management study of 10,000 managers and found that 89.7% of managers "squander their time,"[1-1] meaning that only 10.3 % of managers are using their time to deliver focused results. If 89.7% of managers don't even know what management is, how can you expect your reaction-driven team to deliver high-performance results?

Directive leadership: The directive leadership style now dominates the corporate world, and companies are continuously developing and refining their rules, processes, and systems to find the *right* way to do things. While a good worker should always follow the rules, keep in mind that the complexity of business will always increase faster than the rules, processes, and systems can be updated, meaning that the directive system itself will at some point become the barrier.

Tell-Repel: Telling people what to do is the essence of business management, and a *Tell-Repel* communication style uses deadlines, rules, and compliance to drive action, on the assumption that instilling fear produces results. But while the Tell-Repel style compels workers into action, it also pushes them into a low-performance corner. You can easily avoid this trap by developing the Ask communication style of the Q Model, and this is the first step in building a team that can deal with complex challenges.

The Directive Style: Almost every corporation is grounded in a directive style of management and leadership, and it is correlated with generating results in a factory setting, where managers assign workers specific tasks and it is easy to measure productivity. There is nothing wrong with this top-down style, and it is the most effective way to control low-performance workers.

Don't Be Lite: Many companies suffer from *Coaching Lite* and *Agile Lite*, and across the globe there are Agile teams just going through the motions and missing the spirit and mindset of Agile, just as managers in many companies use the word "coach" but have no idea what coaching is, treating it as a synonym for "telling." Managers in companies suffering from Agile Lite use the weekly stand-up meetings as standard project management sessions with lots of tell, direction, and deadlines, and many people have lost faith in Agile and coaching for this reason.

Trust-Based Leadership: The main issue with Coaching Lite and Agile Lite is the inherent addiction to the "tell" or directive style of leadership that comes with it. Breaking these addictions requires trusting your team to come up with effective solutions and realistically manage themselves. It is natural to wonder, "If I am not telling everyone what to do all the time, how will I maintain my self-identity as a leader?" Give yourself permission to be an Ask Leader, remembering that leadership is nothing more than finding the right people, asking them good questions, and giving them the space they need to deliver great work.

- System Based Leadership:

Great companies like Microsoft, GE, or SAP are built upon great systems, but even great systems must be frequently adapted in response to changes in the business landscape. Systems can be slow to adapt; for example, many companies use an annual bonus system that locks the firm in a yearly change cycle. An annual change cycle is too slow for the world of continuously accelerating competition.

Death by KPI: Every CEO wants to be able to track the success of the company with a single metric. But quantifying success into a single KPI or revenue number only tracks past performance, and these oversimplifications block discussion of more complex problems and solutions. When big companies die it is often because the systems they design for efficiencies of scale have locked them into a *fixed* point of view.

Stuck Systems: Too much focus on the system becomes the problem. As companies grow and the business landscape becomes more complex, the processes that once *enabled* growth can become a *barrier* to growth. Below are some typical examples of system-focused problems:

- Ineffective work-flow between business areas
- Fragmented work with no understanding of the big picture goal
- Silo mentality and conflict between business areas
- Following a process with no ownership of the result
- "It's not my job," aka deferring to management
- A blame mindset displaces solution-focused thinking
- Too much internal focus with little regard for the end-user
- Lack of autonomy and decision-making barriers
- A system that becomes fixed and immovable

Freedom versus Control: A high-performance manager is someone who consistently exceeds the results they are asked to produce. Provided they stay within a given set of operational norms (such as not breaking the law), how they produce those results is up to them.

Breakthrough Performance Needs Freedom: People expect a basic level of autonomy, and breakthrough performance requires free-thinking people to come up with novel approaches and solutions. Freedom will always be at odds with the parts of a company that need control, and the strain between freedom and control can either be a healthy tension or a dysfunctional tug-of-war.

> Pay enough to take money off the table; then focus on Autonomy, Mastery and Purpose. - **Daniel Pink, Drive**

Question: One of my direct reports, Joe, seems to be stuck in low-performance mode. I keep trying to support him, but nothing seems to work. How do I use the Q Model to improve his performance?

Everything in the Q Model is carefully designed to improve performance. However, some people just want to go to work, do their job, and go home — you can't make someone engage if they just want a job. Other people may be nearing retirement, and their vision for life might be one of simplicity and stability, while others may simply not have the thinking skills to engage. Considering that only 9% of the people who survive a heart attack change their lifestyle to avoid a second heart attack,[3-3] this resistance to change in the workplace is not surprising.

Most people will engage if you keep trying, and typically about 80% of your team will engage in a company transformation that is carefully structured according to the basics of the Q Model. Provided you consistently demonstrate your commitment to supporting your team in *their* success, their trust in you, and their engagement in company transformation is almost inevitable.

On the off chance, things are still not working, you may need to buck up, put your boss hat on, and explicitly tell Joe what you need him to do in a short boss conversation. Afterwards, leave Joe alone for a little while and then come back and ask him some Q Model questions to help him achieve the desired results.

One of the best tools here is the qTeam system as outlined in Chapter 14. Start to treat your team as self-directed equals, and when the majority are collectively engaging and building a strong vision of success, it will become almost impossible for the low-performers to resist. And anyone who does resist — those who wish to stay in the old low-performance mode — will have to separate from the group.

- Q is Ask Leadership:

Q is an Ask Leadership Model: You can reduce the entire Q Model to one simple idea: *ask a lot of good questions.* But scaling Q into an operational model of question-based leadership will require additional layers of specific questions, tools, and systems.

Engage: Humans need to engage with a challenge to understand it, and it bears repeating that as complexity increases the level of engagement must also increase. Asking someone to do a *task* is not enough — a powerful Q leader engages people in the challenge by asking great questions.

Engagement is Messy: Tell-focused managers do not enjoy engaging with a problem via the messy process of open-dialogue because it violates their desire to control a clean mental-map of the workspace. But you have to dig into a challenge to find the root cause of a problem, taking it apart piece by piece so you can examine all the elements. Just as a car cannot be in first gear and reverse at the same time, you cannot have *messy engagement* and *command and control* at the same time.

Own it: Ownership is an identity-level transformation where a leader or team becomes 100% committed to a breakthrough in their results. The more you engage in developing a solution the more you own it, and your team will only have the courage necessary to face a great challenge if they have a stake in developing the solution.

Ownership is not Authority: Authority is *narrow* but *influence* is wide, and ownership of business results can be shared across reporting lines and over business unit barriers. Broad ownership of a company breakthrough project is a critical inflection point in any enterprise transformation process, and an engaged multi-silo team gains tremendous influence as they *become* the owner of a breakthrough project or a company transformation.

When the best leader's work is done the people say,
'We did it ourselves.' - **Lao Tzu**

- Ask versus Tell

When to ask? Moving to an *Ask* model of question-based communication is remarkably effective. It is a skill and mindset that is easy to learn, and you can begin by simply applying the Q Model to company breakthrough projects, where leaders can directly experience the "when, why and how" of using an Ask Leadership style:

- A boss tells, a leader asks
- It only takes one inspiring question to engage a team
- Ask leadership is a basic skill
- Ask Leadership requires facing the unknown with confidence
- Ask Leadership is inherently transformational

When to Tell? There is nothing wrong with telling someone what to do, and the rules, deadlines, and KPIs will not go away because you are becoming an Ask leader. The trick to this is learning when to *tell* and when to *ask*, and keeping these two styles of communication very separate. Don't try to be a "nice" boss, as this will confuse your staff. When you need to be the boss, be the boss. Paradoxically, as you get better at *asking* your capability for *telling* effectively also increases. Clearly separating the ask and tell functions will allow everyone to focus on the result, not the personalities.

In teams, separating the functions of *collaboration* versus *direction* is essential. When a team or project is in crisis, it is critical to know who is in charge, and as a leader, you need to know when to tell. Himalayan mountain climbing groups without a designated single leader are more likely to suffer deaths,[3-4] and everything from racing teams to military platoons have a hierarchical command structure; high-pressure decision making requires a single leader.

Low Performance Needs a Boss. There will always be some people who are unable to operate outside the traditional structure of rules and consequences where they feel safe and secure, and they may get stranded on the island of low performance. Some may never leave that island, while others may need nothing more than a little *boss kick* to rescue them.

Question: How do I use the Q Model if my team just wants me to tell them what to do and doesn't want to have any more conversations?

This is a common issue. It triggers several answers:

Telling trains people not to think. A lot of people don't want to answer complex questions because it requires them to think and deal with challenging issues. They would prefer you to keep giving them all the solutions.

As yourself, is this a *tell* or *ask* issue? Simple issues are often best handled with a tell; go ahead and give them the answer or point them to existing guidelines or solutions.

Ask yourself, is this a learning moment? Short Q Model conversations give your team the power to solve problems independently because the questions shift the focus from the problem to the solution. Asking questions forces them to think through a solution, and this is how they develop an independent problem-solving capability. As a Q Model leader, you must spend time developing your team, but carefully pick the right moments since your time is limited.

Complex = Ask: Complex issues usually require switching to *ask mode*. Developing a *long-term* solution to a problem instead of a *quick-fix* requires a shift in mindset. You have to ask yourself, "Is this an Ask Leadership moment?" If it is, you must take the time to ask some difficult questions.

Ask Contract: One of the best tools here is the *conditional if* contract: "I will show you my solution *if* we first spend 10 minutes exploring your approach to solving this problem." One VP at GSK was a master at this approach and used it to drive their entire coaching culture transformation.

- Change is Broken

How Do You Change a Company? The Q Model systematically challenges the flaws in the traditional approaches to company change.

Between the Org Chart: Every new CEO likes to mess with the organizational chart and flattening the hierarchy or moving reporting lines is an ideal way to make your mark. It is also an ideal way to disrupt all the established team relationships and lines of communication. You could write many books on the wisdom or folly of tinkering with the org chart too much, but the Q Model mainly operates *between* direct reporting lines and hierarchical command structures.

Breakthrough Projects: In the Q Model approach to change, we care more about the relationship between the parts than the parts themselves, and the Q Model Enterprise Transformation process envisions a future where breakthrough projects and breakthrough teams are the fundamental unit of business organization. These projects and their teams are almost always multi-silo, multidisciplinary, or cross-functional, and as such, they begin a transition away from "the company as org chart." It is best to approach this transition in small stages, validating the new model with success stories and measurable business results.

Another Useless Leadership Training Program: The problem with training is that the concepts introduced in most lecture-based training and leadership programs rarely link directly to an employee's day-to-day managers, and the concepts themselves are so abstract and theoretical that it is even rarer for an employee to retain them long enough to ever put them into action. Leaders and their teams must also set their work aside to attend training, and this time away from critical projects can only come at a significant cost. But the biggest risk of all is that teams and leaders themselves will reject the idea of training altogether, and perceive any developmental program as "just another useless leadership training."

Tell-Based Training: In 1946, Edgar Dale's Cone of Experience Pyramid[1-5] showed that lecture-based training achieves only a 5% rate of knowledge retention, while the immediate application of new skills in a real situation resulted in a 90% rate of retention. These findings have been culturally generalized and today *Experiential Learning* or *Action Learning* now seems to be everywhere, but it is rarely well integrated or effectively executed. You can read more about this in Chapter 20. The fundamental problem is that most talented leaders or smart information professionals have come through an academic education and still expect a teacher to *instruct* them. It makes no difference if the learning and development manager in the companies recognizes that you *can't tell* someone how to become a strong leader, if all the expectations of *tell-based* training still pervade.

Embed Transformation: By introducing and using the Q Model you embed a hands-on experiential style of learning coupled with an invisible leadership-development process directly into your project delivery process. This nested integration quickly turns ideas and tools into new habits and makes learning the Q Model as compelling as it is productive. When we run external programs in companies, we document a consistent adoption rate of 78%, meaning that over three-quarters of managers have fundamentally changed their habits. Teams that implement the Q Model on their own often report similar levels of behavior change, and this makes the Q Model 15 times more effective than traditional lecture-based training with its 5% rate of knowledge retention.

Coaching: Hiring an external executive coach can be effective but it can also be slow and expensive. The privacy it requires makes it difficult to monitor, and there are many styles of coaching that do not link to business results or high-performance leadership. It can also take six months to know whether the relationship between the coach and the executive is producing the desired result.

Internal Coaches: The Q Model first began life as a system for teaching *manager-as-coach* skills. This is a powerful approach, but we must always acknowledge that managers don't *care* about coaching — they want results. Thus, when introducing any new skill, model, or process, a *clear link* between the new approach and an increase in business results must be demonstrated.

Invisible Coaching Culture: With the Q Model we start by focusing on solving the most pressing problem rather than developing new skills. Begin by focusing on business results rather than coaching. This approach allows team members to model each other, utilizing the uncanny ability of the Q Model to teach the Q Model itself to other members of your team by osmosis.

Rule 16: Use the Q Model to teach the Q Model

Consulting: External consultants have many great models and tools, and hiring one can certainly be useful. But consultants demand even higher prices than coaches, and over the years the big consulting companies have expanded, employing junior consultants who have a formulaic "one size fits all" approach to projects. Even if this approach happens to be suitable for your team and your project, the consultant's role as the "smart external expert" often leaves the company unable to actively execute the consulting results, since as soon as the consultant introduces the new strategy they become the de facto "owner" of the project. This hierarchy remains firmly in place until the consultant leaves, charging you a great deal of money for the "report" which promptly gathers dust. The most important question for external consulting is "What happens after the consultant leaves?"

Create Internal Consultants: Develop your leaders to think like and become a world-class internal consultant. The Q Model empowers internal leaders and managers with a consulting mindset. Its questions drive innovation and strategic thinking, and its tools and processes support your team to analyze project challenges and generate innovative solutions. Best of all, with the internal consultant mindset, your leaders will own their projects and be perfectly positioned to manage their execution.

An Innovation System: Using questions and visual thinking tools that bring out fresh solutions, the Q Model cultivates a collaborative mindset in your team that encourages the co-development of solutions. Because even an average team of passionate people will always exceed the performance of one talented consultant, your team already has the internal resources needed to ignite a company transformation— it just needs a spark. The Q Model is the catalyst that will recast your average team into an elite internal consulting team.

Empowering this new strategic capacity, agility in thinking and a culture of collaborative solutions are extremely valuable. But ultimately it is individuals and their teams who will own the solutions they develop, and ownership is a requirement if you wish to accomplish something meaningful. The Q Model is a structure for the hands-on leadership required to deliver game-changing results.

> **Rule 11:** The people with their hands on a problem
> are the best people to solve it

You don't have to hire an external company to do this — just start small with one breakthrough project team and build out from there, moving swiftly along from one small success to another.

How Q Drives Alignment: The Q Model is a high-alignment system providing leading-edge management tools and leadership skills. Practical and efficient, the Q Model can be introduced organically by doing-it-yourself or formally through top-down projects. Your team will "get it" quickly as you use the tools, and if the breakthrough projects are carefully designed you will see a quick return on your time and energy investments.

Q is Fast: Every high-growth company has a fundamental need for speed, and Q is the quick way to implement a strategy, providing an accelerated way of spreading high-alignment habits and actions throughout an entire enterprise

Emotion at Work: Many leaders view passion in the workplace as a defect leading to poor judgment and decision-making, and in the past 30 years the dry, analytical tone of the directive leadership style has largely supplanted it. But realizing that passion is an energy source that can be harvested to drive engagement and results, major corporations are now creating start-up labs that stimulate the passionate state of high alignment inevitably resulting from the early stages of a team tackling a new breakthrough project.

Engage Passion: Active engagement driven by inner passion is what induces high performance in individuals, and the Q Model *visioning* and *missioning* tools will bring out this passion. *Visioning* is the process for building a clear picture of the desired result. *Missioning* is knowing why that result matters, and you will read more about them in Chapter 12 and 17. The passion these processes generate will give your team the meaning in their work and purpose in their lives that human beings now crave more than ever.

High Potential is Made, Not Found: HR Leaders try to identify the high-potential people in their employee pool or find and hire them externally, but these approaches lack a deeper understanding of the nature of high potential, which can only emerge naturally given the right conditions. Like a heat-seeking missile, the Q Model can locate high-potential team members and create the *ideal* conditions in which they can step into their potential and express their hidden talents. In the Q Model organizational projects, we consistently measure that 27% of team members become project champions who demonstrate the qualities of a transformational Q leader.

Rule 17: Don't hire talent, make talent

Career Alignment: It is very easy to get stuck in a transactional relationship with work, where trapped in a low-performance mindset you see your employment as just another J.O.B. However, if you see it as a stepping stone to your career development and getting what you want from life, everything will shift. Q Model conversations are very effective for building this alignment between your work, career, and your bigger goals for your family or life. Still, many managers simply don't have the skills or mindset needed to establish the trust and respect required to have these conversations, so the relationship breaks down to a state of complaint. This further drives low performance. In studies of why people quit a job, 32% of their decision to leave is based on a lack of trust with their boss.[3-5]

As a manager, it is your job to maintain a basic level of trust and respect in your team. A short Q conversation with your direct reports works wonders for aligning the work and career goals of a team member, and having this conversation once every three months is usually sufficient to keep the relationship growing.

Internal motivation: External goals and incentives are useful, but motivation that lasts comes from the inside, and nothing can replace it. So how do you inspire it in your team members? Internal motivation is embedded throughout the Q Model, and by leveraging the power of "why" questions you gift your team members the power to build and maintain the internal structure of motivation that is the key to unlocking high alignment. Motivation ultimately comes from the *inside*, but it first begins with a few Q questions from the *outside*.

Chapter 4 - Universal Agility

Tabula Rasa: Let's begin with a clean white page. Pretend that you have never heard of Agile and we are starting from scratch, setting out on a journey of discovery in which we will build a new domain of universal agility. To be fair this won't be an empty page for long, as we will carefully bring in selected elements from the past, reducing and simplifying each part until it can fit into a cohesive whole we will call Universal Agility. Foremost, Universal Agility is a mindset for breakthrough results.

Works on Anything: Universal Agility encompasses any methods or processes that will produce breakthrough results with any type of business or project challenge. Agility *Leadership* is the skill required to support Agility projects and teams. We go beyond the world of Agile as *project management* and present Universal Agility as a system of *continuous transformation*. We weave in the Q Model as a simple iterative conversational process that is the elementary particle of Agility.

Q Model = Universal Agility: Of course, we consider the Q Model to be the ultimate system to achieve Universal Agility, but we also respect that the movement toward Universal Agility is already well underway and that many principles and tools will naturally emerge. There are already many *versions of* and *visions for* Agility in existence. In this chapter, we will define the core elements of Universal Agility and then demonstrate how the Q Model is an ideal system to deliver them.

- Which Agile?

Before we build this ideal system we must address the current state. We cannot build the future of Universal Agility without telling the truth about the confusion of Agile in the present day. There are so many versions and usages of the word Agile today that some say the term has become meaningless and destined to become fragmented into obscurity.

Take heart, as underneath the competing *visions* and *versions* of Agile there is a resilient core. We must cut through the noise to find its immutable essence, upon which we will build our shared future of Universal Agility. The Q Model as presented herein, is a force that will unify and transform Agile into a cohesive whole.

Competing Versions of Agile Today:

agility: Agile with a lower-case *a* often refers to general business agility. This might include anything to do with corporate flexibility or business transformation. Many people in the corporate world are now rallying around the business agility concept. Unfortunately, the big consulting firms have discovered that using the generic term 'agility' is a great way to sell more consulting, and are running its meaning into the ground. When *anything* can be agility, *nothing* is agility.

The other problem with this kind of generic agility is that it doesn't come from a Do It Yourself (DIY) social movement. What makes agile powerful is its use by technical people faced with complex challenges. Unless this grassroots force comes from the bottom-up, agility becomes an externally imposed *top-down* corporate thing.

Agile Umbrella: To Agile evangelists, Agile with a capital *A* is a specific term for a small family of Agile *methods* that fit under the Agile umbrella. This *big tent* version of Agile has been codified from the endless wars between competing standards for training and certification. The camps that fit under the big umbrella can include methods like *Scrum, Kanban, XP,* and many more. There are related practices like *Design Thinking* and *Lean start-up* that do not officially fall into this Agile family. However, in reality, this big Agile tent is still dominated by software development and Scrum.

Pure Scrum: As the founding member of the Agile camp, Scrum has a special status. When people say 'Agile' they are often, in fact, referring to Scrum, and much of the Agile world is still focused on Scrum artifacts. For years, the Scrum purists maintained that *Agile done well* was the perfect solution to every software development challenge. This has since shifted to the new reality of *Agile is not working*, where it has finally become clear that Agile needs to go through its own iterative development process.

Beyond Project Management: Here is a little secret that most Agile evangelists would hate to admit: Agile *is* project management. We hate this idea because when most people think of project management they think of project managers with perfect *waterfall* plans displayed in Gantt charts they built in isolation. Agile began life as a *push back* against this flawed style of top-down project management. Even if Agile is a revolutionary approach to project management, it remains entrenched in that domain, and that limits its scope and impact.

As we take Agile beyond the domain of project management into Universal Agility, we can use the Agile philosophy and principles in a broad and transformational way. We need to step outside of project management and include people, design, strategy, and business results. With Universal Agility our goal is a single iterative process that can scale up from small project teams to bring the entire enterprise into a state of continuous transformation.

Agile as Design Thinking: Another force that is transforming Agile, Design Thinking is all about stepping into the customer's mindset and point of view. To do this it uses many team facilitation, visual thinking, and whiteboarding models to address some of the weakest flaws in Agile: strategy and design. In traditional Agile, design is nothing more than a backlog of features managed by a product owner. Likewise, stakeholders hand a fixed project to the Agile team, but they have little room to push back on the general strategy or project goals. When we include Design Thinking as an Agile method, we vastly expand the range of what Agile teams can become. If you jump to the end of Chapter 12 you will find how these principles are baked into the Q Model.

Agile as Lean Startup: Lean Startup, which evolved from Lean Manufacturing and bootstrapping, is critically relevant to Agile. After the collapse of the bloated dot com movement in 2001, small internet startups were left with no financing and no way forward other than bootstrapping. The *doing more with less* mindset evolved into the Lean Startup movement. While Agile project management addresses the constraints of limited resources, Lean Startup goes much further by empowering startup entrepreneurs to *challenge the frame* of product, design, customer expectations, business model, marketing, and launch. Taking this startup mindset to the enterprise-scale, the Lean Startup mindset is fundamentally transformational. If you view Lean Startup as a set of breakthrough questions you will find it fits perfectly into the Q Model. Jump to the end of Chapter 9 for more on this topic.

Agile Transformation: Most people think of Agile transformation as *everyone will do Agile all the time*, but this is only a *method level* transformation. Likewise, people will look for digital transformation, but this is rarely anything more than a new technology or internet approach. As you will note throughout the Q Model, we always use the word transformation in the broadest possible context. Therefore, an Agile transformation should change everything about a company, from the mindset operating at the highest levels down to the day-to-day behaviors and actions of the rank and file employees.

Agile as Q Model: Of course you can view the Q Model as another Agile method. We have already discussed how to integrate the Q Model into projects and teams and use Q Model conversations to keep iterative project cycles running smoothly. However, this is only a tiny fragment of the Q Model's potential for transforming organizations. To understand this, we must face our next Zen koan:

> The Q Model is an Agile Method, Agile is a Q Model Method

With this paradox, we locate the Q Model within Agile as an Agile methodology. The Q model is an effective structure for managing Agile conversations and projects. Conversely, we also view the Q Model as the very idea or context of company transformation. The highest point on the Q Model triangle is *vision*, which represents the quest for a system, process, or model to transform all business ideas and actions. In the Q Model quest for the *one transformation* that transforms everything else, we can include Agile as one of the tools for bringing about that transformation. Metaphorically, you could place the *Q Model within Agile* or *Agile within the Q Model*, but in the end, you just have to roll up your sleeves and get to work on the business of transforming the company.

No one cares: Finally, we must come back to the result and address the reality that no one cares about Agile. We also don't care about Design Thinking, Lean Startup, or even the Q Model itself. Any transformation is pointless if it does not deliver *faster-better-stronger* results. We need to stop acting like process evangelists and become stakeholders in the result. We must embrace the reality that finding the best process is irrelevant unless we deliver a dramatic increase in results.

- Agile Challenges:

Just as we can only generate a breakthrough after we *tell the truth* about the current state, we must confront the *good, the bad, and the ugly* parts of Agile before we are to build this new domain of transformation.

Pure Agile: The problem with pure Agile is that it is either *the truth* or it doesn't exist. If you think it is the truth then you must deal with the old Agile saying that goes like this:

If Agile isn't working, you must be doing it wrong.

This turned into a self-fulfilling prophecy whereby Agile became the perfect solution to every problem. An army of Agile purists would state that if your Agile project wasn't producing results, something must be wrong with *you*, because Agile is fundamentally perfect and the truth. As intoxicating as this kind of thinking may be, it violates the core premise of Agile, that being *agility*. In stepping into the Agile world, we agree to experiment and refine our approach in stages. Thus pure Agile — which discourages experimentation and deviations from the plan — is not Agile at all.

Fake Agile: Another Agile challenge is so-called "fake Agile," which is any version of Agile that contradicts *someone else's* understanding of what real Agile is. The opposite of fake Agile would be real Agile, which we will not even endeavor to define. What is missing here is flexible Agile, *you know Agile that is... um...* agile. We must let go of the idea that there is one true Agile and embrace any Agile that is a repeatable process that delivers a breakthrough in results.

Agile Lite: Why go 100% into Agile when we can go halfway? Why go halfway when we can stop at 10%? We must address the elephant in the room, which is that many Agile projects are poorly planned and often *peter out* or end up with an isolated Agile team. There are dozens of reasons why Agile projects fail, but the most common is a lack of commitment. A great example is *stand up meetings*, better known as the last remaining fragment of a failed Agile initiative.

What is missing is a step-by-step process for transitioning to an Agile culture that addresses the need for a top-level buy-in and ROI. As we will endeavor to provide this, we urge you to join us in committing to push back against the practice of Agile lite.

Agile as Software: Agile methodologies began with a focus on software development in technical teams. Today we are presenting Universal Agile as having the potential to transform any project in any industry. However, this potential presents many challenges. The software development legacy of Agile can make it difficult to implement in other environments. Jargon-heavy concepts like "product backlog" or "user stories" must be adapted to other industries. Agile faces many challenges for acceptance in the broader world of management and leadership. The Q Model reimagines Agile as a universal business transformation system. This legacy of Agile as software-exclusive should be considered a *technical debt*, one that we as Agile evangelists must deal with and overcome.

Isolated Agile Teams: Often companies end up with Agile teams in small pockets that have a high level of internal trust and are strongly committed to following Agile methods. However, these teams are often disengaged from the senior leadership and not broadly integrated into the company. Many Agile teams end up in self-imposed isolation. There are two main root causes for this. First, Agile is viewed as a process-only methodology that can only be applied to the development team environment. Second, the Agile project is not well connected to the general business goals and strategy. A classic example would be dealing with technical debt or legacy code. No one but a small group of techies care about this issue and so you end up with an isolated agile team.

Friction between Agile teams and leadership: Most companies are still dominated by the legacy of scientific management or an MBA style of directive leadership. Real Agile transformation requires self-directed teams to work in an open manner across an organization. The problem is that many directive leaders aren't willing to give up the culture of command and control, so Agile becomes, "You guys go and do that Agile thing over there." As such, many organizations end up with an *oil and water* layer of separation while others end up with isolated teams in Agile *air pockets*. This is clearly not an ideal outcome — for Agile to work it must scale across an entire organization. This means that top leadership must recognize the inherent value of Agile Leadership and Agile Strategy, and embrace the skills and mindset required to achieve success in these systems.

Question: Our company has introduced a set of Agile projects. I am working part-time on this as part of a cross-functional team, but my boss does not support the project.

> **Answer:** Your situation reflects a lack of executive alignment with the Agile project. The people who introduced Agile have done a bad job of demonstrating "what's in it for your boss." Otherwise, he or she would support you and allocate time and focus on the Agile project.
>
> Someone must do the difficult work of designing a strong link between your boss's operational goals and the Agile project. If this is not addressed, there is a good chance your Agile project will fail.

- Universal Manifesto of Agility:

Agile History: While most people think Agile began with the Agile Manifesto in 2001, its roots go back much further. In the Space Race of the 1960s, scientists and engineers developed an incremental design process culminating in the success of Project Mercury, which launched the first American humans into space. Many of these engineers were employees of IBM on loan to NASA, and after the Apollo program wound down they continued to spread the idea of incremental development throughout IBM and the computer industry at large in the 1970s.

My own experience of software development began as a teenager with a small team of friends building games in the 1980s. Although we had never heard of iterative development, we quickly developed an iterative process because it was the only way we could build functional products. Today, looking back at the business landscape of the 1990s, it is easy to see that the self-evident necessity of iterative development was on a collision course with the top-down mindset of scientific management and its growing domination of business culture.

Stop the Madness: The early Scrum movement of the late '90s was a clear reaction to the overly directive "tell-based" management culture. All the factors leading up to the 2001 Agile Manifesto — when a rebellious core group of techies decided it was time to push back — makes it seem inevitable.

We will now take extreme liberty by editing the original Agile Manifesto as part of our quest for Universal Agility. Of course, editing this text is about as sacrilegious as chiseling a few revisions into the Ten Commandments, which were literally written in stone. However, as with any waterfall process, you cannot expect the project leaders to get it right on the first try. In lieu of a community-driven iterative update process, let's have a go at updating the Agile Manifesto into a Universal Manifesto of Agility.

Four core values of Universal Agility:

1. Individuals and Interactions *Over* **A Fixed Plan or Process:** This first core value stands the test of time and remains mostly unchanged. Essentially it states that *we the people*—who are doing the work and have our hands on the challenges—are empowered to discuss, engage, and collaborate. Furthermore, our breakthrough interactions are more important than blindly sticking with a flawed plan, procedure, process, or set of tools.

2. Working Solutions *Over* **Hierarchy and Authority:** Previously this was Working Software Over Comprehensive Documentation. Here we are boldly expanding from software development into a Universal Agile context. We suggest that in the world of accelerating complexity, *working solutions* are the ultimate currency. We do not wish to overthrow all hierarchy and authority, but simply state that they will always be *less important* than a working solution to a challenging problem.

3. Customer Collaboration *Over* **a Fixed Product Mindset:** Previously this was Customer Collaboration Over Contract Negotiation. This one was always a little awkward because it assumed that *everyone* was an outsourced software development team working on a fixed contract. In transforming this principle we must attack the idea of a fixed product mindset. You can expand the idea of a fixed product to include any fixed process, strategy, or service. We are really attacking the fixed mindset itself, and we have to state that *people won't know what they want until they see it*. A key principle here is the concept of *emergent* solutions. This is the idea that innovative solutions *emerge* naturally when a committed team faces a challenge.

Next, we have to ask, "Who is on this team?" Are we playing an *us vs. them* game and isolating ourselves from key collaborators, stakeholders, or end-users? This is a good time to reference the basic principle of Design Thinking, a shift in point of view that allows you to experience a product or service through the eyes of the end-user — your customer.

4. Responding to Change Over Following a Plan: Like the first, this last core value stands the test of time and remains unchanged. That is not to say every plan must be discarded or that we reject the very *idea* of planning. This is about knowing when the plan is no longer working and putting an iterative process in place to synchronize the plan with the reality of the current state regularly.

The Twelve Principles of Universal Agility are:

1 – Agile Planning: We agree that any plan can change and all plans must be open for periodic reassessment. We agree that high-quality planning requires open dialogue with a team of stakeholders.

2 – Customer's Point of View: We agree that stepping out of the corporate point of view and being able to take the customer's perspective is a core principle of Universal Agility.

3 - Sprint and Iterate: We agree to go fast, as long as work is conducted in short team-directed iterative cycles that have a measurable end state.

4 – Collaboration & Alignment: We agree that open discussion, team collaboration, and alignment between key people and stakeholders is the foundation for high-quality work.

5 - Support, trust, and motivate: We agree that supporting each other, building trust, and developing a strong structure of motivation is the foundation for great results.

6 - Face-to-Face Interactions: We agree that text-only communication destroys collaboration and that authentic communication requires face-to-face interactions or voice-based dialogue with key people and stakeholders

7 – Team Solutions Measure Progress: We agree that dealing with non-linear complexity requires team-developed solutions to challenges and that these solutions are the basic measurement of progress.

8 – Realistic Speed: We agree that *speed* will always balance against *reality*, and that going fast requires pushing back on unrealistic deadlines, stopping work to deal with challenges, and investing time to develop a smooth and repeatable process.

9 – Quality and Design: We agree that everyone owns quality and design and is responsible for dealing with problems, technical details, constant improvement, and sustainable changes.

10 – Simple: We agree that simple solutions and systems are worth the effort required to work through all the challenging requirements, constraints, and complexity that come with doing hard things.

11 - Self-directed teams: We agree to fundamentally respect the principle of self-directed teams, where motivated team members have decision-making power, take ownership, communicate regularly, and share ideas that deliver quality results.

12 - Regular reflection and improvement: We agree to regularly engage in team dialogue to reflect and improve our process, skills, and effectiveness.

- Universal Agility Culture:

As we build this new domain of Universal Agility, we should preserve selected elements of Agile's technical legacy, which spans more than forty years. As we go back in time, we will grab the best parts of Agile culture and mindset and include them in our quest for a Universal Agility system. Keep in mind that everything here also fits into the Q Model and can be expressed in the day-to-day actions of a team or leader.

In Tech We Trust: In 1978, Microsoft's core team of 11 people created a company rule essentially stating that team members could only ever report to a manager who was better at programming than they were. A kind of proto-Agile Manifesto, in effect they were declaring "We do not trust any manager unless they are a talented programmer first and foremost." In the modern world, this sentiment seems misguided, but it remains a critical guiding principle that we *must* trust the people who are most deeply engaged in technical challenges.

Respect Experts: Like it or not, all companies are now tech companies that are dependent on highly technical experts often engaged in non-linear work. The key value word we need here is *respect*: we respect the talent and judgment of technical experts, and we assume that they know what they are doing and can manage themselves.

Realistic: Another key value word of the Agile movement is *realistic*. The early Agile evangelists were rebelling against externally imposed deadlines that had no connection to the reality of the work at hand nor the required resources. A core Agile question would be, "What can we realistically accomplish in the next 14 days?"

Flexible: Agile was a push-back against the *waterfall* style of planning, where you map out everything in advance and follow the plan exactly. Command and control and waterfall planning are fundamentally non-Agile; it is understood in the Agile universe that plans must be open to discussion and periodically adjusted.

Iterative: A waterfall project plan has a single cycle of project planning. This only works in very static projects, where everything is linear and can be predicted in advance. For non-linear projects, you need a more frequent cycle of feedback and adjustment, and many Agile teams have settled on a 7 or 14-day cycle time. This links to the idea of reducing the cycle time to achieve a continuous development process, which is a key goal of Agile.

From Roles to Hats: The distinct roles of product owner, Agile coach, and development team member facilitate unique perspectives that encourage collaborative discussion. But to use Agile in non-software industries the roles must be customized, while still maintaining their original intention. We also recommend *hats* rather than *roles*,[4-2] whereby the whole team assumes the role of product owner, Agile coach, or end-user as the needs of the project demand it, allowing people to practice looking at issues from *many* points of view.

Increments: Another key element of Agile is breaking large projects into smaller increments. Every project is unique so this is always a challenge. It requires you to have a clear *definition of done,* which is an agreed-upon measurement of when each increment will be complete.

Backlog: Managers usually have a plan (or product roadmap) for how the next three months of a project will go, but most of these lack detailed ways of measuring progress. A *project backlog* is a list of upcoming product features or project elements. It is important to go beyond a simple *list of features* approach as this limits us to the software or product world. To build an effective project backlog, you must do the difficult work of breaking the workload into standardized increments and prioritizing each element. In the world of Universal Agility, give yourself permission to call your backlog a plan or roadmap if that will help you to communicate with other humans.

Push Back on More: Every enthusiastic manager or entrepreneur wants more: more features, more results, more speed, more everything. Asking for too much destroys trust in the team and the project, creating unrealistic expectations and pressure to perform. Curbing this enthusiasm is about having the courage to push back. Start early and build a team culture where stopping for a *reality check* is always supported. See Chapter 18, *1hourCEO* for a lot more on this topic.

Iterative Negotiation: The reality check needs to take place in a formal ritualized manner. *Grooming* the backlog is what normal humans would call negotiating the product scope or roadmap. This includes the challenges of openly discussing the reality of resource constraints and deciding which project elements get prioritized and worked on.

Limit the Whip: Contrary to accepted wisdom, whipping your team with deadlines doesn't actually improve performance. But in this case, we are referring to *limited WIP*, which means limiting the total Work In Progress at any one time. For example, Kanban often sets a limit of five active work elements per iteration cycle, as its creator Taiichi Ohno reasoned that there is a limited supply of attention or focus in any one team. An Agile leader is someone who fights for such limits.

Product & Customer: Another core Agile idea is to focus on the product and customer rather than the plan or documentation. This naturally interlinks with the customer viewpoint in Design Thinking. Plans are always going to evolve toward complexity, and at some point, you have to ask some very basic product and customer-focused questions, such as: "What is the actual customer experience?" and "How does this really help the customer?" and most importantly "Do they care?"

Face-2-Face: Agile emphasizes face-to-face dialogue rather than following a preset plan or pre-built documentation, asserting that authentic face-to-face communication is the only way to resolve many issues. Consequently, it discourages tell-based management, email-only communication, and remote teams.

Visual: Often utilizing whiteboarding and Post-it notes, Agile methods tend to be highly visual. For example, in *Kanban,* the movement of Post-it notes in a matrix tracks a team's real-time progress through a project. This also links to Design Thinking and the Ideation Post-it Note *craze*, which themselves broadly link to many of the Q Model whiteboarding principles we will explore in-depth in Chapter 13. But beyond this, technical people like to explore ideas visually, and any kind of drawing triggers fresh thinking.

Agile Powered Teams: Because Agile is powered by self-managed teams, many companies end up with Agile teams in small pockets that have a high level of internal trust and are strongly committed to following Agile methods. However, since these teams are often disengaged from the senior leadership and not broadly integrated into the company, many Agile teams end up in self-imposed isolation. This is one of the big challenges with scaling up an Agile transformation. The solution is Agile leaders who can align teams with the overall strategy and goals of the company.

All these Agile culture elements are useful, but this does not quite explain how you *do it*. We are not advocating a rigid structure like traditional Scrum, but rather an open model in which self-directed teams can collectively decide how best to implement the system. This is what we call Q Model as Agile.

- Q Model as Agile

Now that we have introduced the world of Universal Agility, we must now reintroduce the Q Model in a more traditional Agile team and project setting. In this context, we are working with an Agile team and will use the Q Model as another Agile method or set of Agile tools to keep the project on track. This is the Q Model *as* an Agile method.

Q Model Agile Methodology: The Q Model provides an ideal conversational structure for Agile coaching and Agile team conversations. If you are part of an Agile team that has a stand-up meeting every day, use the Q Model as a check-in meeting structure. Likewise, if you have an Agile project review meeting at the end of every two weeks, you can follow the basic Q Model structure:

1 - Current state: What did we complete in the last 14 days?
2 - Desired state: Where do we want to be 14 days from now?
3 - Action: What are we committed to produce in our next 14-day sprint?

Each question is a doorway to a larger domain of big ideas like Universal Agility, Agile Leadership, and Enterprise Transformation that we will explore throughout the remaining pages of this book. Just remember that all the big ideas we're discussing must be applied at the foundational level of teams and projects.

How do you do Universal Agility? It may be self-evident at this point that the Q Model is the most efficient path to spreading the principles and actions of Universal Agility throughout a team or company. The short answer to the question "How do you do Universal Agility?" is "Read the rest of this book, it's all Universal Agility."

- Agile Leadership:

Agile Leadership: The Q Model is an ideal Agile Leadership system. Before we can unpack this statement, we must deal with the fact that Agile has traditionally been an *anti-leadership* movement. Historically Agile advocates have equated the word *leadership* with the old "command and control" or "waterfall" management styles that we rally against. However, in the world of Universal Agility, leadership is a quality that everyone can share. For example:

1 - An Agile coach takes the lead by introducing Agile ideas to a team.
2 - A manager uses an Agile leadership style to transition a team toward Agile.
3 - A group turns into a self-directed Agile team and owns their results.

All three of these are examples of Agile leadership, which also express the *quality* of Agile leadership.

What is Leadership? Many senior executives seem to confuse the concepts of *leader* and *leadership*. A leader is a *person* and leadership is a *quality*. Any leader can fall into the trap of wanting the power and prestige that accompanies their role. Yet the myth of the great leader pervades, and we easily become blind to the poor strategic thinking and low-quality decision making that is baked into the role of a top leader.

Command and Control: The world of Universal Agility will be weak unless we push back on the culture of command and control that pervades corporate management. The MBA leadership style is an echo of an earlier movement called *scientific management.*

Just as economists in the 1950s believed all financial activity could somehow be explained with a simple formula akin to Newton's laws of motion, CEOs and managers in the '50s thought the same about their every business decision. The idea of the smart leader who makes every decision based on data-driven analysis is seductive, but we now know that we cannot rule out the emotional bias that is wired into every decision.

Unfortunately, it is hard to find absolute truths in the postmodern world presented by accelerating complexity and competition. Non-linear challenges come in clusters that present *wicked hard* problems. In comparison, consider how adding each additional destination to the classic *traveling salesman* math problem[4-1] introduces orders of magnitude to the challenge of finding a solution. These are the kinds of problems you must face if you wish to deliver breakthrough results. Solving these kinds of problems requires a unique *thinking approach* which in turn must be supported by an Agile leadership structure.

Open Leadership: Open leadership is a quality that anyone can develop and own. Any person on a team can ask a transformational question or challenge the team to step into the domain of agility. However, the trap of *my idea is the best,* or *I should be the leader,* is always ready to snare us, so this quality of open leadership can be fragile in the beginning. It must be protected by team agreements and a collective decision-making process. The reality is that open leadership must co-exist alongside *I am the leader*, and each approach is needed depending on the context and level of risk.

Talent Needs Freedom: Agile is all about the power of self-directed teams. Leaders and technical experts need autonomy to deliver results. This is critical when teams are dealing with complex challenges. Breakthrough results take place in self-directed teams, but self-directed teams also present organizational challenges. Foremost, Agile Leadership is a system for aligning project roles, interests, and execution in such teams.

Us versus Them: Don't get caught in a battle between team empowerment and command and control leadership. As long as you choose your battles carefully and avoid becoming stuck in an "us vs. them" game of complaining about management, most leaders will often grant autonomy, provided they see that projects are well-managed and align with strategic priorities.

Agile Strategic Alignment: What separates the Q Model from other Agile approaches is the critical function of strategic alignment. Most Agile projects fail because they are not aligned with a company's operational needs or strategic goals. Agile coaches may present an "Agile for the sake of Agile" mindset. HR leaders may present the project as training, learning, or people development. But in order to achieve strategic alignment, operational leaders *must* see how an Agile project will help them achieve their business goals. If they don't, the project will seem like a distraction and will face a lack of resources and support. For this reason, aligning any Agile project with the corporate strategy and key business results is critical.

Alignment is Agility: Ideas like team alignment, leadership alignment, and strategic alignment are baked into the Q Model, and the more you ask Q Model questions and produce team-generated whiteboard solutions, the more people move toward a common understanding of the issues and commit to the implementation process.

Agile Strategy: The Agile mindset often addresses business strategy from a narrow perspective, and an Agile team being handed a new project might say, "We have been handed a difficult task and now we must close ranks and find an Agile way to produce this result." This is a relic from the time when the Agile team was a tiny bubble in the monolithic command and control company, and this limited point-of-view does not offer enough freedom to challenge the goal or strategy, leaving little room to broadly engage and integrate the strategy with other teams across the organization. In the Q Model, anyone can engage in strategy development simply by asking good questions.

Agile Vision: While Agile creates a role for the customer as a product owner, respecting the customer's right to influence a product's development late in the project cycle, it does not go far enough in engaging everyone in the product or project vision. In the Q Model, we open the visioning process up to everyone, adding many more tools and resources for linking the project goal to the company strategy and a larger *vision of success*. The Q Model then turns this vision of success into an *engine of motivation*.

Process Transformation: When some Agile adherents talk about the transformation of a company, they usually mean, "Everyone will use Agile methods, all the time." This is fine at the process level. For example, *Lean* manufacturing can be approached as a purely process-level transformation. Scrum is very effective for managing a software development process. But pure-process misses the best parts of a company transformation: strategy, people, products, customer experience, mission, vision, values, culture, and business results — the latter being the most important part of all. The principles of transformation are *holographically* encoded into the Q Model. This means that as you use one part of the Q Model, all the other parts naturally emerge. Just ask Q Model questions and transformation will be automatic, so long as you keep going.

Agile + Team Coaching: The Q Model is a team coaching system that provides the missing *last mile* for Agile transformation projects. Team Coaching, also called facilitative leadership, is a process for empowering self-directed teams to produce high-performance results. The principles of team coaching and Agile are highly aligned. Both approaches use the power of self-directed teams to cut through the barriers to robust decision making and project implementation.

Agile Q Model: Agile is an iterative project management system. It uses a framework of structured roles, a unique mindset, and specific tools to deliver continuous project results. The flexibility of Agile is ideal for dealing with the accelerating complexity of today's business challenges. The Agile mindset promotes healthy communication within a project team. However, Agile does not exactly specify how that communication should happen. This is where we introduce the power of the Q Model and its system of structured questions and conversations that are ideal for Agile project review meetings and daily check-ins. The Q Model is also structured to integrate the needs of many business stakeholders across an organization, introducing strategic alignment to the world of Agile project management.

- Enterprise Scale Agility:

Where to Tap? A very good question to start with is "Where is the best place to introduce a Universal Agility Project?"

The Boss is not Evil: In the Q Model, we respect that a directive style of command and control leadership can be the best approach in some areas. For example, having a rigid accounting system is often a good idea, if you don't want the money to suddenly disappear. Business systems, rules, and processes develop over time to stabilize a company and provide security, while Agility projects are often best focused on high-potential initiatives critical to a company's efforts to drive the innovation and growth needed for future success.

The Agile Transition: Show me a car that can go from 0 to 60 MPH in *zero* seconds. The laws of physics dictate that you cannot accelerate an object in zero time. For this reason, the *big bang* style of organizational change to Agile is rarely successful. Developing an effective transition process is critical for organizational success. With the Q Model Agile mindset, we take a very skeptical approach and assume that most business leaders will not invest time and resources into an Agile transformation unless they can see traction leading to a strong ROI. As such, the first job is always to deliver strong results in an initial pilot program.

Breakthrough Projects: Agile transformation cannot happen in isolation or as a stand-alone exercise. It must take place within a real strategic breakthrough project. Many companies implement Agile projects, but few of these projects are built on a real strategic breakthrough. Breakthrough projects are the "secret weapon" of the Q Model. Selecting and defining a set of breakthrough projects is a critical part of our program intake.

Multi-silo Teams: People talk about the power of cross-functional or multi-discipline teams, but most companies still suffer from frequent outbreaks of silo warfare. Carefully selecting the *right people* from the *right areas* when assembling a breakthrough project team is the key to cutting through the silo mindset that slows strategic initiatives. However, multi-silo teams will always create friction as they rub against the direct-reporting structure of an organization. This can be a healthy friction or a destructive dysfunction. Aligning breakthrough project aims with the most important goals of each business area is the key to a successful Agile transformation roll-out.

Top-Down and Middle-Out: Agile projects can begin from the top-down as initiatives driven by senior leaders. Likewise, Agile projects can begin organically from the middle of an organization, as initiatives driven by functional teams. However, to achieve scale both approaches must achieve traction. Senior leaders won't really believe that Agile will work unless they can see real results and a visible change in the people and mindset. Likewise, functional teams must see that they have broad support or they risk becoming an isolated Agile pocket in the company.

With freedom comes responsibility - **Eleanor Roosevelt**

Many companies have overcorrected and ended up with too much freedom and an *open everything* culture. People need structure and not everyone can function with the risk required to be a startup entrepreneur. How do you find the right balance between the freedom needed for high-performance and the responsibility needed to manage risk? The perfect tool is a portfolio of projects.

- The Project Portfolio:

What is senior management's role in all of this? A great way for senior leaders to approach the world of Universal Agility is through the lens of project portfolio management. You can use an investment model, in which every potential initiative or breakthrough project will require time, energy, and resources.

Early-stage projects have a high risk and many projects or ideas lead to a dead end. This creates a declining risk curve, where risk is reduced as projects deliver results and gain traction. Senior management's role is to manage this risk and support teams through the process of *de-risking* their project.

OK to fail: Early-stage teams require a protected space in which they can invest the time and resources needed to gain traction. The goal is to mature an early-stage project until a clear ROI path can be identified. However, to achieve this it must be accepted that many projects will fail or reach a dead end. Management must accept this idea so that talented teams can recycle themselves for the next breakthrough idea, even if their last project did not produce a "hit."

Internal VC Model: I have worked with many corporate executive teams to introduce an internal VC model. We begin by asking the teams to pitch their project ideas to the executives. Senior leaders take a VC-like funding role and make supportive suggestions. Before long, the executives start to think of themselves as venture capitalists deciding which projects to "fund," ultimately upgrading some projects from side initiatives to formally supported projects with expanded teams and budgets. It is important to note that this approach is highly aligned with the principles of Lean Startup.

Domob Pitch Day: We used this internal VC model extensively during our successes at Domob that we explored in Chapter 1. Working onsite with the project teams, at the end of each day we had them pitch the CEO and COO, who would make suggestions and approve resources. This started as a fun game that slowly became *deadly serious* as winning projects were approved for expanded budgets and staff. One team expanded from 8 to 30 full-time staff based on the success of a single *killer* presentation.

But the potentially high rewards of this internal VC model does not come without risk. By default, most senior leaders are *terrible* at giving supportive suggestions and will offer instead all the reasons why the project will fail. In every organization, there seems to be one CEO, COO, or CFO who is an expert in killing budding team enthusiasm. This is a challenging habit to break.

How to Tell the CEO to Shut Up: In facilitating these kinds of events, I would spend many hours negotiating the terms of engagement in advance. I would work with the senior leaders and frame the benefits of holding back any "telling" or negative advice until the teams had developed momentum. I would even get them to agree in advance that I would pick a strategic moment to humorously tell them to *shut up* in front of all the teams. This would help the teams to relax and deliver a breakthrough result.

That's one more little Q Model joke — I fly around the world and get paid to tell CEOs to shut up. Armed with the power of Universal Agility and the Q Model, before long you will be telling CEOs to shut up, too.

Chapter 5 - What is qDrive?

What is qDrive? A simple, practical, and powerful *set of questions* that can be used in formal or casual business conversations, qDrive is a coaching-style leadership system that has been introduced to thousands of executives, managers, and business leaders over the past 15 years.

Adding seven conversation stages to the Q Model but retaining the three foundational corners of *Trust, Vision,* and *Action,* qDrive is a universal system that can be applied at many levels: individuals, teams, products, companies, and customers. An ideal tool for developing solutions, motivation, and engagement, it is a highly efficient way to create a culture of high alignment in your enterprise and drive business results.

High-Performance Communication: Most people are not very aware of their communication habits or style, but the qDrive process challenges managers and business leaders to ask insightful questions and use high-performance conversations to drive breakthrough business results. qDrive is a cognitive model of high performance — a model of the mind and how people naturally think when they are in a high-alignment state.

Where? Everywhere. The nine qDrive questions can be used everywhere, from casual day-to-day chit-chat to formal business planning. And because the questions are used in real projects to produce results, they quickly *stick* in the mind and become habits, each question triggering a key conversation area that naturally builds broad situational leadership skills. Using a simple and powerful conversational model with seven core stages, the qDrive Model is a highly effective structure for one-on-one and team conversations.

Each Stage Builds to the Next: You can view each of these seven stages as elements in a conversation, but also consider them as *qualities* that must be present for a high-alignment state to occur. For example, *trust* is critical for high performance, and it must be present not only in the current state section of a conversation but also maintained throughout an entire breakthrough project implementation.

- How qDrive Works:

Each of the nine simple questions below trigger an entire domain of a conversation. For example: "How is the project going?" includes all conversational elements relating to current state analysis, which drives trust and relationships. Once you use these questions in a few conversations, their utility becomes self-evident and you naturally continue to integrate the Q Model.

qDrive Integration: qDrive ideas and tools interlink to self-reinforce sticky learning and rapid leadership skills development. This fully integrated approach is the key to the consistent delivery of high impact results in a short time.

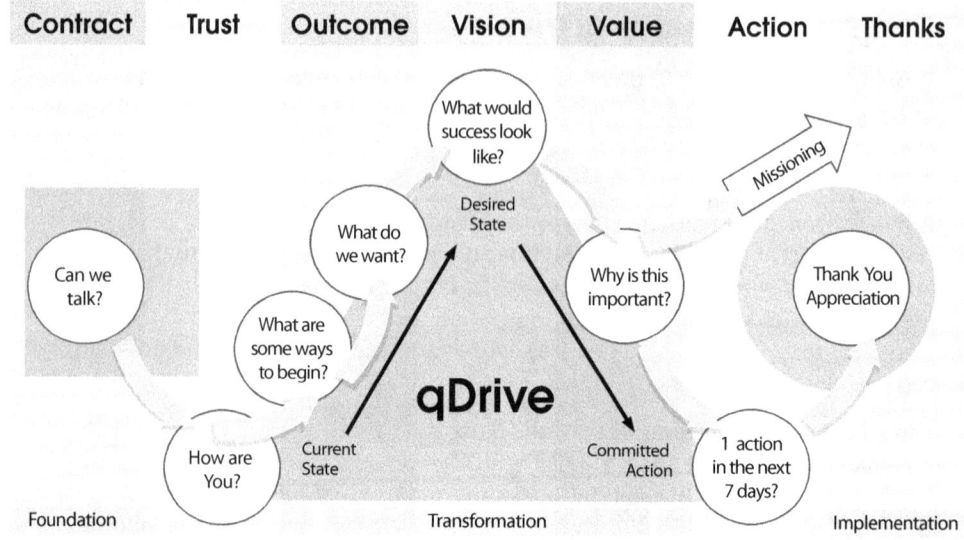

Nine qDrive Questions:

1 - Can I ask a question?
2 - What is the challenge?
3 - How is the project going?
4 - What are some ways to begin?
5 - What do we want?
6 - What would success look like?
7 - Why is this important?
8 - What is our mission?
9 - 1 Action in the next 7 days?

Key Tools:

Contract, agreement, permission
Focus on the hard part
Current state, listening, trust
Questions, brainstorm
Clear outcomes, goals, measurements
Vision, a picture of success
Value, engagement, motivation
Passion, big picture, contribution
Clear, focus, commitment
Finish with appreciation

The qDrive States:

Tool	State	Key Questions
1 - Contract	Agreement	Can we talk?
2 - Current State	Trust	How is your project?
3 - Questions	Open	Some ways to begin?
4 - Outcome	Clear	What do we want?
5 - Desired State	Vision	What does success look like?
6 - Value	Motivation	Why is this important?
7 - Missioning	High Energy	Who else benefits?
8 - Action	Commitment	What can we do in the next 7 days?
9 - Thanks	Appreciation	Thank you for being... (value word)

- qDrive: *Questions* that *Drive* Results

Below are some more qDrive question examples. As you read them, you will get a sense of the overall structure of the conversation. These are generic questions, so you will have to customize them for each type of conversation or project focus, but this is easy to do with a little practice.

For most questions, you will have to add some project-specific challenge keywords. For example, "How is the *project* coming along?" would become "How is the *data optimization* coming along?" As you move through the conversation, collect keywords, and use them to form the next question.

> Q: What is the most challenging part of your project?
> A: Data optimization (this becomes the next challenge keyword)
> Q: How is the *data optimization* coming along?

The other format shift is moving from *one-on-one* conversations to *team* conversations. For example, "What do *you* want?" would become "What do *we* want?"

qDrive Conversation Stages and Questions:

1 - Agreement: At the very beginning you are looking for permission to have a conversation and build a consensus on the focus of the conversation. While we probably won't discover the true focus of the discussion until we address the current state, a basic focus or topic is all we need to get the qDrive conversation stages up and running.

> Can we talk?
> I am curious, may I ask you a question?
> Can I ask you some questions about your project?
> What are some of the critical issues?
> What are some of the main challenges?
> Can we take 10 minutes to discuss your challenges?
> What should we focus on for the next 30 minutes?
> What is the best use of our time?
> What is the main result we want from our conversation?

2 - Current state: Operating from a frame of non-judgment, we try to be curious and keep a light and playful emotional tone as we root out the real challenge of the current state, and uncover how our team member is tackling it. Remember to collect challenge keywords.

> How are you doing?
> How is your team doing?
> How is your project coming along?
> What is the current state of your project?
> How is your primary goal coming along?
> How are you doing at dealing with the challenges?
> What is the most challenging area?
> How are you doing at dealing with *that* challenge?

3 - Open: At this point, we don't need to solve the challenge, but we do need to warm up to a solution-focused mindset, coming up with fresh ideas that introduce new ways of thinking. Whether one-on-one or in groups there's always room for a little mini-brainstorming session.

Can we explore some possible solutions?
I am curious, what are some other solutions?
What are some ways to begin to...? (use keywords to finish the question)
What are some better approaches to get there?
How might you begin to solve this?
What would an ideal solution look like?
How might you begin to produce this result?
What are the critical elements of the strategy?
How could you turn this solution into a system?

4 - Outcome: Now we are addressing the main goal, strategy, or result. But often we can't see what we want because the goal is not clearly defined, and we may need to deal with an underlying challenge that is blocking project movement.

What do you want?
What is the primary goal?
What is the real issue?
What is getting in the way of project success?
What is the plan to get there?
What is the strategy?
What are some parts of an ideal strategy?

5 - Vision: Here we are looking for the sudden increase in engagement, energy, and passion that comes when you and your team form a clear picture of the end result. This vision could be a picture in the mind's eye or a visual map of the process for getting there. People automatically visualize success when they get engaged — vision is natural — and if all the previous stages were structured well, your team members will be excited enough to automatically engage and build a vision.

Is this result even possible?
What would success look like?
How would you know if you produced this result?
How would this actually work?
What would success look like in three months if you made this work?
What would the system look like?
What would this look like as a business process?

6 - Value: To increase motivation in your team, link externally measurable results to internal motivation. We need to find out why this success is meaningful to them so that they can connect with a strong internal drive.

Why is this important?
How can we measure this result?
How will this support you and your team?
How will this help the company?

How can this result help our customers?
How would success support the impact on the bottom line?
Why is producing this result important?
Why is this meaningful for you and your team?
How will dealing with this challenge make a difference?

7 - Missioning: We can amplify motivation by imagining even more project success. We are also expanding the project value by including more stakeholders. The Missioning process should usually be conducted over a longer period of time, but it can begin with tiny steps.

What would long-term future success look like?
What would even more success look like?
How will this success help your career?
How will this success help your Team? Your Project?
How does this benefit our customers?
How can our project success benefit more people?
How can we scale up this success even further?
If we were very successful, what would it look like in 1/3/5 years?

8 - Action: By making a promise to carry out one essential action step, we build a stronger connection to our vision. Action makes the vision real, and by establishing the implementation details with tracking and check-in conversations we can stabilize the vision by linking it to a real plan.

What are some small action steps to get this going?
What are some first steps to get this moving in the next seven days?
What is the most important action in the next seven days?
What does the implementation plan look like?
What are the key steps and milestones?
How do we track results? How can we stay on track?
What might get in the way?
How can we deal with the challenges?
Can we set up a series of meetings to stay on track?
Are we 100% committed to this result? Is this a promise?

9 - Appreciation: In this final stage we whole-heartedly thank people for their commitment to making this project happen. Rather than thanking them for their *action,* we thank them for who they are *being*, appreciating their inner strength and their drive to make it happen. You can also thank them for being their *value words*, as explored in Chapter 16

I appreciate your determination to make this happen.
Thank you for being... (their strongest positive quality or value word)
Here is what I specifically appreciated about your commitment...
Thank you for your commitment.

- Where to use qDrive:

Using a universal set of tools that can be applied to many types of business challenges, qDrive creates simple yet powerful daily habits that stimulate high-alignment communication in your team.

qDrive Conversations are highly effective for:

- Problem solving
- Dealing with project implementation challenges
- Powerful one-on-one conversations
- Developing high-potential employees
- Generating employee engagement and passion
- Developing high-trust relationships
- Generating team engagement
- Driving fresh thinking and innovation
- Effective project planning
- Designing a high-alignment culture

Trust is the Foundation: For qDrive questions and conversations to work a basic level of trust is required, and other approaches may be better-suited when faced with a long-term low-performance employee, a toxic manager, or a conflict between company silos. Sometimes the best way to deal with these challenges is with a boss conversation, an HR intervention, mediation, or some other more formal approach. Remember: qDrive cannot solve every business challenge and sometimes you have to use a directive leadership style. We call this being the *boss*.

Question: Can I use the Q Model on my boss? How do I ask my boss the Q Model questions?

Here is a good analogy for approaching your boss with Q Model questions: How do porcupines make love? Very carefully.

First, you have to assess the level of trust in your relationship with your boss. Some leaders are stuck in "tell mode" and are uncomfortable with any open discussion. Realistically, it is not always possible to ask Q Model questions with every boss in every situation.

Start with a few good questions, remembering to ask permission; "I am curious, may I ask you a question?" is a simple but polite opener to get you started. If your boss engages with the question, ask permission to ask the next question. If your boss is getting value from the conversation, they will continue to engage.

It always takes time and energy to build a high-alignment, trust-based relationship with your boss, but hundreds of people have used the Q Model to swiftly achieve this exact result.

Question: I don't need to start another project. I just need to achieve my KPI numbers.

Achieving your KPI numbers is an ideal Q Model breakthrough project. Don't pick some abstract "pie in the sky" project — find the issue or challenge that is the most important thing you are focused on right now. That way the Q Model will provide the most useful and relevant results.

- Everything is a Project:

How to Define a Breakthrough Project? From existing projects and initiatives to key strategic goals, anything can become a breakthrough project.

Where's the Breakthrough? Adding a breakthrough element means abandoning *business as usual* and adding a big stretch or an unexpected result to a project or goal. As you proceed you will have to come up with a realistic plan or strategy to produce this result. Remember, you can always explore a breakthrough scenario and later fill in the implementation details. The most important thing is to add a breakthrough element so you shift away from your regular planning habits.

Pick a Project: In the Q Model, we recommend that you pick or create three breakthrough projects. You can select an immediate short term project or business result that you are currently working on, or you can craft a formal company project where you are only part of the team. Likewise, provided you stretch the intended result into a breakthrough, you can take any personal or business goal and turn it into a project.

Problems into Projects:

Consider that people don't have problems. They have projects. Anything you do can be linked to a higher-level business result, which is also a project. Setting a *project frame* in a conversation is a simple and powerful shift that will almost always foster a higher level of commitment.

Advanced homework: Generate an agreement to ban the use of the word "problem" in your team. Instead, replace it with the word "project" and your team will quickly discover they have many projects!

If you complain about a problem, by default, you are promising to turn that complaint into a project, which you will manage until the issue is resolved. You will discover you must be very careful about what you complain about, or you will end up being very busy. If everyone on your team agrees to play this game, complaints will disappear and ownership will increase.

Chapter 6 - Trust
- Hoerbiger China

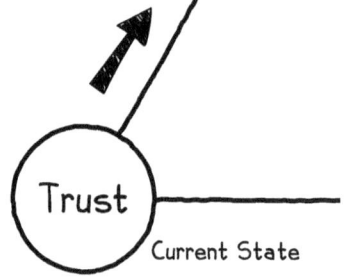

Trust

Current State

Having just closed the largest deal in his company's history, Mr. Chi was facing a crisis of extreme growth: how could he scale up production by seven times?

Mr. Chi was the chairman of Hoerbiger China, the Chinese arm of a global German engineering company. While globally Hoerbiger manufactured everything from reciprocating compressors to explosion protection solutions, the Chinese branch specialized in high-end transmissions and components.

2016 saw a tremendous change in the Chinese automotive market when Made in China brands, like BYD and Great Wall, migrated to German drive-train technology in their vehicles. Consumers realized that these Chinese vehicles now offered European quality for about half the price, and China's total industry volume of passenger vehicles increased by 19% in one year.

7x Production: Back at Hoerbiger this translated into a swelling order book, with their largest single order exceeding one million transmissions. On the production floor, this translated into a sevenfold increase in manufacturing volume in less than 12 months, as well as many more types of transmissions to contend with, many of which required customization.

Mr. Chi brought in a Chinese Q Model team to run a company transformation program led by myself, Paul Gossen. We engaged the key technical leaders and business unit heads to address these scaling challenges, following the standard Q Model process and using a customized intake process to analyze the current state. Working with the GM and several business unit heads, we identified a series of technical challenges and turned them into breakthrough projects. We then organized multi-silo teams to work on the most critical breakthrough projects in a series of strategic Q Model implementation sessions. There were a lot of big issues: engineering bottlenecks, barriers to ramping up production, a partially completed lean transformation, and an SAP ERP (enterprise resource planning) system customization.

Speed Needs Trust: We quickly discovered that all these issues came back to trust. As we worked through the key challenges, we kept encountering engineering vs. production conflicts and finger-pointing. The level of trust between the engineering and production departments was insufficient for the scale of growth.

The real issue wasn't the total manufacturing volume. It was the number of new products and all their customized specifications for different orders. This is what was happening: Engineering would design a prototype and hand it to production. Production would discover that a tiny adjustment to the design was needed before volume production could begin, and they would send the prototype back to engineering. Engineering would make the adjustment and send the prototype back to production, but inevitably production would discover another tiny adjustment was needed, and they would send the prototype back to engineering again. This revision and testing cycle was where every customized product order would get stuck.

We named this challenge of getting from the prototype stage to the volume production stage the *valley of death*; customized production orders would go into the valley of death and never come out. It quickly became clear that getting this number of products from prototype to volume production required a level of collaboration and process systemization that was missing.

Stress Kills Planning: Typically, German engineering companies excel at this kind of process integration. But if you take even the most talented and experienced engineers and production managers and put them under enough workload stress, planning will break down and reaction will take over. At Hoerbiger China, long-term planning and process integration had given way to short-term reactive firefighting.

The Q Model is ideal for this exact kind of extreme-growth technical challenge. Because a project breakthrough always begins with trust, we had to get the teams talking to each other using Q's structured conversational process. Facilitating open dialogue with the multi-silo teams to address the current state challenges was the foundation, and during the intensive phase, we ran many of these multi-silo strategic sessions in parallel.

Solution Focused: From there we engaged the teams in building process integration models using the whiteboarding tools, carefully managing the process to keep dialogue respectful and conflicts under control as we focused on solving the most challenging issues. The engineers and technical managers proved to be highly adept at whiteboarding, and once they could collaborate and see the challenges from a systemic, company-wide level, their natural problem-solving instincts took over.

The teams quickly began to shift into a more collaborative, solution-focused framework. They came up with crazy team names and designed detailed implementation plans for the new collaborative solutions. And the breakthrough projects became real for them.

Twelve months later the company still faced many challenges, but they had achieved their primary growth milestones. Anyone who has worked in manufacturing will recognize what it means to scale up a production line volume by seven times, and that is what Hoerbiger China did in 2016, using the Q Model.

- What is Trust?

Trust is Low: Most employees in organizations operate in a low-trust business environment only half of global professionals trust their employer, boss, or team.[6-1] We have become used to this, to the point where it is now normal.

Speed of Trust: Trust is the foundation for high-performance, and there are simple steps you can take to quickly establish it. Once you have trust, everything else speeds up.

Trust is Open: Open dialogue is a must if we want to bring trust into our teams, projects, and one-on-one relationships. It will be difficult to build trust if you are avoiding talking about the *elephant in the room*, and positive thinking that ignores the elephant will kill trust even quicker.

Trust is Respect: You may be 100% sure you are *right* or have the *best* idea, but you must find a way to respect other points of view. You don't have to agree with every idea or implement every strategy, but you must respect dissenting opinions if you wish to earn trust.

Golden rule for building trust: Respect other peoples' points of view

Trust is Earned: The human mind is easily confused by words, but the emotional system is infinitely wise. Tending to be past-focused, it asks, "Overall, based on my experience, do I feel safe and respected around this person?" If the answer is no, we withdraw from authentic engagement and go back to *pretending* to be happy and compliant.

Trust is Face-to-Face: Trust is something that happens in a conversation. You can build trust in a one-on-one conversation or a small team meeting. You can build trust on the phone, in a small virtual meeting, or in a voice conference call. But trust is almost four times more difficult to build via email or text,[6-2] and using lots of happy face *emojis* will not make it any easier.

Trust is Multifaceted: Trust is highly contextual. The many facets of trust relate to the specific situation or project you are working on with an individual or team, and together these facets generate an overall experience of trust. You can ask the following questions to understand the broad scope of trust:

- What level of trust do you have in yourself?
- What level of trust do you have in your problem-solving capability?
- What level of trust do you have in your team?
- What level of trust do you have in your project?
- How confident are you about the success of your project?
- What level of trust do you have in your relationship with your boss?
- How safe do you feel in your work environment?
- What level of trust do you have in the stability of your company?

Trust is a Sensitive Issue: You might get uncomfortable if your boss asked you all the questions above, and if they were asked with a harsh tone your level of trust might decrease dramatically or be outright destroyed. While the good news is that you don't have to ask all these questions to establish trust, you must always be careful and respectful as you approach the subject of trust.

Digital vs. Analog Trust: Often we think of trust in binary terms, believing you either *have* trust or you *don't*. When people are under stress or stuck in a cycle of low-performance, the reactive system tends to dominate their thinking, habitually preferring a "yes or no" mode of thinking that hinges on fight-or-flight responses and defaults to a low-trust state of mind. But if you resist this impulse and examine the specific situation, you will notice that your current level of trust is often not a binary black and white but an analog grey that fluctuates up and down over time.

Current State Builds Trust: The golden rule of trust is elementary. In the Q Model we repeat it over and over again:

Rule 1: Trust comes from an open dialogue about the current state

To build trust you must have a non-judgmental, open dialogue about the current state of a project and the challenges you and your team are facing. The more you can get the key challenges out in the open, the more trust you build.

Work in Progress: You are always building more trust. There is always more trust to earn. Building trust is never done. But as you move through a conversation, there will be times of high trust and times of low trust.

Trust Account: At the beginning of a discussion, the person you are talking to may fear your judgment. At this stage the trust is low, so you listen to them without judgment as they describe the current state and together you begin building trust. As the level of trust increases, you might try asking a difficult question. At this point, the trust level may drop, but if you have built up enough of it, the other person may have the cognitive resources to answer the question. If you have not yet established enough trust, you may get no response, and to earn it you may have to go back a few steps in the conversation. Trust is a bank account you can draw upon in times of challenge, so never stop accumulating it.

Trust Cycle: Your team needs to trust that the plan will work to fully engage with it, but as you move through a project cycle there is also a cycle of high and low trust that naturally accompanies it. At the beginning of a project, the team builds a strong plan and the trust in the plan is high. But at some point in the execution of the plan, the project hits a wall OR runs into a challenge, and the trust in the plan goes down. This shift is normal, and you will be able to quickly rebuild the plan and restore your team's confidence in the project's success if you anticipate it.

Over time, if you engage in a series of current state conversations, you can move the project or team towards a state of long-term trust. Establishing trust is the key to high-performance states and high alignment, as well as the key to instilling the confidence your team needs to deal with most challenges.

Four Components Required for a Foundation of Trust: There is more to trust than just the current state, and the Q Model pinpoints the four critical elements required to build trust in a conversation or project:

1 - Contract or Agreement: We need to agree on what we will talk about
2 - Warm-up: We need to feel comfortable and safe so we can relax
3 - Current State: We need to know where we are at now
4 - Clear Conversational Goal: We need to know what we want to get out of the time we are investing in the conversation.

Adding in each of these elements will build trust in a relationship or team. You can view these elements as a section of a conversation, or you can think of them as a state or quality that needs to be present in a high-performance project or team.

1 - Contract or Agreement: People cannot engage unless they know what they are engaging in — every conversation needs a focus or purpose. If you wish to establish trust, it is much better to get this focus through agreement rather than authority. If you are engaging in a project, you need to know your role in the project and have some idea of the scope of it:

- Do we have a clear agreement on the discussion topic?
- Does the conversation have a clear focus?
- Do we know how long the conversation will last?
- Do we have a clear intended result for our conversation?
- Do we have clear roles and responsibilities?
- Do we have clear agreements about who does what?
- Are the agreements for action natural or are they forced?
- Do we have a relationship of equals?

2 – Warm-Up: It takes time to warm up in a conversation or a new project. In a team conversation, it might take 5-10 minutes, while in a new project it might take a few days or a few weeks. Talking about the current state and the challenges is a good start, however the *tone* of conversation in the warm-up is as crucial as its *content*. Since words account for only 7% of communication,[6-3] your body language and overall demeanor are worth far more than your words in assisting your team to relax and start thinking. Rapport is the science of getting people on your wavelength so they can relax, understand, and engage with you. Start with the basic act of *being curious*, which is the simplest form of mirroring.[6-4] Building rapport is essential for you and your team to succeed.

3 - Current State: We will circle back to the current state many times:

- What is the current state of the project?
- Where are we now in the project?
- Is the project stuck in some area?
- Are we clear about the main challenges?
- Are we trying to look good and avoid an honest discussion of how the project is actually going?

4 – A Clear Conversational Goal: Unless people have a clear outcome or goal to move toward, they cannot fully engage. The problem is that defining a project breakthrough can be challenging: everyone has sat through meetings where the discussion keeps looping around, nothing gets resolved, and the team seems to lose sight of what they want to achieve and falls into a state of confusion. Trying to figure out what you want to achieve at the beginning of a conversation can be difficult, but a basic conversation goal — while not the same as the final project goal — is enough at this stage to get your team talking enough to build trust and delve into issues that are most important to the success of your project.

- What should we focus on in this conversation?
- What is the purpose of our conversation?
- What are we trying to achieve in the next hour?
- How will we know if we achieve this basic conversational goal?

Why build trust? At a basic level, building trust is about getting everyone on the same page. This means having an *explicit* shared understanding of the challenges you are facing, the roles you are assuming, and the goals you are pursuing. The reason we must invest time and energy to build trust is that we are always working against the force of *emotional reaction*. When problems occur, the root cause can often be traced back to a simple misunderstanding or assumption about the challenges, roles, and goals. However, after a problem occurs it is very easy to assume that the other party had a negative intent, and this can begin the cycle of emotional reaction that leads to the breakdown of trust.

- The Reactive System

To understand trust we will need to delve into some neuroscience. We will also touch upon some parts of the Q Model neuroscience *philosophy* which is based on research but as a whole has not been proven in a controlled setting.

Trust is governed by emotion, which in turn is governed by the reactive system. The reactive system is linked to the reticular brain area, which is a little enlargement in the brainstem at the top of the spine, right between the ears. Commonly called the "reptilian brain" in the 1970s, modern neuroscience has shown that the reticular brain area links with brain chemicals like adrenaline and cortisol to trigger a pattern of reactive responses.

Your reticular brain area and reactive system have developed over millions of years to protect you. They manage your body and habits and take over control of the body in fight or flight emergencies. Reaction is beneficial for immediate action or a response to potential danger: if you accidentally put your hand on a hot stove, it is the brain system that automatically pulls your hand away, without conscious control. You don't have to ask yourself, "Should I move my hand?" The hand just moves. The reactive system response is a self-protection survival mechanism.

My Reactive Habits: Everyone has their own reactive habits, and certain people or situations in your life will trigger you to react in unique ways. Notice these reactions throughout your workday, particularly those in response to the sounds of your phone: you hear the ring of an incoming call or the ping of a new email or text message. Perhaps an urgent issue needs to be dealt with, so you respond by jumping into action and your attention shifts. In business, interruptions and emergencies come at you all day long. Each time you respond, you further entrench your existing habit to respond, until eventually, your reactive responses become hardwired into fixed habits.

The Emotional System: Working closely with your reactive system, the emotional system (often called the limbic system) encircles the reticular brain area like a small glove. It reacts with adrenaline and cortisol which we experience as negative emotions, and it triggers serotonin, dopamine, and endorphins which we experience as positive emotions.

The Emotional System:

It is a *sameness* system. Emotionally, we like to maintain long-term habitual patterns and often want things to stay the same as they were.

It is dualistic. This means responses are "either/or," "yes/no," or "black/white." Emotion can operate quickly, like a light switch.

It is auditory and tonal. Emotion is linked to sound-based communication. We communicate emotions with the tone of our voice.[6-5]

It is group-based. Since we tend to synchronize emotions with people we work closely with, our emotional system encourages trust in small teams.

Your Safety Response: The emotional and reactive systems interlink for self-protection, taking control of our attention in times of stress or danger and shutting down our long-term thinking. This allows our immediate reactions to take over: black or white, yes or no, the field of our potential responses narrows and becomes simplistic. Because the emotional system codes safety and survival as *failure = death*, we often never explore all our options. Instead, we make impulsive decisions, based on a negative emotional reaction.

To produce results, people require a foundation of safety, trust, and security. In other words, we need to relax so that we can "turn on" the visual brain and move into a high-alignment state. Once this foundation of trust and security is in place, the executive function of the brain can stop worrying about safety and begin to engage in developing solutions.

Agreement = SAFE: From a neuroscience point of view, *agreements* play a critical role in providing safety. Agreement is the foundation that allows us to step into the world of high performance. However, before we can create a world of high performance we need to understand the world of low performance, which is held in place by the reactive system.

Scanning all incoming stimuli for any potential threat to our safety, the reactive system is the part of our brain that responds to danger. Imagine you are a primitive human, walking in the forest. Suddenly a large creature with big teeth appears and wants to eat you. How do you react? There are three options:

Option 1 – Run: Fear takes over, and we flee. The body is flooded with adrenaline. We get in action and move fast.[6-2]

Option 2 – Fight: Get angry and attack the creature. A rush of adrenaline hits the brain, and our warrior response kicks in.

The third option is a little tricky:

Option 3 – Hide: Find a safe place and don't move — the best way to hide is to be very still. A predator will track movement, so we must be completely still. We are under intense fear and stress and cannot seem to move. Our mind goes blank, and we can't think of anything. We call this *Brain Freeze.*

Hard-Wired: Our fight-flight-freeze responses are hard-wired into the human body and ready to take over whenever you need to make a decision instantly. The reactive system is perfectly designed to keep your body safe, and it also responds well to food, money, and sex, but that is another story. As you go through your day, your reactive system is scanning all available data for anything that could be a threat.

While easy to understand as an external scientific idea, it is critical to address this concept from your own unique point of view. What triggers your reaction? How do you react? What are your reactive habits?

Override Manual Control: The key point is that the reactive system can take control of your body: imagine touching a hot stove as a child. How would you react? Your brain would not have time to process the decision the conventional way, using internal dialogue and logic; there would be too many thought processes involved, and this would slow the decision-making. Meanwhile, your hand would start to burn. Instead, your reactive system takes control of your body, and the hand moves. No conscious thought is required. The body moves the hand.

Negative: The reactive system tends to respond well to negative language. After you touch the stove, the brain issues a system-wide memo: "NEVER touch the hot stove." Even if you didn't say this to yourself, chances are your mother said this to you a hundred times. The reactive system needs and loves this negative language, and it encodes the hot stove into the list of known threats. We then begin pattern matching all experience, watching out for anything that produces feelings similar to the hot stove. This list of perceived threats gets longer as we grow older, and naturally we become more cautious and hesitate before taking action. This response is natural and usually beneficial. However, this can also keep us in a box of low performance.

Reactive Action: Epitomized in the Nike slogan "Just Do It," the reactive system provides the little jolt that moves you from thinking to doing. If you need to take action, you must involve the reaction system. But sometimes the system can become overwhelmed and trigger brain freeze instead, which results in mental confusion and inaction. The key issue is that there are two main routes to engage action: we can be *moving away* from a negative or *moving toward* a positive. The human mind is less resourceful and more easily overwhelmed when we are moving away from a negative. To stay resourceful we need to be moving toward a positive, but this requires some basic security and a vision of success that we can proceed toward.

How do humans make decisions? There is an old tale of a monkey riding an elephant through the jungle. The monkey says "turn right," and the elephant turns right. Feeling like a king because apparently he can command the elephant, the monkey doesn't notice that the elephant had already turned right *before* he told it to do so. He thought he was commanding the elephant, but really he was only commenting on what had already happened. This is the nature of emotional decision making.

Emotional Decisions: We think we are rational and that every decision we make is well thought out and logical. However, consider that many of our choices are merely reactions, where we have already made a decision emotionally and only later seek to justify it using logic and internal dialogue. From our point of view, we are right and every decision we have made is perfectly logical, but in reality, the logic has been bent to fit our emotional desire. The only way out of this bind is to build awareness of our reactive habits and step back from emotion in our decision making.

Humans Need to be Safe: The best way to stay safe is to successfully predict the future. In many ways humans are very good at this; it's what sets us apart and allows us to thrive over other animals, develop civilizations, and keep ourselves largely fed and sheltered. The act of planning our day or figuring out what task we are going to do next is based on our expectations of the future. This need to *understand what is going to happen next* is hardwired into our brains and can also be a detriment.

Throughout our day we have a set of expectations for how we think things are going to go. These expectations are mostly based on our experience of how things went in the past and provided nothing unexpected happens it is relatively easy to keep our emotional reactions in check. Our day can also go the other way, and we can get stuck in a loop of over planning or anxiety. This becomes even more challenging as we move into the world of accelerating change, and the volume of unforeseen events keeps increasing.

- Deadlines Destroy Trust

Deadline = Death: There is a line in time, and if the required action doesn't happen before you reach that line in time, you become dead. That line is the core feature of the deadline, and every manager knows that the best way to get a project moving is to introduce a deadline. Speaking directly to the reactive system, the deadline is *the* great tool for driving your team into action.

> If you *don't* take this *action*, by this *time*, you are *dead*.

This wording might seem extreme, but this is the kind of language that the reactive system needs to hear: negative language that demands immediate action under the threat of death. All of this gets encoded into an imperative *must take action* central command.

Deadlines: Perhaps the most abused traditional business tool is the deadline. Of course, you don't actually become dead if you miss the deadline, but humans can't help but process the specter of a looming deadline using the same survival-based reactive system as a life-and-death situation. In this respect, deadlines are an ideal way to generate activity, and thus they have become one of the dominant management tools of the 21st century.

What is the Cost of Deadline Driven Action? Why don't we just keep pushing the deadline button and getting more and more action out of our direct reports? What happens if we do this? Remember, the reactive system is grounded in survival. Survival is the oldest and most central instinct. As a mature adult, you can manage a certain level of stress, but there is always a cost; a threat to survival is inherently stressful. It is a bit like drinking 13 shots of espresso per day. The release of adrenaline and eventually cortisol can lead to long-term burnout.

Remember that the reactive system thinks in fight or flight, yes or no, black or white. It is a binary system, and any computer programmer will tell you that working with a binary system is hard. Have you ever traveled to a foreign country and tried to communicate using only the words yes and no? In my first trip to Russia, all my communication was composed of "da" and "nyet," followed by an assortment of hand gestures. Conveying any higher-level ideas with only yes or no communication is impossible.

Stress kills creativity: Harsh and reactive thinking pushes people into a narrow band of yes and no responses. Stress kills creativity, and the moment when we most need our higher-level problem-solving capacity is exactly when the stress of a situation causes us to lose it. Many people are resourceful enough to regain their solution-focused thinking capacity in a few minutes, but in a world of constant interruptions, it is easy to become stuck in a reactive style of thinking and action. Remember the number 2617, which is the average number of times we touch our smartphone per day — reaction is a long-term habit that is difficult to break.

In the old model of management, all we wanted from our workers was direct action, so the deadline was the most effective tool. But in the new model of accelerating complexity, we need people who can think and work collaboratively to deal with difficult challenges.

- What are your deadline habits?
- When and where do you habitually operate in deadline mode?
- Catch yourself creating deadlines for yourself or others.
- Stop and consider how to develop a plan or solution.

- Brain Freeze:

Deadline Without Solution = Brain Freeze. Here is the catch-22 that leads to low performance:

- Your boss gives you a big project with a big deadline
- You automatically say yes
- Perhaps you have some solution or plan for how to accomplish this result, or maybe you have no plan at all
- You get to work. You encounter an unexpected problem at some point, or you hit a cluster of complex issues
- Suddenly it seems like there is no way to move the project forward
- You lose trust in yourself and the success of the project
- You don't have enough trust with your boss to have an open discussion about the challenges
- You react by isolating yourself as you search for solutions
- You keep looking for a way forward but everything seems stuck

If you work in the modern world, this scenario should seem very familiar. This scenario is precisely what managers, leaders, and information professionals confront every hour of their working lives.

Complex Solutions: Naturally, the way forward is to come up with a solution or an effective strategy that you can put into an operational plan. But this requires clear thinking, and human beings don't tend to think well when they are stuck or under stress. Another way to say this is that you must have a basic level of security and trust in yourself to function well in stressful situations. The more complex solutions require team thinking, which itself requires effective communication and open dialogue. If the level of trust in a group is too low, effective communication becomes difficult. Projects get stuck.

Manage Quality, not Time: A core feature of the world of Agile project management is a general disdain for deadlines. Thus you manage your projects based on *quality* rather than *time*: quality in Agile is fixed, while people, features, and time become variables. Conversely, in classic project management, these variables are all set in stone. As a result, *quality*, the only remaining variable, is often secretly cut to meet a deadline.

Agile ≠ Deadlines: While Agile and Scrum cultures are a defiant response to the world of deadline-driven action, it only takes one frustrated senior leader to begin the slide back into the old habits of reactive leadership. At the end of every Agile cycle, there is a push to demo working code or completed features. This can easily create a team culture of *demo or die*, which itself mounts into a subsequent push for *ship, ship, ship,* where quality is forgotten altogether in the name of shipping the product on time. This is the most common way *real* Agile gets subverted into *fake* Agile.

A $4b Deadline: A classic example of *ship, ship, ship* comes from my friend Charlie Pellerin, who led the team that sent the Hubble Space Telescope into low-earth orbit with a flawed mirror.[21-1] In analyzing this four billion dollar mistake, NASA cited a toxic culture of deadlines and a low level of trust with subcontractors as the primary cause. Undoubtedly, a lack of trust coupled with inexorable deadlines is a blueprint for astronomical expenses.

This story ends well, as Charlie worked behind the scenes to arrange a repair mission that ultimately fixed the flawed mirror. Many researchers now consider the Hubble Space Telescope to be most important scientific device ever created by humankind.

Chapter 7 – Agreement

Option 1: War
Option 2: Agreement

Key Agreement Questions:

Can we talk?
I am curious, may I ask you a question?
Can I ask you some questions about your project?
What are some of the key issues?
What are some of the main challenges?
Can we take 10 minutes to discuss your challenges?
What should we focus on for the next 30 minutes?
Can we take an hour and explore a project breakthrough?
What is the best use of our time?
What is the best result from our conversation?

- Oxy: 150k B/D

Facing a room full of Arab men yelling at each other, it appeared that my highly professional program was about to turn into a bar room brawl. I sensed that we were about to have a breakthrough.

More Barrels per Day: The year was 2010, and we were working with our global partner Erickson Coaching International. The task was to deliver a project in Oman for Occidental Petroleum (Oxy), the American company that manages all oilfield operations for the Sultanate of Oman. Oxy gets a small percentage of each barrel they pump, so any increase in production goes directly to their bottom line.

They brought in a team of 20 oilfield engineers to develop their strategic thinking, and while the initial focus for increasing oilfield production had been agreed upon in advance, the exact goal had not been specified.

We introduced some basic coaching and Q Model ideas, asking the team to agree to spend four days exploring their processes and developing systems for increasing production. Culturally they looked and dressed like Arab men, with long white gowns, full beards, and each one sported an expensive watch. However, underneath this exterior, they were all engineers, highly technical experts in process and systems thinking.

120 to 128: We started with the current state, asking "What are some of the main challenges you face?" Most of the engineers were local Omanis. They would spend their 14-day shifts in the dusty fields, managing teams of 30–40 untrained Indian laborers in the overwhelming heat. Although their official KPI was 128,000 barrels per day (128k B/D) in twelve months, due to equipment shortages and machine failures their current production was at 120,000 barrels per day (120k B/D).

120 to 200: With only four days on-site, we needed to energize the discussion on the morning of day one. So we introduced the concept of exploring a breakthrough in oilfield production, asking the engineers to throw out some possible breakthrough production targets. Several of the younger ones suggested 200k B/D in production, and this number caused an immediate uproar among a group of older engineers. The problem was their relationship with the Oxy KPI system that the company had structured. KPIs are not fun: if you make your KPI you get a bonus, but miss it and you get a punishment. KPIs are serious.

Death by Stretching: Every experienced manager has played the stretch goal game. Your boss asks you playfully to explore an increased KPI number. At the end of the "exploration," the boss makes your stretch goal into your new KPI. You now have more work and more risk for the same reward, and you realize that you have fallen for what has become another toxic term in many companies: the old KPI *stretch goal* trick. Conversely, lots of experienced managers play the opposite game, introducing problems and risks to negotiate a *lower* KPI. Unfortunately, neither of these approaches will produce a breakthrough in strategic thinking or business results.

120 to 180: Back in Oman, the 20 engineers had split into two camps. The younger group of engineers had aligned on 180k B/D as *possible* and were excited to use the Q Model to explore how they might design a breakthrough in the required systems. Meanwhile, the older group was sensing that this entire Q Model program was just a secret *trick* from the OXY executive team to make them agree to a higher KPI. Despite this, introducing the idea of a breakthrough in production with a specific number had at least gotten everyone paying attention, and it was clear our day was not going to be another boring lecture on abstract leadership theory.

At this point, the older engineers voiced some strong concerns about managing performance expectations. A heated exchange lasting more than an hour erupted, wherein I had to define the exact meaning of the word *explore* several times. I also had to play traffic cop, making sure everyone had a respectful chance to voice their concerns as we negotiated the exact terms and scope of the engagement.

The keyword was "realistic." The older engineers needed to know that they could challenge the process and address any unrealistic ideas. I insisted that we push most of the skeptic challenges to the end, agreeing to spend the final day focused on the implementation challenges. This way our breakthrough plan would have a realistic scope.

150k Breakthrough: In the end, everyone agreed that we would spend four days exploring the process and systems required to achieve 150k B/D in 18 months. We had achieved a *contract* for a specific *result*, one that allowed everyone to engage fully. This process took us almost three hours, so the engineers were now late for their midday prayers. We finished the morning as a single aligned team with a clear *result contract* for a breakthrough.

- Agreement = Trust:

Structure of Agreement: Companies run on a structure of agreement. Although some leaders may get into disagreements, any conflict sits above a lower level of agreement, for example, the company agrees to pay you and you agree to work toward the interests of the company.

Rule 19: Agreement is the foundation of trust

What is real? All of these tiny agreements form a foundation for cooperation. In life, we operate within a structure of agreements that governs our relationships and society at large. In the extreme, you could say:

Objective reality is an *agreement* about what is real

Frame of Agreement: High alignment takes place inside a larger frame of agreement. This framework is a critical foundation for every breakthrough project, and how the agreements within it are defined and set up is essential for the success of any breakthrough program.

Permission: Asking permission is a small and simple way to build the frame of agreement. One of the most potent Q Model questions is, "May I ask you a question?" If you are the boss, you don't actually need to ask permission to ask a question. However, asking this question shows that you respect the autonomy of your team member. When you show this respect, it helps people to relax and engage.

Conversational Goal: A contract is the goal of the conversation, not the goal of the project. If the project goal is a breakthrough in business results, the conversational goal could be to spend an hour exploring the strategy for a breakthrough in business results.

Contract = Trust: Trust is often perceived as a *fuzzy* emotional thing. It seems counter-intuitive that this very *formal* contracting process is one of the best ways to build trust. Trust is not about being nice or soft. It is about respecting people. You show respect by quickly dealing with the key issues and getting to a solution. No one wants to sit through endless meetings where nothing moves forward. With a result contract, everyone agrees to respect each other's time and work toward the specific result.

Reactive System: If people don't feel respected, they don't feel safe. The result contracting process speaks directly to the reactive system, building a set of rules that satisfies the human need to feel safe. Once this need is met, people can relax and engage.

Scale up the Breakthrough: Again, it is counter-intuitive that a *small* contract is one of the best ways to scale up to a *big* project breakthrough. Adding a breakthrough challenge to a project goal is inherently risky, and a result contract lets people know that the project breakthrough conversation is taking place inside a frame where *possible* plans can be safely explored.

Not too hot, not too cold: In the story of the three bears, Goldilocks liked her porridge to be not *too hot* and not *too cold*. Setting the scale of the breakthrough is a tricky balancing game, one where you need to respect the new challenges that arise as you test the limits of your endeavor.

Frame of Exploration: A breakthrough often begins with a contract for exploration. *Explore* is a wonderful word that permits people to step outside of the scarcity thinking and resource limits that constrain most business planning today.

- Result Contracting:

What is a Result Contract? This is not a legal contract, per se. With a result contract, you spend 5-10 minutes at the beginning of a conversation to make an agreement about how you will use your *time* to *focus* on a set issue and create a specific *result*. This is a simple set of agreements that allow people to relax and engage in the conversation. The word *contract* has been used in the world of coaching in this very specific way for more than 25 years. In the Q Model, we utilize result contracting as a universal tool for getting a *small* result out a conversation, which can build towards a *large* transformation. There are three ingredients in a result contract:

> **Time:** How much time are we going to spend?
> **Focus:** What are we going to focus on?
> **Result:** What do we want to get out of the time we spend?

Contract Scale: While contracts in coaching typically apply specifically to a single agreement for one conversation, a result contract can encompass anything from a single question to an entire project life cycle.

Result Contracting is the process of defining any initial *frame of agreement* required to begin a conversation or planning process. A great contracting question for a one-minute Q Model conversation would be "May I ask you a question?" If the other party says yes, it sets a *frame of permission* for *one* question. In this sense, the general principle of result contracting can be applied broadly to many different scales of interactions or projects.

Here are some of the agreements in a result contract:

1 – Time: We agree on the conversation length at the beginning
We agree to start and end on time
We agree to maintain momentum

2 – Focus: We agree on the focus at the beginning
We agree to get back on track if we go off-topic

3 – Result: We agree on an end result from the conversation
We agree that this end result is possible
We agree to work toward this end result

> These points may seem completely obvious, but consider how many *business as usual* meetings don't follow this path. Note that these are implicit agreements. You do not need to make each agreement out loud in a check-box style.

Contracts are Permission-Based: As the boss, you can use your authority to make people say yes and do what you want. Power is a subtle issue: your employees or team may seem enthusiastic and agree with you, but at some level, they are responding to a perceived threat. By asking permission you respect their time, you respect their autonomy, and you put yourself in a support role, which invites people to bring their best solutions to the table.

Remember to ask permission. As a boss, you might be able to force people to do things, but this may also entrench low performance. High performance, however, is grounded in agreement.

Contracting Transformation: The Result Contracting process can be quite technical and detailed, as you are negotiating directly with the reactive mind to design an agreement for a safe space where people can explore a breakthrough. This can be a difficult negotiation, akin to pedaling a bike uphill. Here is why it is so important—when you hammer out a strong result contract, 80% of the work of building a transformation is already done. The moment an individual or team says "yes" to a strong contract, they are declaring that a breakthrough is possible. From this point onward, you are riding the bicycle downhill.

Result contracting is a mastery process, so get technical and become a Q Model geek. Here is a more detailed breakdown of the result contracting process:

1 - Time:

How much time do we agree to spend having this conversation? Most people agree that there is not enough time, so time is a useful negotiation tool to keep the discussion on track. Agreeing on the conversation length is easy, but you are also agreeing to manage the time and keep the process moving forward quickly.

How much time do we have today?
We have 20 minutes to talk, is this enough time?
We only have 10 minutes left, what should we focus on?

Remember: managing time is not just about agreeing upon when to finish. You may have to be active in the way that you manage time to keep moving toward the intended result. In your role as a Q Model facilitator, you may have to *interrupt* a story or introduce a *visioning* or *whiteboarding* process. All this links to your agreement to use the time as effectively as possible.

2 - Focus:

What is the focus of the conversation? What do we agree to talk about? At this point the process gets more complex. First you need to widen the range of topics to pull out the key challenges, then later you will need to narrow the focus down so that you can close the contract with a clear agreement on the conversational result. This focus segment makes use of the *current state* and *keywords,* both of which we will go through in detail in the next chapter.

What project do you want to discuss?
What should we focus on for the next 20 minutes?

Go Wide: As you get into a conversation and uncover the broader issues, the focus tends to sprawl into many topics. Give people a little space to complain about the current state, but don't let them get too negative. As you get into the details of the challenge it will bring out many sub-issues, each of which can be dealt with as another challenge. Any big challenge usually has *three more* challenges hiding inside of it. Below are four questions that will help you reveal them:

What are some of the issues?

What are some more challenges?
How are you doing with that?
Why is that a challenge?

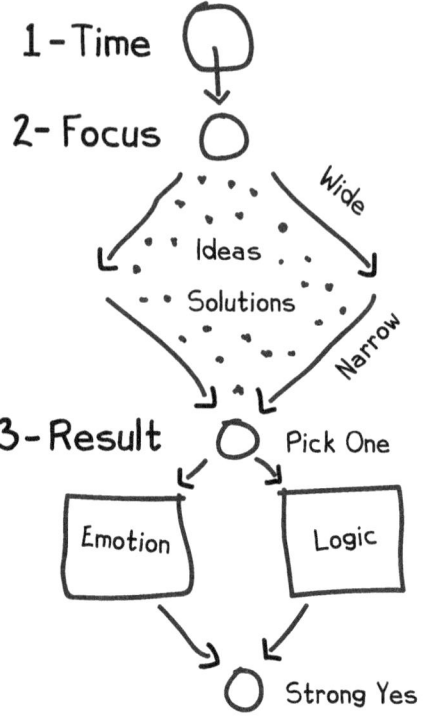

Capture each challenge on paper, a flip-chart or Post-it notes. Go wide and let the challenge and solution focus sprawl a little, remembering that the goal is to create a shift or transformation *later* in the conversation, and therefore *anything* that gets discussed in the broad focus will be included when a shift occurs in the main issue.

Go Narrow: At some point you must begin to narrow the focus. Previously we were looking for more challenges, but now we are looking for the biggest ones. The following three questions will begin to funnel the conversation toward a single main issue:

What are the biggest challenges?
What is the most challenging part?
We only have 60 minutes, so which one of these issues is the *most* difficult?

Pick one: It is critical to pick one issue as the focus for the discussion, as it is easy to get overwhelmed by all the sprawling sub-topics. As well, in case you go off-topic, make sure you have a pre-set agreement to either bring the conversation back to the main issue or have the freedom to explore any subtopics that come up.

3 - Result:

What do we want to get out of the conversation? You can think of this as a *conversational goal.*

What do you want to get out of the conversation?
What would be the best result from our discussion?
What would you like to achieve in this conversation?
Where would you like to be at the end of the conversation?

Soft: People tend to freeze in the face of a challenge, and sometimes we need soft questions to warm up the brain. Words or phrases like *begin, first steps,* and *explore* create a safe thinking space to get the conversation going. Here are some *softener* words that reduce the risk of engagement.

Begin Small   Tiny Explore   First Steps   Next Steps

Here is an extreme example: "Can we *begin* to *explore* some *tiny first steps* to *start* to get this project back on track?" This question may seem overly wordy, but when people are under extreme pressure this kind of language is needed to help them explore solutions.

Specific: A good conversational result will have a specific and measurable outcome that satisfies the logical mind. People need to see that the specific conversational goal aligns with larger issues and overall business needs.

Logic and Emotion: A good contract must satisfy both the logical mind and the emotional system. While a detailed plan or specific number can often satisfy the needs of the logical mind, to meet the requirements of the emotional mind we need to find the *value word* that represents the end result. First, ask what your team member wants to achieve in the conversation, then listen for the key emotional word that represents the value of that result. Finally, say this value word back to them and test to confirm that word. Catching a value word is a learned skill that takes time and practice. We will explore value words thoroughly in Chapter 16.

> We agree that at the end of the meeting we will have a clear plan.
> To confirm, if we have a solution to this issue we will be satisfied.
> You would be happy if we came up with a realistic plan.
> It will be a good use of our time if *everyone* can *agree* on the next steps.

Get a Strong Yes: Closing the contract is critical, but how do you know if you have made a firm agreement? The most effective test is to summarize all of the *time, focus,* and *result* keywords into a closed question:

> OK, so if we spent the next 60 minutes *(time)* working on a breakthrough in data optimization *(focus)* and we are clear *(value word)* on the next steps *(result)*, would that be a good use of our time?

As you summarize, it is critical to vocally emphasize the *tone* of the value word that links to the result of the conversation. You can do this by shifting your voice tone slightly to highlight that word. If the tone is strong when your team member says yes or confirms the value of the result, you have a firm agreement. However, if the tone is weak then something is missing, and you may have to ask more questions about the time, focus, or result to build a stronger yes.

Question: The CEO told me I *must* produce this result. How do I ask permission to negotiate this deadline using the Q Model?

> **Answer:** You have to be careful. Some executives give very direct orders and might be under extreme pressure and looking for compliance. To ask any questions at this moment could be a CLM (career limiting move).
>
> One of the best responses to this question came from a VP at American Express. In response to a challenging demand from his SVP, he asked, "Is this a non-negotiable request?" This response is a negative closed-question that speaks directly to the reactive mind. Apparently, in response the SVP's eyes bulged out and after a pause she laughed. They then had a real conversation about the implementation challenges.
>
> Essentially, you are asking, "May I negotiate this?" If the answer is *yes*, you have a basic contract to ask questions and carefully challenge the frame of the request.

If the answer is *no*, you may just have to agree and begin doing it. However, you can always come back later and ask again for permission to ask questions, using Q Model questions to test the scope and parameters of the demand.

Dead Language: Meeting Agenda. While meeting agendas may have a *time* and a *focus* element, they almost never have an intended result. The entire idea of a meeting agenda has emotional baggage from every unproductive meeting you have ever attended. Stop using the term altogether and introduce the idea of result contracting instead. Simply explain the process and agree to set a result contract in advance for all meetings.

Transform your Meeting Culture: Unproductive meetings are one of the most significant sources of wasted time and frustration in an organization, and many companies have used the result contracting process to transform their meeting culture. Start with your team by building a set of agreements with them to result contract your meetings. If you are invited to a meeting, ask what the intended result is before you accept the invitation. As a rule, if you don't have a result contract, don't have a meeting. In some companies, you cannot book a meeting room without first providing a specific time, focus, and intended result for the meeting.

Why is Apple called Apple? Here is an old story that demonstrates the power of result contracting. Back in 1977, Steve Jobs and Steve Wozniak were in their garage trying to come up with an ideal name for their new computer company.

After two days of arguing and rejecting potential names one after the other, an exasperated Jobs yelled, "If we can't agree on a name in the next two hours…" He looked around for the closest available random object he could find and grabbed it. "We are going to call the company apple," he said. This word was the most stupid name Jobs could think of in the moment and represented his utter frustration with the whole affair. He and Wozniak continued arguing for their *result contracted* two hours, but when their time was up and they were no closer to agreeing, they had no choice but give the company the "stupid" name of Apple Computer Inc.

Chapter 8 – Current State

Key Current State Questions:

How are you doing?
How is your team doing?
How is your project coming along?
What is the current state of the project?
How is your key goal coming along?
What are the challenges?
What is the most challenging area?
How are you doing at dealing with the challenge?
What is the real issue?

- Coastal – We Care About our Team

We knew it was impossible. We needed to rank in the top 50 best employers in Canada, and in our prior year, we hadn't even cracked the top 1000. We had only ten months to do this and the clock was ticking.

We Care: Coastal Community Credit Union, a regional bank in Nanaimo Canada with 700 staff, had a long history of a caring and employee-focused organizational culture. Although these company values proved to be an essential foundation for our coaching culture program, too much "employee wellness" was also seen as a distraction by some of the more ambitious executives. Many employees also felt that the whole "we care" thing was just a trick to make them work harder, and together these misgivings had given rise to ongoing disputes between the union and the executives over employee wellness issues.

Hoping to attract talent, drive growth, and support long-term stability, a key company goal was to land a spot on the Top 50 Best Employers in Canada list, which was run by Aon Hewitt. Utilizing a balanced scorecard to assess each employee's satisfaction with their workplace, a company can only score well on the Best Employers survey if almost all of their staff is actually satisfied in their job. With only ten months to go, we knew there was no quick fix. Every employee had to genuinely feel respected and enjoy working at Coastal.

The VP of HR, Deborah Lang, had already recruited a few senior executives to help her shape a company-wide coaching culture transformation. Several executive sponsors also envisioned a tipping point whereby a caring culture oriented towards revenue growth would be created.

The credit union presented a happy face of harmony to the world. However, in staff surveys, many employees made it clear that they did not feel respected. There was an older leadership culture of command and control at Coastal, featuring many senior leaders who were comfortable in their habits and did not really want to change. There was also a well-entrenched low-performance culture in some areas of the company, such as the front-line bank-tellers, who often complained about a lack of respect.

Intensive: Working with Deborah and her employee data, we developed a comprehensive plan to use a coaching culture to drive organizational growth. First, we conducted interviews to get a clear picture of the current state, then in the first round we ran a series of two-day Q Model *Manager as Coach* programs for all leaders, managers, and a group of high-potential staff. These programs included staff from administration, human resources, marketing, operations, branch managers, assistant branch managers, and most of the executives and directors. More than 15% of the total company staff was involved, and half of these people engaged in a six-month follow up peer-to-peer program to broadly integrate their skills and spread the coaching culture.

Ongoing: The aim was to create strong trust-based direct reporting relationships. The intensive programs were supported by a series of on-site follow-up sessions where each participant promised to conduct three formal weekly coaching conversations and engage in casual conversations throughout the day. We supported this with games, visual reminders, and integrated an ongoing progress check-in from senior leaders. This included a formal company-wide shift from periodic performance reviews to ongoing coaching conversations, and we organized an extensive tracking system to test the results and address any program breakdowns. After this six-month integration period, a select group of 30 managers engaged in a second round of the Team Coaching Facilitative Leadership program to help integrate their skills at the team level.

No Fake Coaching: What made this program so effective was the depth of the ongoing program. Every week each person had to document a series of coaching style conversations, and Deborah was very rigorous in making the distinction between *authentic* relationships and *fake* coaching compliance. Many people in the peer-to-peer teams naturally became internal champions and one manager documented 110 coaching style conversations in one month. There was no place to hide from the coaching culture in such a small company, so we quickly made a big impact.

The Secret Game of Trust: Toward the end of the first round, we worked with a group of 35 managers to create the *How are you?* 30-day challenge. A secret game intended to create a breakthrough in trust, it dared managers to ask "How are you doing?" to five new people in the company every day. Agreeing to stop and be authentically curious about how that new person was actually doing, each manager would take a moment to listen and be present to that person's current state. This could include their relationship with their workload, projects, deadlines, or anything related to how they were doing in general, including their well-being. We decided to test the results by monitoring employee wellness, employing one of the project coordinators to track any shifts in the trend line of absenteeism over 60 days.

Authentic Curiosity: The tricky part of the 30-day challenge was to consistently be authentically curious. With the small number of staff at the head office, people there might be asked "How are you doing?" up to eight times per day, and it wasn't long before news of the secret 30-day challenge leaked out and people would simply laugh if you asked them how they were doing. This was where the real breakthrough occurred.

Although many people knew about the game, the program champions persisted in asking "How are you doing?" with authentic curiosity, and over the 60 days, we saw a small decline of 11% in sick days. However, the real shift was in the employee experience: if you are frustrated or complaining and your boss who you trust gently asks you "How are you doing?" you ultimately have no choice but to recognize that they do indeed care about you and your day-to-day challenges.

Results: Based on their tracking numbers, we saw a significant shift. After 60 days, 74% of participants had integrated basic coaching culture skills into their day-to-day behaviors, and 22% of those participants had shown a *champion-level* skill adoption. Building on the existing culture of caring for employees, Coastal had begun to develop a true high-performance coaching culture. As the team had aligned, many of the small disputes between the union and the executives had disappeared.

The Top 50: The real prize of the entire program was the result of the Top 50 Best Employers workplace culture survey. One year prior, Coastal had not even ranked in the top 1000 employers. Now they discovered themselves in the top 50.

- How are you doing?

This is always the first question. If the answer is *fine*, listen carefully to the tone. If it is flat, you may need to go deeper to find out what is really going on.

"How are you doing?" is the ultimate current state question, the single most powerful question for creating rapport and trust. But its power is lost when the other person replies with *"Fine"*, which is usually a sign that you have a business-as-usual relationship of low-trust. Consider that there is a *quality of listening* that you could bring to the conversation that would encourage the other person to share their authentic current state. Try getting authentically curious about how people are doing and see where it takes the discussion.

We can't transform a company unless the employees feel safe, and "How are you doing?" is the crucial question that earns the trust needed to build this foundation of safety. We can use this question to check in on an employee's level of rapport, comfort, and well-being, and we can also check in on the current state of their work or how a breakthrough project is proceeding. However, the magic of "How are you doing?" goes much deeper than this — we are looking for a transformation in trust. And this kind of transformation defines the first corner of the Q Model.

"How are you doing" is a domain of questions. Consider the following chain of sub-questions:

How are you doing?
How is your well-being?
How are you doing with your work?
How is your project coming along?
What kind of results are you getting?
How are we doing as a team?

How is our team performing?
What is the current state of our project?

Turn to Face the Challenge: As you build rapport, we can turn and focus on the most challenging parts of the project with the following three-question sequence:

First Question: How are you doing? The first answer is usually "fine." Be warm and curious. Broadcast that you *really want to know* how they are doing.

Second Question: How is the project coming along? You usually have to dig a little to find out what is really going on.

Third Question: What is the challenge? This question is where the conversation builds traction.

- Challenge:

Why do people climb mountains? People climb mountains because they enjoy the challenge. *Challenge* is a magical word in the Q Model. When a project or team is stuck in a problem state, success seems impossible. But when you ask the question "What is the challenge?" you reframe the *problem* into a *challenge*, and your team member cannot process your question without also presupposing that a solution is possible.

You need to bring out the challenges so that people can see them and deal with them. You need to isolate the most difficult part of the problem so we can focus on it. Here are three questions that will get people talking in terms of challenges:

What is the challenge?
What are some more challenges?
What is the *most* challenging part?

It might seem quite repetitive to ask three questions in a row that seem almost the same, but digging for the *real challenge* is a critical element of the Q Model. Many people get stuck in the *spin of busyness* and won't even hear the question until the third round.

Always Move Toward Your Enemy: In medieval Japan, only samurai could carry weapons and wear armor. The martial art of Jiu-Jitsu developed as a secret discipline that allowed non-samurai to fight back. But how does an unarmed person defeat a fully armed samurai? There is only one rule: always move toward your enemy. At very close range, the samurai's weapons and armor get in the way, giving his unarmed opponent an advantage.

Rule 20: Always move toward the challenge

Many people habitually start with the easy things first. As busy managers, we might tend to avoid dealing with complex or challenging issues. But *always move toward the challenge* means that you look at all issues and pick the most challenging one to focus on first.

Focus on the Most Challenging Part: 89.7% of all managers put their energy into dealing with ineffective activities.[1-1] To have power, you need to work with the most challenging high-level issue first. We call this the *real challenge* or *real issue.* Once you create a breakthrough in the real issue and hone in on it, many lower-level problems will automatically shift, disappear, or become irrelevant. You can begin this by digging down with current state questions and getting good at listening.

- Listening:

Of all the leadership skills, listening is the talent most often ignored. A fundamental communication skill, everyone should be good at listening, but other forces are constantly working against it. Good listening requires a renewed awareness of the basic perceptual patterns that you have developed over many years. Try to recognize your pattern in the following list of thinking habits that set you up for *bad* listening:

No Time: You perceive that you don't have any time, so you stop listening to people unless they provide an immediate solution.

No Solution: You perceive that there is no solution to the problem, so why bother listening to people?

No Talent: You perceive that other people can't produce results independently, so you don't bother listening to anyone and do it all yourself.

Only Me: You perceive that only you can solve the problem, so you filter out any ideas that didn't come from you.

No Trust: You perceive that someone does not respect you, so you cut short your communications with them.

My Idea: You perceive that your idea is the best so you ignore other solutions.

Recognition: You operate in a scarcity of recognition, wanting others to recognize your ideas and solutions as the best. (This one applies to me, Paul Gossen)

Achievement: You perceive that you must be successful, and you fail to link your success to the success of others.

Be Interested in Them: It is actually easy to shift these habits. The trick is to *actually* be interested in people and their *subjective* experience of a given issue. Somehow you must decide that their point of view is the most important thing in the world; presuppose that you have a large red LED display on your forehead that will let people know immediately if you are displaying *fake* interest. When you dig a little deeper you discover that every human is unique, and every business challenge presents an interesting puzzle. Treat it as a game and take on the challenge of being authentically interested in other peoples' experience of the current state.

Be Curious: There is a light and playful tone of curiosity that will open even the most well-guarded bank vault of a human being. Curiosity starts with your mindset and naturally extends to the tone of your voice. Likewise, this mindset of curiosity fundamentally affects the way you listen.

The Art of Listening:

1 - Is your mouth moving? If your mouth is moving, you are not listening. It is impossible to listen and talk at the same time.

2 - Let them finish: Never say *'Yes but'* again for the rest of your life. Chewing off the end of a person's sentence is a sign that you think the *"what you have to say"* is more important than the *"what they have to say."* For the first five minutes of a conversation, pretend that what your conversation partner has to say is the most important thing in the universe.

3 - Wait before Asking: Ask yourself, "What did they just say?" then pause and take a breath, making sure you understand what they said before you ask them your next question.

4 - Ask, Then Wait: A great question can take 60 seconds to mentally process. Give them some time to reflect. Wait in respectful silence.

5 - Give up a Judgment: Is *your* version of the story so loud you can't hear *their* version? Give up your judgment for a few minutes and replace it with a brand new one, such as "I am committed to understanding their experience of this situation."

6 - Get Comfortable with Silence: Great salespeople and negotiators understand that silence builds the emotional intensity required for a shift or transformation to occur. So let that silence build-up, especially before speaking or asking a question.

Who Blinks First: As children, we all played the game *see who blinks first.* With listening, the game is: *whoever makes a sound first loses.* Don't talk. Get comfortable with the sound of silence and harness its transformational power.

Listening without Hearing: It is not that people don't listen at all. Of course, we all listen at a basic level. The problem for so many leaders is that they are addicted to quick-fix solutions, so they fail to slow down their pace and focus on identifying the real issue. If you are not listening in a focused way, you will miss the signal that it is time to delve deeper and uncover the real issue at play.

Sense the Real Issue: It is not unusual to see beginners rush through the Q Model process. However, when they see myself or some of the other elite Q Model professionals go through the process, the most common observation is the way we continuously *loop back* around, sniffing out the challenge like a bloodhound and listening for the real issues. Often people are "too busy" to do this, but somehow you must carve out a block of interruption-free time to explore the real challenge in depth.

Give up a Judgment: Our internal judgment is what is really standing in the way of our ability to listen and be fully present to other people.

Our judgment of *ourselves* is based on our internal positive *intention.*
Our judgment of *others* is based on our external *interpretation* of them.

If you judge people based on your past experience, you will only see limitations. If you judge people on the possibility of *who they are becoming* you will only see expansion.

Coach Position: A key idea here is the concept of taking *coach position*.[8-1] Imagine you are standing outside the situation as a *judgment-free* observer. From here you can see the current state from many angles. Standing in coach position, our viewpoint can range across a time frame that includes the past, present, and a *future of success*. A magical tool, coach position was developed by Marilyn Atkinson and integrates many ideas from Milton Erickson.

- Keywords

Confirm Data Exchange: People often think of listening as a passive thing but is actually a very active process. Good listening takes energy and focus — people need to perceive that you are listening or they will not bother to tell you what is really going on. The old way to do this was to throw in an occasional "Um-hum" or an "I understand," but these tiny sounds will only break your conversation partner's focus. It is much better to wait in silence until they finish and then confirm their keywords.

Keywords have power. Of all the tools in the Q Model toolbox, keywords are one of the most powerful. A foundational building block of the entire Q Model, many other Q Model tools, such as *open-ended questions* and *value words*, run on keywords. You won't be able to build useful questions or run the whiteboarding process unless you first confirm a set of keywords to represent the key ideas.

What is a keyword? Keywords are always:

A Single word: Listen for a single word that represents the issue or idea
High Energy: By energy, we mean a shift in emotional tone or emphasis
Important: These words are at the heart of what is most important
Repeated: They tend to get repeated several times in the conversation

How Dogs Hear: There is an old *Far Side* comic by Gary Larson in which the master says to his dog,

"OK Ginger, I told you to stay out of the garbage. Understand Ginger?"
All the dog hears is: "Blah - **Ginger** - blah - blah - blah - blah - **Ginger**."

How Q Model Leaders Hear: If you start to listen carefully for keywords, you will hear them everywhere. All communication will sound like this:

"Blah - blah - blah - **keyword** - blah - blah - blah - **challenge** - blah - blah."

This example is a little Q Model joke. You do have to listen to all of the other words. However, with practice you will start to filter for keywords, and the conversation will begin to sound like the above text.

How a Master Q Model Leader Listens:

"Blah - blah - blah - *Blah* - Blah - blah – blah - *Blah* - Blah - blah."

This third example is a little subtle. The point here is that it is easy to get lost in all the words, but with practice you begin to focus on the *emotion behind* the words. Paying attention to the sub-frequency *carrier tone* of emotion and emphasis is a subtle listening skill that allows you to sense the real issue and pull out the keyword that represents it.

Close the Loop: It is critical to confirm the keywords. You can formally say "What I heard was that X is important, correct?" or "X is important to you?" If they say "Yes," listen to the tone: if the yes is strong, the keyword is confirmed. This act of declaring "Yes," closes a tiny loop in the mind. In this conversational *transaction*, we agree that many ideas and emotions will get condensed into a single word. This also builds trust as this is the moment where the mirror neurons in both your brains actually synchronize.[6-4] You can also casually confirm the keywords, with a simple *Recap* and you will get the same result.

Recap Keywords: With a Recap, you simply pause and carefully say back a few keywords to your conversation partner, adding a little rising inflection to your voice to indicate a question. Sometimes they may say "Yes" and formally confirm it, and other times the conversation may just move on; as long as there is no objection, the keyword is established. Working with a team, one person may confirm the keyword on behalf of the team. This begins to build a group consensus, even if everyone has not formally agreed to each keyword.

Simple & Clear: This whole business of keywords may seem to be *too simple,* however establishing keywords can spark a tiny but fundamental transformation. Complex problems always come at people in an overwhelming and fragmented way. As you establish a set of keywords, the world begins to get *simple* and *clear* again, and this supports people to reclaim their inner resourcefulness for finding solutions.

Don't Word Switch: Many people have a habit of paraphrasing or switching keywords. Don't do this. What happens when you recap the exact keyword precisely? People sense that you *get them* and they begin to go deeper into the conversation. Conversely, a word switch is jolting. It is a sign that you are not listening.

> What is the difference between *joy* and *happiness*? Aren't they the same?
> The difference is that they said the word *joy*.
> If they say joy, you say joy back to them and they know you are listening.

- Complaint

Something is Wrong: Humans like to complain. Getting stuck in a "something is wrong" mode is easy. The basic formula for getting *stuck in life* is to make a long story in your head about how "something is wrong" and repeat it over and over again. This works with 100% efficiency. It is part of the human condition, and each of us is engaged in our *hero's journey* to break free from our own version of the "something is wrong" story that governs our lives.

Something is Wrong *with Them*: People like to gossip about other people. The real statement you make when you gossip about someone is, "Something is wrong with them and they are *fundamentally broken* and can *never improve*." Should you ever need to destroy trust in your team, gossip is the most efficient way to do it. Don't be evil — gossip creates a communication triangle where you ask your co-conspirator to agree that the individual you are gossiping about is a *bad* person. To *untangle* this bind, you must break the triangle and address the issue directly with the person you are complaining about.

The Narrow Path: As a powerful human, start by promising to yourself that you will only speak directly to the person you have a complaint with, and if you cannot do this you agree to drop the complaint altogether. Making this promise seems restrictive, but this will set you upon a narrow path that will bring more power to your words.

Interrupt the story: If the story keeps going or people seem to be stuck in a loop, you will have to interrupt. Knowing *when* to interrupt is a key skill. As a rule, let people complain for a few sentences before you interject. A great question here is, "May I interrupt you?" Ask this gently and people almost always say yes because at some level they know they are stuck and genuinely want a way out.

Give up Your Right: As a powerful human you must give up your right to complain unless you are committed to a solution. If you complain, *by default* you are promising to fix the problem. Try this and you will quickly stop complaining. Likewise, if you ask people if they are willing to find a solution or turn their complaint into a real project, they will probably stop complaining.

A complaint cannot survive in the presence of the question "What do you want?"

Interrupt Complaints: It is easy to get hooked into a looping story of complaint that will keep people and projects stuck in a low-performance, *problem state* mindset. Here is a tricky point: in a Q Model conversation, to get an understanding of the current state you must bring out the complaints. But let people complain too much and they will become *even more stuck.* The danger is that the more they complain, the stronger their story gets. At some point, you *must* interrupt the complaint by beginning to explore solutions, but first you must get the key issues out so that it can be seen. While they are complaining, listen very carefully for the challenge keywords, then confirm or recap them. A small but powerful shift will occur if they sense that you are listening to their challenge keywords. People complain *because* no one will listen to them, so demonstrating that you are listening is another way to break the cycle of complaint.

Keywords Transform: Humans can easily get stuck in a negative internal story that tends to become their perception of *the way things are*. This perceptual filter is how people get stuck. However, the moment you put a name to the main grievance of your story it transforms into a standalone thing. The act of naming it with a single word breaks the looping pattern of the story, externalizing it into a "real thing" and from there you can choose to deal with it or not.

Divide, Name, & Conquer: To deal with confusion and complexity you have to divide and conquer. You must break up the largest, most challenging issues into smaller parts. To begin working towards a solution, first name each critical part of the problem with a keyword, then use the keywords to ask questions and give each solution a keyword of its own. Whiteboarding is the process of getting the keywords out in front of you, where you can see them as a system. This process is fundamentally transformational.

Make the Complex Simple: Words represent ideas. When you confirm a keyword, you condense many ideas into a single word. Keywords are the ultimate tool for dealing with complexity. They allow people to see the issues they need to address more clearly. Later, when we use the Q Model tools to transform a keyword issue, everything associated with the keyword will come along for the ride. In practice, this kind of transformational *ripple effect* can move quickly through a project team.

Keywords Drive Speed. When you give something a name, you create a word that encapsulates all the discussions you have had about that subject. When one keyword represents many ideas it allows the conversation to move much faster, and this effect is amplified when you work with complex projects and large teams. Since conversations are a driving force in any team effort, keywords will also accelerate the speed of your breakthrough project.

Keywords accelerate conversational *speed.*

Harvest Keywords: To build trust and set the stage for the next level of the Q Model, you need to collect a set of keywords that encapsulates the main issue. Working with a CEO or executive team, I will often collect 20-30 keywords and try to boil all this down to a good benchmark of five main keyword issues.

Technical Keywords: Many people first think of keywords as emotionally rich words like *trust* or *success.* However, keywords can take any form and some of the best ones can be very technical. Everyone knows that engineers love *efficiency*, but fewer people know they also love *drainage.* The keyword approach is one of the reasons why the Q Model works so well for technical people, who tend to use specific and detailed language. You can earn the respect of your engineers and other technically-oriented team members by showing them that you are listening to their exact words.

186 Questions: When I was working with a group of engineers at Oxy in Oman, they kept repeating the number 186. I didn't really know what they were referring to, but I could tell from their tone that it was important. I started asking "186" questions.

How can we get 186?
How are we currently doing at achieving 186?
How do we test that we have achieved 186?
How can we improve our ability to maintain 186?
How can we develop a system to consistently achieve 186?

The engineers engaged in each question and began to develop a systematized solution. I later discovered that 186 degrees was the temperature required to keep the crude oil flowing efficiently through the pipes. My favorite part of this story is that after I asked all these questions they were convinced that I was an expert in oilfield optimization even though I explained several times that I was just asking good 186 questions.

- The Real Issue

The Challenge Loop: The real issue is often hidden. It usually takes some exploration to bring it out. The following is a simple loop, a two-step process for going deeper and bringing out the real issue:

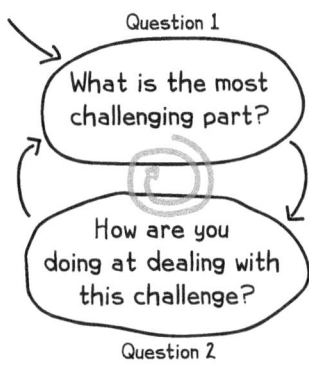

> Question 1: What is the most challenging part of this project?
> Question 2: How are you doing at dealing with that challenge?

With question one, you are breaking the problem into many parts to find the most challenging part.

With question two, you are trying to bring out the current state of how your team member *is* doing at solving the problem. You may have to go around this loop 3–4 times to dig into the real issue. This is a very good universal conversational skill to master, as unearthing the real issue is a key step in unlocking a breakthrough.

Question two often causes the main issue to branch into several subtopics. Ask "What is the most challenging part *of that?*" and you can take each subtopic back through the loop again. Often each subtopic will also branch into more issues and the whole process can seem a little overwhelming. Write each issue down and deal with them one-by-one. At some point, remember to go back to the initial project challenge and try to find the thing that is *most* challenging from *everything* you explored. This will lead you toward the root cause.

Root Cause: People often talk about issues in an abstract or dissociated way, as if the problem is external or *over there*. If you let people complain about an external issue that is beyond their control they will end up with a diminished sense of personal autonomy or power. Instead, we need to work toward identifying a root cause that is within their control. Notice that question two is "How are *you* doing at dealing with this?" Phrasing the question this way makes it personal. There is a hidden or implied question here:

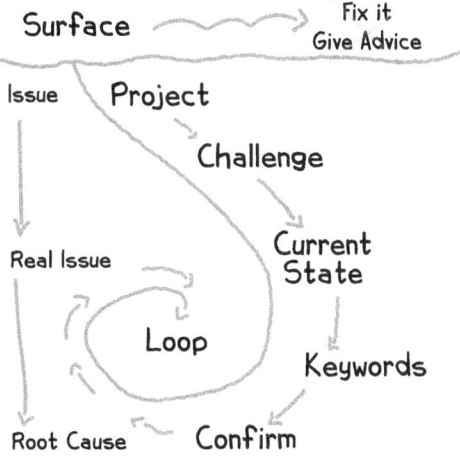

> What is your emotional "reaction" to the challenge?
> How well are you dealing with that emotional reaction?

Emotional Reaction: Humans are pretty resourceful when it comes to solving problems, but even the most effective people can become confused and overwhelmed by too much complexity. When you put people under enough stress, everyone loses their thinking resources.

People don't get stuck by problems.
They get stuck by their *emotional reaction* to the problem.

The real challenge is staying resourceful in the face of a challenge. But you cannot tell people to do this — they must arrive at this conclusion on their own to build inner strength needed to face it. At the same time, the ability to catch your emotional reaction to a challenge and shift it into solution-focused action is a step on the journey to building *your* inner strength in life.

In a team context, you could ask, "How well are we dealing with this challenge as a team?" This question encourages learning via self-reflection and self-assessment, and opens the door for potential growth. From here you could design a new developmental challenge, such as *becoming* a team that can deal with these kinds of challenges.

Climbing the Mountain: You can think of the Q Model triangle as a mountain. The bottom left of the mountain is the problem-focused current state. This corner is a state of low energy and low trust. The peak of the mountain is the desired state, which is a high-energy state of *vision*. How do we assist a person, project, or team to achieve this? We must support them to climb the mountain. But it takes a significant amount of energy to scale it, especially when you are in a low-trust state on the bottom-left corner. While it may feel like you are rolling a giant rock up the mountain as you try to make progress, set a firm contract with yourself and keep going, remaining focused on the essential elements of trust.

Trust is Multifaceted: This is a two-way street; you build trust with your team and they build trust with you. Everyone must work together to build trust for a project to succeed, but this happens in tiny steps and stages. As much as people need to see a solid plan, they also need to feel respected, and trust is something that is earned over time. However, you will never have 100% trust in your team. People need to be safe, so they will always keep an escape hatch in case they need to withdraw. The reactive system always reserves the right to take control of our body for survival. In a business setting, people can always retreat to "Just tell me what to do, Boss." Trust is slow to build and easily broken.

Question: I went through the trust model with my team, but my staff still don't seem to trust me. What should I do?

> **Answer:** Trust is tricky. Many managers pretend to be supportive in a fake way. It is probably better to be a nasty boss than a fake "nice" boss. With trust, you can say all the right things but if people don't authentically sense that you are supporting them in *their* success they won't ever open up. People won't automatically trust you after a single current-state conversation — trust is earned, and only by observing you over time can people determine if you are someone safe and genuinely supportive.
>
> There is an old story about a seagull and a clam. The seagull wants to eat the clam, so he pecks at the clam with his beak. The harder he pecks, the more the clam squeezes his shell tight. The seagull pecks, the clam squeezes. That's the end of the story. It is not a very good story.

Most managers act just like the seagull. They keep pecking and pecking, and as they do the trust they receive in return diminishes. As a manager, how will you gently support your team to engage and build trust?

Question: How do you work with someone who has just been laid off? Currently, I am working in the oil patch in Alberta and there are major layoffs. How do you use the Q Model when someone has just lost their job and has no money for Christmas for their kids? Is this something we can approach using the Q Model? And if so, what is the strategy? What are the pitfalls?

The Q Model is an ideal tool to deal with the rough patches in life. I have experienced my own dark periods outside of the business world, and I always come back to the three basic Q Model questions to get me out of them:

1 - Get present to the current state: How much money do you have in the bank? What are your job prospects? Don't add negative meaning to the past or future or you will build anxiety. Just be present to exactly where you are at right now The more you can be present to your current state, the more you will generate an ability to be OK with the bad news.

2 - Desired state: It takes courage to ask "So now, what do I want for my life?" and begin to rebuild a vision of future success. This question is often the beginning of a three to six-month journey, and it is useful and much more effective to have a conversational partner who can ask you these questions.

3 - Next Action: I had a marriage end and a company fail at the age of 30 and was naturally distressed. I kept adding negative meaning to my life story to the point where I would often freeze in moments where decisions needed to be made and action needed to be taken. At some point, I started to rebuild my life vision, but I still faced many challenges and would get stuck in negative emotions. "Stay in action" became my mantra. Making a small promise for the next action was my way to move past the negative story. Perhaps I might be nervous about making an outbound business development call, but I would say to myself, "stay in action" and then make the call. It was these tiny action steps toward my vision that made all the difference. in my confidence.

Summary of Chapter 8 – Current State ideas

Current State: You need to be clear and present to the current state before you can create a breakthrough.

Where are you? A map is useless if you don't know where you are on it. The current state is about finding out where you are at right now.

The Foundation of Trust: Ask simple and gentle questions to explore the current state of the project and trust will emerge naturally.

The Golden Rule of Trust: Trust comes from an open dialogue about the current state.

Don't Fix It: Many managers need to prove that they are good managers, so they jump into Mr. Fix-it mode. But this behavior short circuits the trust model. Don't try to fix the problem. Don't give advice or offer your solution. Just explore the current state.

Open Dialogue: The better the quality of open dialogue about the current state of a project, the more you build trust. You must authentically explore the challenges the team is facing.

Non-judgment: Explore the current state of the project without judgment, using the analytical or dissociated tone of a passive observer.

Find the Challenge: Bring out the main challenges and then try to isolate the most challenging area.

Face the Challenge: Somehow you must find the courage to turn and face the challenge.

Chapter 9 - Strategic Implementation

Key Strategic Implementation Questions:

What do we want?
How do we get there?
What is the plan to get there?
How do we achieve this result?
What is the strategy?
How do we align on the best strategy?
How do we break through the strategic challenges?
What are the critical elements of an ideal strategy?

- What is Strategy?

A business strategy is traditionally defined as a long-term plan of action designed to achieve a given set of company goals or objectives. The CEO, executives, and senior leaders set the strategy, and the middle managers execute the strategy. The key idea is that the strategy should *cascade* down the hierarchy of the organization, from middle management to the front-line staff. [9-1]

There is nothing inherently wrong with this model. In a stable, unchanging business environment this can work quite well. However, when confronted by accelerating competition and complexity, the cascade down system falls apart.

What is Your Strategy? Over the past 15 years, the Q Model has been tested with hundreds of companies and executive teams. We always start with the same set of questions:

What is your strategy?
How will you achieve this goal?
What is the overall goal of the company?
How are you doing at rolling out this strategy?
How is the strategic implementation coming along?
What are the challenges? What is slowing down the strategy?

Executive teams often cannot answer these questions in detail and instead they respond with a generic statement such as "Our goal is to achieve X result." But keep asking these questions and they rapidly reveal a layer of strategic confusion that lurks beneath the confident but simplistic responses you will receive; several executives have even fired us for asking them such difficult questions.

Too Much Strategy: The world is full of great ideas for improving your business results, and most companies are drowning in too much strategy. Whether you copy industry leaders, read the Harvard Business Review, or hire Mckinsey Consulting, you will end up with more strategy than you could ever possibly implement, so voluminous is the supply of great ideas in the world of business.

Strategic Competition: Ask any executive team, "Is everyone aligned with the strategy?" and the answer is always yes. To be perceived as a team player you must always appear to be aligned with the team. However, if you interview each executive individually and ask them their thoughts on the best way forward, you will discover that each one has their own version of a given strategy. Strategic competition often ends up in a zero-sum game where opposing internal forces cancel out all forward movement.

> "It's hard to get people to even agree on what
> *strategy* means." **- Robert Keidel, The Geometry of Strategy**

Strategic Silos: Another form of strategic competition takes place between company areas or departments, where people in one area of the company all agree on the best way forward and become hardened in their point of view. It all comes back to the basic idea of falling in love with *our strategy* or *my idea.*

The real challenge is to find that *one* strategy that everyone can agree on.

My Idea: By default, everyone thinks their "great idea" is the best. People get attached to their strategy, and this leads to a push and pull between conflicting points of view. But if there are competing strategies, the transformation process will get stuck. The real challenge is not coming up with a great idea, but getting the team to fully align on executing a single strategy. Achieving this is a critical first step in any breakthrough program, as unless the executive team can see a single clear path to success, they will not be able to engage fully. To get there, the team must pass through the cloud of strategic confusion.

- Strategic Confusion:

Dealing with Ambiguity: In 2009 we ran many Q Model programs for Aditi Technologies, a global technology outsourcing company with offices in Seattle, London, and Bangalore. Working with the entire leadership team, their sales channel, and most of their software architects to define the program goals, they identified the ability to deal with *ambiguity* as the one leadership trait that was most needed. As we delivered our programs the Aditi top brass rallied around this, understanding that only leaders who could deal with confusion and uncertainty in the accelerating world of technological change would reign supreme. After the Q Model project, the company maintained its aggressive growth rate and was later purchased by Microsoft in a series of acquisitions.

The Cloud of Strategic Confusion: Before a leadership team can align on the strategy, they must address the current state and work through all the options until they agree upon a systematized strategic model. Finding the strategic focus to rally around is the heart of the transformation process.

How do we break through the strategic confusion?
How do we align everyone around the best strategy?

People resist change, so never assume the new strategy will trickle down. Business as usual is comfortable. If the new strategy is competing against *comfort*, comfort will usually win because you are fighting against the comfort of *no change.*

It is Moving Slower than Expected: The idea that the new strategy will trickle down is fundamentally flawed. The problem is the low-performance model that is dominant in most companies. Here is an extreme scenario that contains a kernel of truth:

Say Yes: An executive tells a manager to execute a new strategy or project. He agrees but has no idea how to actually integrate the new strategy into all the other parts of the company. He might start to implement a change, but in thinking about the complex implications of changing all the necessary business processes, he rapidly hits a bunch of barriers and freezes.

Look Busy: The manager waits, hoping to come up with a solution as they remember to look busy with a flurry of other activity. While they are waiting, they look around and ask themselves, "Is anyone else implementing this new strategy?" Everyone else is also waiting, so the manager assumes it must be a fake strategic project.

Hide Problems: The executive asks for an update on progress a few weeks later. The manager replies, "We are working on that, but there are a few complex issues, so it's moving slower than expected."

Repeat: Later the executive comes up with a new, even better idea that displaces the old strategy. The manager knew this was going to happen all along. They relax and wait for the next impossible project. The cycle begins again.

Fake Projects: Every company has a set of *real* projects and a set of *fake* projects. No one seems to know how to tell them apart. How can you tell the difference?

Isn't every company project a real project? Real projects are the priority initiatives in which people are investing their energy and getting results. Fake projects are the initiatives where people seem busy but nothing is happening. While there's a secret code that managers use to indicate the priority projects, even the most crucial project can turn into a fake one if it stops moving forward. Indeed, all it takes is 30 days of no results to turn a real project into a fake project, and this insight highlights the harsh reality of project implementation.

This business of real projects and fake projects might seem like an unnecessarily harsh way to view the current state of project implementation in a company. However, take on this point of view and you will begin to see strategic implementation in a very different way: there is a freedom that comes with declaring that your project is a fake project, an honesty that facilitates open dialogue and creates the space to either abandon it or do what is needed to generate a breakthrough.

- Strategic Implementation:

What is Strategic Implementation? Coming up with *the brilliant idea* is not the point. The purpose of asking the Q Model questions is to engage your team to own the project entirely, which will give them the strength to fight through the implementation challenges.

Four Strategic Implementation Steps:

1 - Turn the strategy into a set of projects.
2 - Focus on the implementation of the strategy.

3 - Focus on the challenges. Do the hard part first.

4 - Track ongoing implementation. Address the barriers.

The Last Mile: Because we live in the city of *now* and we want to travel quickly into the city of the *successful future*, you can think of the company strategy as a ten-lane superhighway connecting these two cities. Most companies invest a lot of time and energy in building these strategic superhighways, but they forget to create the on and off-ramps that connect them to the local areas in each city. To build these last crucial miles of the strategic breakthrough superhighway, you need to address the strategy at each layer of the business. This requires designing real strategic integration projects for each part of the company.

- Layers of Business Strategy:

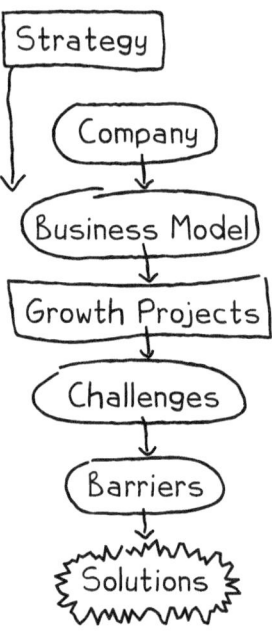

You can think of strategy like a layer cake. Most leaders think a lot about the top layer, which is the company strategy. But they don't think much about all the layers below, which include everything else required to implement the strategy within the company and in the external business landscape.

- How do we express the strategy at every business level?
- How do we integrate the strategy into each area?
- How do we translate the strategy into real projects and low-level actions?
- How do we implement this strategy with our customers, suppliers, and stakeholders?

Company Strategy: As mentioned, general company strategy lies at the top of the cake, and therefore often already exists. However, good strategic thinking can move up or down. There are often implementation barriers at the lower levels which may require a shift in high-level strategy. Implementation tracking needs to flow upward and downward. It is important to test the general plan to make sure it is still working and on track. We live in a world of continuous strategic transformation, so this work is never *done.*

Business Model: Is the current business model aligned with the strategy? Has the team assessed alternate business models that could accelerate the strategy?

Business Area Strategy: Next it is essential to assess how the big picture strategy is working in each area of the business. For each business unit or business area, the leaders need to get their hands on the planning process.

Project Strategy: Turning the big picture strategy into a series of projects is the next step. The first few that you select are the most critical, so choose your battles carefully. It takes a lot of team brain-power to work through all of the implementation challenges, so be sure to select the leaders, managers, and technical experts who will most ensure success. This is the basic idea of a Q Model breakthrough project.

External Strategy: How do you implement this strategy with your customers, suppliers, and stakeholders? How will it work out in the market, with products, or in marketing and sales? There may be challenges in the external implementation of the strategy that require additional breakthrough projects.

Dealing with the Challenge: A project will always hit a challenge and get stuck. Dealing with the challenge becomes the real project. If general business strategy is a layer cake, breakthrough projects are a Russian doll of overlapping goals and challenges nested within each successive layer. To get things moving and bring focus to your project, you need to uncover the right layer with the right people.

Problem Solving: While the Q Model focuses on solving specific problems, you must know how these problems link to the execution of the general company strategy. If you can't articulate the linkage, no one will allocate resources or make *solving the problem* a priority.

Upward Strategy: Breakthrough ideas and strategic thinking also need to move *upward* in a company. When breakthrough solutions to challenging technical issues emerge from the front line, executive leaders are often so focused on KPIs and "Just do it" that they cannot see or hear them. Another issue is that challenges emerging from front line leaders may require the top leaders to rethink the overall company strategy, which is another reason to ignore them.

Hands-on Solution Teams: Again, the people with their hands on these challenges are the best people to work on solving these issues. For example, if you are developing software and you discover a bug, it's obvious that the person working on that code is the best person to fix it. They are most up-to-speed with the details and have their hands-on the code. However, sometimes, when you are very close to the code, you can't see the error that is staring you in the face. You need someone who knows the code who can ask you some basic questions and walk you through examining the code line-by-line. When you do this the error will often jump out. This is the essence of Extreme Programming (XP), an Agile methodology for *paired* programming.

We can scale this idea up for large projects, but things are often not as simple as a single error in a line of code. When you are deep in complexity, it can be hard to see the forest through the trees. When we examine *why* a project is behind schedule, we often find there are layers of complexity nested together with multiple dependencies between teams. The complexity of these challenges is beyond the capability of a single logical mind. You need people on the team who can ask tough questions that challenge the frame of thinking. Solutions only emerge when you get the people who have their hands on the problem and bring them together in a multi-silo team and challenge them to ask the difficult questions.

The Real Project: A cluster of intertwined issues often blocks a project breakthrough or business transformation, so keep digging until you break through and unearth the root cause. The real project is dealing with whatever is blocking the success of the big project. Finding this root cause often involves taking on a detective role and asking a lot of questions. I often pretend to be the TV character Columbo, the disheveled detective who no one takes too seriously. He was famous for always saying "Just one more thing" and then asking his suspect the innocuous yet critical question.

Hunt for RED projects: Red projects are strategic initiatives that have somehow gotten stuck in implementation but are critical to the future success of the company. For example, in the Domob case from Chapter 1, everyone knew the company needed a breakthrough in Intelligent Marketing and automation of ad optimization. The leaders had launched many projects to produce this result, but each project would somehow get stuck. It wasn't until we carefully assembled all the best technical experts from around the company to focus on the challenge in a carefully orchestrated *breakthrough session* that we got any traction on this project. At the end of that team conversation the CTO famously stated:

> "We just made more progress on this in the last two hours than we did in the last two 2 years."

- Strategic Ownership:

Everyone Owns Strategy: In the Q Model, we define strategy in the broadest possible way because we want everyone to feel included in the development of the plan. Strategic thinking can scale from solving one problem to transforming the entire company's results, and this approach allows your entire team to engage physically with the project, taking ownership of the parts of the strategy that are within their reach.

Strategic Engagement: Unless your team can fully identify with the strategy and collectively engage in it, they will not have the requisite team strength to face the challenges of implementation and take personal ownership of it. Put simply, everyone must own the strategic implementation.

Asking versus Telling the Strategy: In traditional business, the leaders tell you the strategy. In the Q Model, the leaders ask you good questions to root out the strategy. Meanwhile, out in the real world there is always a mix of both methods. Even if the plan is handed down from above, many companies have a culture where challenging your superiors is accepted and encouraged and you can ask questions about implementation. But if you don't work in a company like this, you still have a choice in how to react. Start with a tiny group of trusted associates and work through the strategy by asking good questions.

One Enterprise Backlog: In an Agile context, you could say the ultimate way to *break* the cycle of strategic competition is to have a single prioritized backlog for the *entire* company. You might have dozens of teams working on breakthrough projects across an organization, and each of those projects would be represented in a single, company-wide backlog. A large group of leaders and stakeholders must then do the hard work of prioritizing all those projects.

Since nothing beats a physical representation of this prioritized backlog, a wall of index cards or Post-it notes is the classic approach. [9-2] However, today there are many software tools that allow all the sub-project team members to report progress details in real time; in 2003 I assisted a small US Navy team in utilizing an entire wall of Post-it notes to organize a massively complex dynamic repair schedule for nuclear submarines. When a sub came in for repairs, they would discover dozens of new problems, which would scramble all of their previous planning. They had tried every planning and scheduling approach they could find, but nothing could overcome the dynamic complexity. In the end, physically reshuffling all of the Post-it notes in real time was the only approach tool that worked.

- What is planning?

Ultimately all this discussion of strategy and priority comes back to this most basic question. If you observe the day-to-day actions of managers, you will notice that their behavior answers this question in one of three ways:

1 - Just do it: There is something you need to do so you just *do it* now. As a manager you tell your team it is *urgent*, meaning that they must drop everything and deal with the problem immediately. Everything is perfect until another *must do it now* thing comes along which displaces the first, and soon you have a logjam of urgent issues. This is not planning.

2 - How many shovels? Like digging a hole, there are projects in which the work is completely linear. For example, in mine production optimization, engineers literally calculate how many shovels or tons of ore they can move per hour. Some kinds of projects simply require a lot of *work* and a great deal of *time.* In the world of accelerating complexity, there are few projects that still fit this profile, but many managers still insist on thinking this way.

"Do you want good, fast, or cheap? Pick two."

3 - Theory of Constraints: This quote above summarizes the entire theory of constraints. The reality is that strategy is all about trade-offs. Here are some examples of project planning constraints, and some questions for testing the limits of project scope:

Time: Is the schedule set in stone? What actually happens if we miss the deadline?

Cost: What is the scope for contingency expenses or cost overruns? If the project *value* increases, can the *budget* increase as well?

Features: What is the minimum viable product? What are the *must have* core features? What is the priority level of each of the extra non-core features?

Quality: What level of errors, bugs, or problems which we will *only discover after we ship* is acceptable? How do we test for errors or bugs before we complete each element?

Talent: Who is on the team and what is our pool of talent? What parts could be outsourced? Where do we need specialty skills or unique high-level talent?

Notoriously Difficult: When you look at a project through the lens of constraint theory, you will see that there are many complex decision points and contradictory trade-offs. This is a bit like finding the shortest path in the *traveling salesman problem*,[4-1] which we have mentioned before. When you factor in all the constraints, the entire planning process can be almost impossible for a single person to work through, which is why we always come back to the *breakthrough project team* as the most effective unit of work.

How do you find the *Goldilocks Zone*, the place in the middle where trade-offs balance and the best workable solution emerges? *Open dialogue* is the way to work toward this point, ideally in a *whiteboarding* process that gets all the issues out on the table where they can be examined in detail. There are no easy answers when it comes to juggling constraints and finding the Goldilocks Zone, but you can get your team engaged and get closer to finding that *best possible* solution by asking your team good questions.

- Lean Startup Strategy:

What can Lean Startup bring to corporate strategy? In Q Model breakthrough projects, we have spent many years developing ways to get project teams to think like startup entrepreneurs. The Lean Startup mindset is introduced via questions you can ask throughout Q Model strategic conversations and planning sessions.

Lean Filter: You can view Lean Start Up as a strategic filter. Most companies have many layers of checks and balances that tend to slow things down. The mindset of large companies operates something like "We are the market leader so there is no rush," or "We need thorough research before allocating resources," or "Only well-planned projects get approved." However, when you run a project through the filter of Lean Start Up, these antiquated ways of thinking quickly go extinct.

VC Criteria: A great place to start is with the classic venture capital criteria used to select the one-in-five-hundred companies that get funding. I have personally used this approach with many early-stage companies that went on to attract large rounds of VC funding, but it gets more interesting when you apply this same criteria to a breakthrough in an enterprise-scale company. All of the following elements are also part of the VC funding criteria, and we have used them in large companies as part of the very serious internal funding game. You can read more about how we run the breakthrough project internal funding process at the end of Chapter 4.

Blue Ocean: We always start with the concept of a Blue Ocean, which is a market of high-growth potential with limited competition. Conversely, most companies operate within a Red Ocean mindset, where the market consists of lots of companies with very similar products fighting an endless marketing war. Getting everyone on the team engaged in the Blue Ocean strategic process is the key to breakthrough results.

What are some possible ideas for high-growth projects?
How can we develop a new offering that will have high growth and low competition?
How can we build a moat to protect our new product from competitors?

Scalable Model: Nothing scales like software, which has a digital replication cost of zero. However, even if you are firmly in the brick and mortar world there are always highly scalable growth models. Projects must be designed from the ground up for extreme growth. This is a mindset that must permeate product design and your overall business model. Extreme growth requires a little luck and a lot of planning.

How could we scale this project up?
What would it look like with 10x results?
How could we use other business models to scale this up?
How can we develop breakthroughs in production or distribution?
How could we develop an industry platform where everything goes through us?

New and Unique: One more blockchain start-up will not attract investment. Breakthrough projects must be hot and fresh and lead the industry somewhere new. Rather than playing catch-up copying everyone else, your team must anticipate where the industry will be in 2–3 years and build a product that will lead the industry to that place. You may get this wrong, and this is why companies have a portfolio of many projects.

What could be a completely fresh way to approach this product?
Where will our industry be in two years? In five years?
What are some silly or crazy ideas that we have never discussed?
How can we develop the next insanely great idea?
How can we transform our entire industry?

First Mover: Companies need to show they have the potential to achieve a first-mover advantage in their industry. This is a big push back against the slow and incremental product development mindset that dominates most large companies. It is important to note that when a big company achieves first-mover traction, their market momentum and access to capital can give them a big advantage. It is not just about getting there first, but also about using your resources to dominate the new market segment. For example, Apple often offers products that are late in arriving on the market, but they are always well-integrated and have the best quality.

How can we launch the first product in this space?
How can we quickly build market momentum?
How could we use networks or partners to accelerate adoption?
How can we use our strengths to own the product space?

Lean: The mindset for rapid testing of minimum viable products is critical for speed. Companies must test many innovative products to find the one that attracts growth. Small teams can often move much faster than a large company division, so it is important to scale your development down to something that could be built by 5–10 people in three months.

How can we develop this with minimal resources?
How could we make this work with a very small team?
How can we bootstrap our development process?
How can we test launch this without a big marketing budget?

MVP: This concept of a Minimal Viable Product (MVP) is a central tenet of Lean

Startup. Instead of trying to guess or conduct heavy research to determine what the market wants, you simply build a quick version and throw it out there to see how the market reacts. Rather than fall in love with your great idea, you build many lite products and see which one will fly.

How can we develop a lite version to test this out?
What are the absolute minimum set of features needed to validate whether this works?
How can we quickly test this with real customers or industry partners?
How can we test several alternate versions of this?
How will we measure the results of a quick test program?

Speed: Accelerating the speed of results is the key to success in the world of ever increasing competition. Go back to Chapter 9 and review the segment on accelerating strategic implementation.

How can we streamline our development process?
How can we get this out quicker?
How can we quickly greenlight the approval process?
How can we deal with the barriers that might slow us down?
How can we get an executive champion on board?

Traction: In the Lean world, you cannot dominate the market with brute force, so projects must show real user adoption or industry validation. Focusing breakthrough teams on the key steps to achieve early-stage traction with limited resources is the essence of a Lean Start Up strategy. As you run your breakthrough project development process through many team whiteboarding sessions, you will naturally circle back through many of the above questions. While building a breakthrough project is important, developing a team that naturally thinks from a Lean mindset is even more valuable.

Chapter 10 - Open Questions

Key Open-Ended Questions:

Can we explore some *possible* solutions?
I am curious, what are *some ways* to solve this?
What are some ways to *begin* to...?
What are some *better* approaches to get there?
What is the *best* way to solve this?
What would an *ideal system* look like?
What are the main elements of the strategy?
How can we turn this solution into a *model* or *process*?

Great Questions: When someone asks you a great question, it takes you on a journey. You explore new ideas and consider new points of view, to the point where you might have a completely fresh perspective on a subject when you return from your exploration.[10-1]

Questions Focus Attention: Simply asking someone if they are going to purchase a new car within six months increases their purchase rates by 35%.[10-2] Asking citizens whether they are going to vote in an upcoming election increases the likelihood that they will vote by 25%.[10-3]

Open the Thinking Process: While the process of asking Q Model questions can yield great ideas and potential solutions, the real value is in how it requires you to consider alternative approaches and challenge your prior assumptions.

Flipped Leadership: You can think of the Q Model as a flipped leadership system. In the traditional leadership model, the people at the top set the strategy and the people below follow the directives and deliver the strategy. The Q Model flips this hierarchy around, making it the job of the leader to ask great questions that bring out an ideal strategy. Flipped leadership is also an open model, empowering anyone in the system to ask questions that might potentially improve the overall strategy of the project.

Smart = Fail: Smart people often fail because they don't ask questions. Having a smart brain or a lot of information in your head can be a curse. Intelligent people tend to get stuck in many right/wrong, "best idea," or "my idea" traps, chasing one solution and trying to prove that it is the best or "right" solution until they inevitably get stuck. As Rule 23 states, never say the phrase "my idea" again for the rest of your life. You can't own ideas, and you probably weren't the first person to have that "great idea" anyway. Instead, give ownership of all your ideas to your team.

A Great Company is Built on a Great Question: Every company transformation begins with a single great question. Of course, you may have to work through a hundred questions to find the one that transforms the company but it is worth the effort. Keep going. Think of Google, a company that was founded on the question "How can we organize all information on earth?" This kind of question can sustain the momentum of company growth for years or even decades.

Wisdom of Crowds: The work of James Surowiecki affirmed that having an outsider come in and ask a bunch of stupid questions is faster than getting an expert to build a strategy.[10-4] He also demonstrated that the team intelligence of five average people would almost always outperform one top expert. However, he pointed out that all this would only work within the right context and environment. The qTeam system outlined in Chapter 14 is one approach for developing these kinds of environments, where team intelligence can emerge. But like the Q Model itself, the qTeam system first rests on a foundation of asking good questions, so let's continue to master the art of asking them.

- Ask versus Tell

The first challenge is to remember to ask questions. If you recall from Chapter 3, most business leaders have been trained to "tell" through years of traditional education and on the job demands. When we say "tell" we are referring to a directive style of leadership. When presented with an issue, the default response is to "fix it" immediately, whereby you give your idea or solution without asking any questions.

There is nothing inherently wrong with an automatic tell response or a directive style of leadership. Indeed, there are many instances where telling people your solution is the best approach. At the beginning of an employee development cycle, there naturally tends to be more teaching and directing because your team members need to understand the rules and systems that are already in place in a functioning company.

The Challenge is Complexity: Because we live in a world of accelerating complexity, the idea that one almighty leader has all the right answers simply doesn't work anymore. To deal with complexity, you may need to engage with the subject matter experts who have first-hand knowledge and direct experience with a particular issue. Many complex problems have dependencies that cannot be resolved by one person, so you will need to address these problems in a broader context of interrelated issues. For this, you need a team of people to collaborate and engage in multi-silo team thinking.

Tell is a Slippery Slope: The more you tell, the more those being told will ask for your advice. As a manager or leader, you step into your role and you naturally form your self-identity around the expectations of the job function. You wish to be seen as talented, competent, strong, smart, or some other value word that best applies to your need for external recognition. The structure of the leadership role plays into this system: people want to work for a confident leader because they need security, so you play into this role. Over time, your *tell response* gets stronger and stronger until it becomes the dominating characteristic of the role you play for your team.

Conduct a Tell *Audit* on Yourself: These ideas are not new. There have been many articles and books extolling the virtues of leaders who listen and ask good questions; you can go as far back as Socrates searching for a founder of the Ask leadership approach. We all know that we are *supposed* to ask more questions, but we rarely do it. It takes a long-term commitment to shift a habit, and first we must be aware of our bad ones and their consequences before we can make a concerted effort to shift our behavior.

Tell Repel - Ask Open: The boss "tells" someone what to do, rather than asking them what to do, and this approach assumes an employee doesn't know what to do or how to find the answer. Worse, it never taps the employee's talent and experience, and worst of all the employee takes on very little responsibility or accountability. A directive leadership style does not allow the employee to take ownership of the solution.

More Ask versus Tell:

Tell tends to:

- Control the conversation and shut down the flow of ideas
- Trigger a withdrawal from engagement

Ask tends to:

- Open people up and generate creativity
- Stimulate learning and deepen understanding
- Support people to develop solutions on their own
- Deepen engagement and create a buy-in

To support your team to step into a high-alignment state:

- Ask them how they might solve this problem
- Invite them to commit and take accountability
- Allow them to tap into their own approach or solution

Challenge 1: The first challenge is to remember to switch to ask mode.
Challenge 2: The second challenge is to get very good at asking questions. Asking effective questions is a skill that develops over time with ongoing practice.

Paul Gossen - Fall in Love with Questions: As a teenager, I spent years studying transformational technologies. By the age of 21, I had spent well over 10,000 hours as a student of this discipline. However, when faced with the task of running a high-growth company, I fell into the same trap of telling that plagues even the most seasoned of business leaders for their entire careers.

My second company was a technology consulting firm and throughout the 1990s we would approach businesses and help them develop a complete digital transformation program. Our success depended on providing the best solutions, and as waves of tech disruption hit many different industries, we established a broad knowledge base of the best solutions and leveraged this for our customers. Stepping into the role of the smart technology "whiz-kid" of this company, over time, my self-image as a leader with all the answers reached Herculean levels. I prided myself for apparently knowing all the answers, but at a deeper level, I knew I was faking it.

It was very stressful to be in this role. No human can have all the answers, and there is always a younger generation that is even more integrated with the technology who can inherently "get it" faster than someone only a few years older. I ended up feeling like an actor performing a scripted role. At some level, I knew I didn't have all the answers.

I stumbled upon coaching in 1998 and fell in love with the idea that you can have a question-driven relationship with your team and customers. In recognizing the power of questions, I realized that I didn't need to have all the answers anymore, and this realization lifted a great weight off my shoulders. But breaking free from my old habits was still difficult for me in the beginning, mainly because I did not have the wonderful Q Model tools of today. Although it took me two years to effectively shift my thinking and habits from telling to asking, over the past 15 years I have seen hundreds of managers do this in under 90 days.

- Powerful Questions

We will now dive into the world of asking powerful open-ended questions that liberate your team to relax, listen to themselves, and get a clearer picture of the resources and potential solutions at their disposal.

- Open-ended questions are questions that cannot be answered with a yes or no.
- Using open-ended questions invites a person to respond freely.
- Closed questions are limited to a yes or no response, which tends to shut down the conversation.
- Open-ended questions disentangle your team from either/or thinking, which often leads to looping complaints or negative judgments.

Hyper-Simplistic: Sorry to send you back to kindergarten with this mind-numbingly simplistic question building process, but many people go on autopilot when they form questions. By deconstructing the question building process into basic building blocks, you can interrupt your existing question building habits and start from a clean slate.

Question Matrix: You can think of this matrix as a question construction kit. Simply pick one word from each column and you will quickly get the idea of how to build these questions. With a little practice, you will find yourself developing customized questions that will naturally pop out of your mouth at the exact moment they need to be asked.

Preface	Modifier	Keyword
What are some ways to	improve	Market share
How could we	increase	Data quality
What is a fresh way to	expand	User growth
What haven't we done to	optimize	Pipeline flow rates

This process runs on keywords. Keep gathering keywords so you can turn them into open questions. For most questions, you will have to add some customized keywords. For example, "What are some ways to improve *market share*?" could become "What are some ways to improve *data quality*?" As you move through the conversation, collect keywords and use them to form the next question:

Q: What is the most challenging part of your project?
A: Data optimization.
Q: OK, so how is the *data optimization* coming along?

It may seem obvious that in moving from a one-on-one conversation to a team conversation, "What do *you* want?" would become "What do *we* want?" As you move forward, you can apply this approach to the open-ended question scale below.

- Open-Ended Scale:

The 10 Levels of Open Questions: First developed by Marilyn Atkinson in 2002,[10-5] the open-ended question scale is a system for asking great questions that has been fine-tuned and simplified many times in the years since its creation.

Imagine a scale from one to ten where one is a basic open-ended question and ten is the most powerful open-ended question possible. As you move from one to ten, you can create and test different kinds of questions to see what works. You can also combine the groups of qDrive questions with the question modifiers below, mixing and matching the latter with the relevant keywords to form the best questions. Each level has its own unique character, and a conversation will comfortably flow as you scale up the levels.

Level	Modifiers	Example
Soft		
1	**Open-ended**	How/What/Why... could you... (solve problem X)?
2	**Curious**	I'm Curious...? Explore: Can we *explore*...?
3	**Softeners**	How could you *begin* to...? Small, begin, start, first steps
4	**Plurals**	What are some of the solutions...? Many ways, multiple solutions, brainstorm
Develop:		
5	**Ideas**	What are some other ideas...? solutions, silly ideas, approaches, fresh thinking
6	**Better**	What are some *better* ways we could...? more, increase, improve, optimize, efficient How could you *develop* a way to...? increase, expand, advance
7	**Best**	What are some of the *best* solutions...? best, most, ideal
Model:		
8	**System**	How could you build a system to...?
9	**Process**	How can we develop a process?
10	**Model**	How can we model this solution?

Test drive the open-ended scale: Find two people and come up with a real break-through project where one person asks the questions and the other person is the project owner.

Question Asker: Use the template above to ask questions about the project. Start at level one and work down, rearranging the questions using the project owner's keywords and the relevant project challenges. You can customize each question based on the answer the project owner gives. Try out lots of questions and see which ones have the most impact.

Project Owner: Give short answers so you can test the impact of as many questions as possible. Note in your mind the questions with the most impact so you can debrief them later.

Let's go through each level in more detail:

Level 1 - Open: This is the very idea of asking any open-ended question. If you catch yourself asking a closed-ended question, stop and rephrase your question as an open-ended one, making a habit of starting your sentences with *How, What,* or *Why.* Be sure to pause and give yourself a moment to form the question before you ask it.

Level 2 – Soft: The two classic softeners are *curious* and *explore.* When people are busy and under stress, they tend to react negatively to unusual stimuli, which includes any unexpected questions. Bosses often use questions to trick direct reports into accepting a new project or an increase in workload, so more often than not they are perceived as an attack, which automatically raises defenses. Simply adding "I am curious…" to the front of a question signals that you are safe and friendly and only wish to explore an issue. "Can we explore X?" is a closed-ended contract question that often has a similar result.

I am curious…   Can we explore…

A Curious Voice Tone: When you start a question with "I am curious…?" you are asking the listener's reactive system to lower its defensives. This is a big request, and your listener may not comply unless they sense that you are sincerely curious. This can be achieved by using a light and playful tone that authentically engages your listener.

Light and Playful: People often ask me why I am so effective at engaging CEOs and executives in company transformation projects, and my answer is that it's not so much *what* you ask, but *how* you ask it. I might ask a huge question like, "How can we begin to scale up revenue by ten times?" But I ask it with a playful voice tone that permits the listener to loosen up and explore while simultaneously understanding that I am still asking a serious business question. This is a skill I have seen hundreds of people master, but it takes a little courage to be playful in the face of a big challenge.

Level 3 – Small: If you ask a big question like "How can the human race solve global warming?" most people will freeze. Unless they are a climate change expert, they will not be mentally prepared to answer such a big question. A better warm-up question would be "What are some tiny steps that you could take to reduce your carbon footprint?" Small questions are questions that address only a tiny part of the solution, which is within your immediate sphere of influence and thus easier to approach. The number one reason that MBA leaders and top consultants fail is that they are trained only to ask big questions. Big questions only work if your team is ready for them, so start small and work up to them in stages.

How can we begin?
What are some tiny first steps?
What is the very first action?

Level 4 – Plurals: The human mind is powerful. If you ask for a single solution, you will get *one* answer. If you ask for many solutions, you will get *many* answers. Many business leaders are looking for a single solution, so they stop when they find it. If you search for multiple solutions, you can dramatically broaden the scope of thinking in your team. Keep looking for more solutions, ideas, or fresh approaches — you can always have a little brainstorm with your team member in the middle of a conversation and come up with many possible solutions. This approach dramatically expands thinking.

What are some solutions?
What are some other approaches for solving this?

Soft Questions Warm up the Brain: Levels 1 to 4 are a warm-up section of the conversation. The point here is not to chase the big solution yet, but to ease the team into Q Model thinking in small steps.

You can merge levels 1 to 4 into a single question opener:

I am *curious*, what are *some ways* to *begin*… (to make this work?)
I am *curious*, what are *some ways* we could *begin* to… (solve this?)

This question opener is one of the most useful question-asking tools you will *ever* use. If you don't know what to do, *do this* — tattoo it on your arm so you will never forget it. I have worked with more than 5000 people, and consistently hear that this is the most effective tool in the entire Q Model.

3x: Many leaders become discouraged at this stage because they ask a question and the response is a vacant stare. It is critical to know that most people will only start to process a question after hearing it at least three times. When asking questions, we are always working with the intuitive system, the part of your mind that *pops* an idea or thought into your short-term working attention.

You won't get much of a response from your team member if their intuitive system is running cold, so repeat your question a couple of times to warm it up. Of course, if you ask the same question three times in a row you may look a little stupid. The key is to phrase the question a different way so that it seems fresh. This will fire up your team member's intuitive system and allow them to process the question from a different angle.

Remember: Questions only work once you ask them three times.

Develop: Levels 5–6–7 are about expanding the range of ideas in the conversation and then narrowing its focus.

Level 5 – Ideas: New ideas tend to trigger more ideas. At this point, the conversation may achieve *lift-off* or you may hit a conversational *dead zone*, where you seem to run out of ideas. In either case, you need to track the flow of the conversation and the overall level of momentum, so try to expand the discussion when your team member seems ready. You want lots of ideas at this stage, and the Level 5 questions below will trigger the fresh thinking that generates those ideas. Always go for *quantity* instead of *quality* at this level.

What are some other ideas? What are some new solutions?
What are some silly ideas or fresh approaches?
What are some different ways to solve this?

Level 6 – Better: Level 6 questions offer a range of questions that refine the ideas you have come up with so far, making them *even better* and introducing potential solutions. If you are talking with an engineer, "How can we increase efficiency?" might be an ideal Level 6 question.

What are some of the *better* ways we could produce X result?
How can we improve this? How can we make this more effective?
How can we (improve, increase, develop, optimize, expand, advance) this solution?

Level 7 – Best: With levels 1-6 we have been seeking to warm up the conversation, getting more ideas and expanding our thinking. These levels are about making the conversation *wider*. With Level 7, we are beginning to *narrow* the discussion: when you ask for the *best* solution, you are sifting through the ideas you have generated, *filtering out* any ideas that are not the best. Don't begin this shift until your team has built up their brainstorming momentum, even if you have to re-contract and ask for more time. Shifting to best/most/ideal questions will naturally start to shut down the momentum and narrow the conversation so that it becomes more serious. Senior executives tend to get more focused at this point, as they sense the process is moving towards a tangible strategy or realistic solution.

What are some of the best ideas?
What are some of the most effective solutions?
What would an ideal system look like?

System: With Levels 8–9–10 you are *refining* the best solution into a complete system. These three levels offer the most direct paths toward a well-established *vision*, which is the top of the Q Model triangle. You do this by asking *system-level* questions and displaying the results visually as an interlinked map. System thinking integrates broadly with *visioning* and *whiteboarding*, two tools we will cover in greater detail in Chapters 12 and 13.

Level 8 – System: To design a system you need to be able to visualize all the *parts* working together as a *whole*. Thus when you ask people to develop their best ideas into a system, you are automatically energizing their visual-spatial thinking system. Scientists, engineers, and technical people often have years of experience in this, so they will enjoy and gravitate naturally towards systematic thinking. A great approach is to create a flowchart that explores how you can turn your key idea into a system.

How would this work?
How could we begin to turn this into a system?
What would the system look like?
What would this look like as a flowchart?

Level 9 – Process: From VW to SAP, all great German companies are process-driven. Employees may complain about the lack of flexibility, but a well-designed process is an ideal way to scale up business results. The number one reason most managers cannot turn a *goal* into a *result* is the lack of a *process map*. However, there is a big difference between following an *existing* process and developing a *new* process; well-tested business processes are easy to follow but hard to make. It takes a very different set of thinking skills to develop an effective process.

While getting team members to engage in the development of a process marks a pivotal transition in the implementation stage of a breakthrough project, simply asking "How can we turn this solution into a business process?" may not be enough — just like Lean or Agile, it takes time to internalize the process mindset. Start by asking many questions to *develop* the process and then *implement* and *test* the process to see if it works. Then keep *refining* and optimizing the process over time, until it becomes a *proven* process. Here are the six levels of process development:

Explore:	Ask questions about a *possible* process
Develop:	Build a functional process
Implement:	Use the process in the business
Test:	Track to see how the process is working
Refine:	Improve the process in a series of iterative cycles
Proven:	Demonstrate long term effectiveness, establish it as a protocol

Level 10 – Model: What is a model? When we say model, people often hear "business model." However, any set of ideas can fit into a model, which is a simplified representation of any complex system. A well-developed model is an ideal tool for navigating through challenging problems or decisions. For example, the Q Model reduces all the complexities of business transformation into three ideas: trust, vision, and action. These can be represented visually as a triangle, a shape that is easy to remember and understand.

How can we turn this solution into a model?
How can we improve this model?

Holistic Thinking: A team must think visually when they begin the process of modeling a project or business. Done right, a complete breakthrough model creates a holistic understanding of the entire process, an expanded view that allows everyone on the team to get a complete picture of how the project creates value and why it is meaningful. It also fully commits your team to the project, transforming them into equal owners who are just as invested in success as their superiors.

Once a model is firmly established and owned by the team, they can organize other details into its structure. They can use the model to make many small decisions or resolve *open-loop* issues independently. A well-developed model allows a team to become more self-directed, which increases their speed.

4 Question Types: While our main focus is on positive open-ended questions, there are three other kinds of questions:

Open - Positive:	How can we succeed?
Closed - Positive:	Will we succeed?
Open - Negative:	How can we fail?
Closed - Negative:	Will we fail?

Delay Closed Questions: Asking closed questions early in the process tends to shut down the conversation and the flow of ideas. In general, engineers, scientists, and technology people tend to ask closed questions and challenge ideas perceived as unrealistic. You must negotiate with these skeptics in advance, getting them to agree early on to avoid closed and negative questions. This agreement allows the team to explore and develop their ideas to the point where they can survive harsh external evaluation and criticism. In general, never explore failure at the beginning of a conversation.

0	**Closed**	Can you solve X?
-10	**Negative Closed**	Will you fail at X
-100	**Negative Open**	How could you <u>fail</u> at X?

When to Close: Of course, there is a place for closed questions in the Q Model. But delay asking them until *after* a team forms a strong vision of the desired state and a realistic plan to get there. Once a team has developed their breakthrough plan to this point, closed questions and even negative questions can make the project more tangible, bring awareness to potential challenges, and strengthen team commitment. However, this generally comes much later in the Q Model process, *after* vision and value are well established, and *just before* it is time to commit to action steps.

Q History: Milton Erickson developed the idea of *as-if* questions in the 1950s, asking individuals to *presuppose* or *act* as-if their desired state were achieved. Scaling this up to the level of the group is one of the best ways to develop an unstoppable team.

"Pretend anything, and you can master it." **- Milton Erickson**

Brainstorm the Questions: This approach is outstanding if you are working with a team that is under stress or experiencing conflict. Rather than brainstorm *solutions*, brainstorm the *questions*. Set a firm rule for a timed segment where everyone agrees not to answer any questions but instead brainstorms the *best questions* to ask. Some people call this question generation process *frame-storming* or *question-storming*.[10-6]

Teams often chase content. By searching for the best answer or an ideal solution, they go down rabbit holes and get stuck. Setting a firm rule to forgo solutions and only ask questions allows them to shift to a pure process approach. And by brainstorming the questions, teams naturally challenge their own *groupthink* mindset.

This approach is transformational because it bypasses the habitual conflict of *my idea* versus *your idea*. You end up with a single team working together to find the best questions to ask rather than the best answers, and this is far less contentious.

Chapter 11 - Alignment

Key Alignment Questions:

What do we want?
How do we measure that result?
Is this even possible?
What is within our control?
How do we get there?
What is the plan?

- Oman Airport

Only the King can solve this problem: We are powerless to fix it. This flawed software will mess up the airport for months.

It was 2011 and we were working with the management team of a $1.5 billion project to construct a new international airport in Muscat, Oman that could compete with Dubai for hub traffic. This was a flagship national project, and we were working with a core team of 60 managers, engineers, and project leaders. One group of mid-level engineers were managing the software that controlled the fully automated baggage handling system. An analysis of the current state revealed a cascade of issues, starting with a flawed purchasing process and poor quality software. This was compounded by a shoddy testing process that hid problems until it was too late. With so many potential issues to tackle first, we started asking Q Model questions to identify the root cause of the problems.

Could the Software be Fixed? The engineers had already explored this for months, and all agreed that it was beyond repair. Worse, the cost of replacement was estimated at $20 million USD. They had been alerting their superiors of this issue for weeks, but no one seemed interested in doing anything about it. In a culture where admitting a mistake would mean losing face, no high-level leader wanted to be associated with bringing up a $20 million dollar mistake. Engineers were coming apart at the seams in their frustration, and the problem was at a complete impasse.

Keep Going: when everything seems stuck, *keep going*. Keep exploring the issues and challenging the frame of reference. Keep playing dumb and asking very basic questions, including this series of role and control questions: What is your role? What is within your control? Who do you report to? What is their interest in resolving this issue? Who do they report to?

This group of engineers was accountable for the software, but they had no authority in the decision-making process. They didn't actually know who they reported to; there were five companies jointly overseeing the airport construction project, and there was a well-established pattern of finger-pointing to avoid blame.

Who is the boss? We explored the question, "Who is ultimately accountable for the airport?" The final answer was the *King of Oman*. Only he had the actual authority to intercede on this issue directly. But none of the engineers could ever imagine asking the King to step in.

Authority is overrated: Influence is much more flexible than authority. We started to explore ways the engineers could influence the key players in the five companies, and we asked many questions about those key players' interests in finding a solution. We also asked the engineers, "What is the cost of delaying the decision to buy new software?" This cost was difficult to calculate because it required estimating the impact of the delay on the entire project. The consensus of the engineers was that this was the most significant risk factor in the whole project since it could delay the airport from opening on time.

$1m per day: This issue of project risk triggered the next question: "What is the cost of a delay in the airport opening?" This cost was easy to calculate, and they ended up with a figure of $1 million per day. Suddenly the answer to saving the entire project became clear: Spend $20 million to prevent a potential cost overrun of $1 million per day. The longer we wait to do this, the more the risk of delay increases. If there is a delay, each day we avoid making the decision would increase the project cost by $1 million.

Armed with these questions, the engineers discovered they had tremendous influence. They set up meetings with each of the five parties and asked the very same questions, letting the leaders arrive at the cost overrun number of $1 million per day on their own. Each of the five parties quickly aligned on the importance of an immediate solution. No high-level leader wanted to be associated with such an outrageous cost, and each of the five companies competed to be the first one to resolve the issue.

- The High-Alignment State

As the team goes through the conversational process, they make many tiny team agreements until naturally, they begin to align around key ideas and solutions. When they translate this conversation into an implementation plan, they operate from a common vision and frame of agreement. As project teams reach a momentum phase, this quality of team alignment can quickly transmit through an organization.

The Top of the Q Mountain: These three elements are required to create a high-alignment state in a team:

    1 – **Strategy**: We are clear on what we want and we have a plan to get there.
    2 – **Vision**: We can see success. It seems realistic that we can achieve this.
    3 – **Value**: We know why this is important. We have a strong link to the value.

We refer to these three elements as the top of the Q mountain. Unless these three areas have been vigorously explored, most people, teams, and projects will not be able to build a strong vision of success and function in a high-alignment state. Because it takes a great deal of focus and energy to make it through the cloud of confusion that comes with generating complex business results, you may need to loop around the mountain three or four times. But *keep going* and the team will inevitably plant their flag on the summit.

Team alignment is one of the most challenging issues in any organization. One of the most powerful results of the Q Model process is the increase in alignment that occurs in teams using the Q Model.

Go back to the Bottom: Why do some people and teams never acquire a strong vision of success? This is because the *level of trust* is insufficient compared to the *scale of the challenge*. Strategy, vision, and value cannot be formed without first building a foundation of trust. A lack of vision means you have to go back to the bottom of the mountain and work on trust, addressing the current state challenges, warming up the team, and asking good open-ended questions. You may need to bring a lot of patience and structure to this process; at the enterprise-scale, it often takes two to three months to get a team of executives to answer the big question "What do we want?"

- What do we want?

"What do we want?" is one of those questions that seems simple but is difficult to answer in practice. Ask yourself this and reflexively you might answer "I want more money," or "I want my project to succeed."

> OK, so you want more money: Why do you want more money? What are you going to do with that money? What will that money bring to your life?

> OK, so you want your project to succeed: Why do you want your project to succeed? Why is project success important to you? What will that success bring to your career? Team? Company?

In both these examples, we are asking follow-up questions that dig deeper into what we think we want. If you wish to achieve a challenging goal, you need to delve into the motivation behind that goal and understand it. Long before the Law of *Attraction* became popular, the Law of *Attention*[11-1] a much more scientific concept stated: "Whatever we pay attention to gets stronger." Here is the Law of Attention applied to motivation:

> The more you *explore* motivation, the *stronger* motivation gets.

This motivation will give you the inner strength to deal with all the problems and challenges that will come up when you get into the messy process of implementation. Figuring out what a project team wants always links to a *state of being*. We think we want "things" but what we really want is to "become someone" who can achieve those things. This quality of *being* or *becoming* is the true source of inner motivation and the engine that powers the Q Model.

From Task to Result: By default, most people put things into a "to-do list" context in their mind, where everything becomes more work. This is called *task thinking*, and it can easily trap you in a low-performance state. By contrast, *result thinking* has you looking at the goal first and thinking backwards through the implementation process. This way the achievement of the result becomes the source of motivation, and the task itself becomes a small step in achieving that goal. The difference may seem trivial, but it has a significant impact on performance. Executive coaches and mil-

itary planners will tell you to start with "the end in mind" or a "defined end-state," but in reality, the culture of task-thinking pervade most companies. Remember, elite athletes can improve their performance by 30% by visualizing the result.[2-1]

Strategy is not Enough: Before we fully address the strategy-oriented question "What do we want?" we need to examine vision and value, the other two elements that define the top of the Q Mountain. As you practice and work with your team, you can use their initial answer to the question of "What do we want?" to build a *clear outcome*. This will strengthen their goal, and get them thinking about and taking vision and value into account as they explore their motivation.

Clear Outcome: To be focused and aligned, people need to have a clear outcome or goal. As you proceed, you can test this outcome to see how precise it is. The goal of a project will always have a range of states that can move between fuzzy and clear:

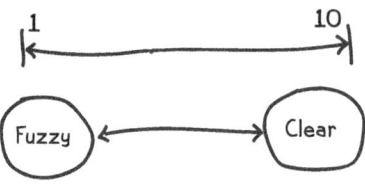

This range is a natural part of any project cycle. At the very beginning of a project, there is confusion, but as you build a plan things become clear. Still, when the project hits a challenge you may lose sight of the goal and things will get confusing again. For example:

At the beginning of a project, the goal is unclear
We make a plan and detailed outcomes become clear
We start to implement and hit some challenges
We face competing priorities and unexpected complexities
The project goes back into a fuzzy state of confusion

3 Elements Required for a Clear Outcome: To deal with this confusion and fuzziness, we offer three main tools. These will dig into the desired state and provide clarity.

1 – Positive:

Stated in the Positive: You need to be able to say what you want to achieve using positive language. When people encounter problems they get stressed and can't help talking and complaining about it because they can't see a solution. This response is a natural symptom of dealing with the challenges in the current state. However, it is easy for people and teams to get stuck in a problem-focused mindset, and at some point, you must *interrupt* the complaint and ask them what they want. Typically you will have to do this many times, approaching the result from different angles, and this can take time if you're working with a group of frustrated executives. But given enough time to explore their concerns, your team will align on a common measurement of success.

Flip the Negatives: Take any number and multiply it by -1 and it will flip — a negative will become positive and vise-versa. You can always interrupt the negative by asking: What is the opposite of that? or: If you didn't have that, what would you have?

Complaint × -1 = Flip

2 – SMART:

Get Specific: Another approach is to get into the details. SMART questions allow people to explore a clear outcome in high-resolution, prompting you and your team to sense which area of the goal is weak or unformed and focus on it. SMART is an acronym for a set of five thinking styles:

Specific: You can think of *specific* as a data-tree where the branches of the big goal are at the top and the roots that dig into the details of implementation are at the bottom. You don't have to explore every root, but bringing out some lower-level details that support the goal can nourish the branches of the tree. Many people love details, especially if they are technically-oriented, and will not trust you if you don't dig below the surface of things.

Measurable: Business runs on numbers. People need to explore these numbers to understand and align on a goal — one good number is enough to bring a goal to life. Measurement can range from a single KPI or numerical goal to a detailed scenario-planning spreadsheet full of numbers. The logical mind needs precise numbers to think clearly, and these future-based planning numbers can later form the basis of a metric or tracking system that will be critical for implementation. Remember, every KPI started life as a number in someone's vision of success.

Achievable: Here is a very normal scenario: Your boss asks you to produce a result that seems challenging, complex, or even impossible. However, from your boss's point of view, the result seems completely reasonable. This scenario is a good formula for producing brain freeze and the classic stuck state of low-performance; but what if you switched roles?

Imagine that you're the boss asking for a challenging result. Your team is stuck, so the only way to move forward is to reassess the current state and re-establish trust. If your team is unable to envision a successful future, asking the fundamental question "Is this possible?" is a simple way to unfreeze their thinking. You can also start by warming up the conversation with a set of "What are some ways to begin?" questions. Once they are engaged, ask "Is this possible?" Most things only seem impossible because we have yet to acquire the thinking resources we need to find a solution,

Realistic: "Realistically, what would we need to produce this result?" Most managers are already very good at managing scarce resources like time and budget, but they stumble when they try to get their team into a new and complex project. Asking *realistic* questions is a great way to get people to engage and get their hands on the result. You can save the detailed resource planning for the implementation phase of the conversation — for now, asking realistic questions reassures your team that a realistic plan is in the pipeline for development. "Realistic" is a simple trigger word that allows even the most number-driven planning people to relax and imagine success.

Timeline: Time is a powerful thinking tool but it can also be tricky. If you have a hard deadline that is causing stress and blocking clear thinking, try moving from a *deadline* to a *timeline* and begin to map out the key steps and stages. Likewise, a big goal may often be floating out in an unspecified time in the future. In this case, ask the team when they might begin to achieve this goal and start to clarify the *time frame*. Working with time is one of the best ways to bring a target into focus. People tend to see things more clearly if those things are closer in time, and hence a 90-day result is much easier to envision than a two-year goal. Simply put, if the goal is too big and too far into the future, you may need to focus on a smaller subproject that could be achieved in a shorter period of time.

3 – Role and Control:

Authority is Overrated: In the traditional authority model of leadership, the boss is in charge of setting strategy and making decisions. They might delegate some issues to a lower level, but often these issues will bounce back up to the boss when they hit a problem. While this model resulted in slow response times and endless bottlenecks, at least everyone knew who was in charge. In the modern world, where people get thrown into new projects and teams on a seemingly daily basis, there is much more confusion among team members and leaders alike. Most companies want everyone to have clear roles and responsibilities, but with so many stakeholders and other people influencing every decision, few can keep up with the web of communication lines. The most effective way to deal with this is at the individual, team, and project level. Asking questions to clarify project roles is critical to project success.

Within Your Control: Want less power in your life? Complain about things that are outside your control. If you would prefer to have more power, focus on what you can control. Start with what is within your control and then ask good questions to work outwards to expand your influence.

Influence: Influence can be much more effective than control. Many people get stuck because they don't have the power to resolve an issue. Even if you have the authority, you can't make people "obey you" if they don't want to. Influence is a much more effective approach, a mindset you can apply to any role or control issue. The secret to building influence is to ask good questions that will help you develop a network of trusted associates and expand your sphere of influence. Many leaders are very good at building their trusted network, and like everything else, it all starts with asking the right kinds of questions at the right time.

What parts of this project are within your control?
What kinds of external dependencies present challenges?
What areas of this project can you influence?

What is your role? To speed things up, you need clear roles and responsibilities. However, the roles and responsibilities model only works well in a slow or static business. In the age of accelerating complexity, "Who is in charge of what?" results in a great deal of confusion. Complex projects may have many stakeholders with competing interests, and the most talented people can end up in many virtual teams, which often have a short project life cycle.

What is your role in this project?
What are you responsible for?
What is your main accountability in this project?

- What is the Real Issue?

Focus: Finding the right point of focus is always a careful negotiation. When people are stressed or excited, their focus tends to jump erratically. If this is happening with your team, go back to the basics of *contracting* outlined in Chapter 7 and renegotiate the terms of engagement in your conversation or project. Likewise, you may have to re-contract to focus on an underlying issue.

The Real Issue: The real issue is always hidden from view. Most leaders expend their energy trying to fix the wrong issue or addressing issues at a simplistic level. As a Q Model leader, you must wade through the surface issue to reach the heart of the challenge. Once you've found it, even a tiny shift in focus can have a huge impact.

Where should we focus?
What is the real challenge?
What is blocking our success?
What area of the project implementation is stuck?

- Breakthrough Confusion

Confusion versus Breakthrough: A group of leaders will not fully align until they all commit to a single realistic strategy. It sounds easy, but aligning on a single strategy is difficult because leaders are often pulled in different directions by competing priorities or groups with different interests. The sheer number of possible strategic options alone is enough to overwhelm leaders and prevent alignment. To combat these forces that are tearing your team apart, we need a stronger force to bring them into alignment. Fortunately, such a force can be generated by working through the following set of questions:

1 - How do we achieve success?	Success
2 - What do we want?	Goal
3 - How do we get there?	Strategy
4 - What is the real challenge?	Challenge
5 - How can we resolve the challenge?	Breakthrough
6 - What is the best strategy?	Single Strategy

A key challenge is the interplay between question 2 - "What do we want?" and question 3 - "How do we get there?"

Here is the classic bind between goal and strategy:

Until you have a realistic strategy, the goal does not seem possible.
If the goal does not seem possible, you can't build a realistic strategy.

I have seen dozens of executive teams get stuck in this catch-22 loop. One team member introduces a solution and then another immediately rejects it because it doesn't seem possible. The more stress or pressure they are under, the faster they reject ideas. The more they reject ideas, the more stuck they get.

An Organic Approach: To deal with this, you must go back to the basics of the Q Model and agree to explore several *possible* solutions. You may have to explore many goals and strategies to find the best ones, but the way forward is to work through the six questions below. You can start at question one and progress linearly, but you may have to take an organic approach, jumping around and looping back to the same question a few times. Only when the team has begun to answer each question partially can they fully engage in a complete solution; building a comprehensive breakthrough must be an iterative process. As such, it can often take two to three months to get an executive team into a state of strategic alignment. For a refresher, re-read the Domob story in Chapter 1, which illustrates this point.

Where to Tap: Building a comprehensive breakthrough plan that everyone aligns on may seem daunting. However, if you can sense which area is weakest, you can work on that area first and get some traction. This is called "knowing where to tap," and it can quickly get your team engaged and building momentum. Combining this with some of the qTeam tools in Chapter 14, you can make significant progress in a few hours rather than months.

---

6 Strategic Alignment Questions:

1 - How do we achieve success? Often the first goal is external. It might be very fixed, such as producing a specific result or KPI. This first question is usually a warm-up question to find out where people are at in the strategic process. We need to get the existing strategy out in the open.

2 - What do we want? Picking the right goal and defining it is critical. "What do we want?" is one of the most challenging questions you can ask, and you may have to explore many goals and strategies to find the best ones.

3 - How do we get there? Coming up with a realistic plan is the essence of strategy. But there are many layers to strategy, and you may need to work through several strategic approaches until you find the right one. At this stage, you don't have to go too far into the planning process, but you do need to bring out some of the difficult issues. The goal is to align on the primary strategy and render it into a visual map.

4 - What is the real challenge? You can't own a strategy until you deal with the hard parts. You could frame it as, "If we take this approach, what are some of the challenges?" You need to get the most difficult parts out where you and your team can see and discuss them.

5 - How can we deal with this challenge? This question can take the team into the domain of a breakthrough. The real strategic *point of focus* is how to deal with the issue that is blocking progress. This question marks an excellent spot to bring in the qTeam whiteboarding tools.

6 - What is the best strategy? As soon as you introduce the word "best," you start to aim at a single strategy. There may be many smaller strategies within the larger strategy, but provided they all link upward to one big goal with one main strategy, it will be perceived as a single approach. From here on, team alignment will become natural and automatic.

Chapter 12 - Visioning

The only thing worse than being blind is having sight but no vision. - **Helen Keller**

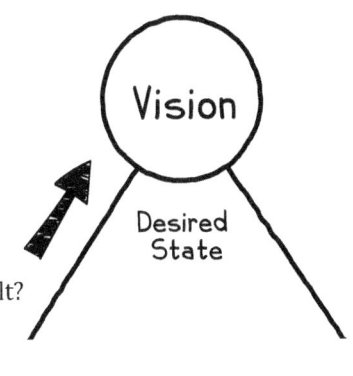

Key Visioning Questions:

Is this result even possible?
What would success look like?
How would you know if you produced this result?
What would success look like in six months?
What would this look like as a system?
What would this look like as a business process?

- IntegraSoft Transformation

Brian confided, "This company is a mess. No one thinks we will ever change. Our projects are always late and most of the code is written in Cobol."

An excellent example of a successful company transformation, in 2013 Brian Hanna used the Q Model to accelerate the development of a cloud-based digital transformation program at a small software company called Tech Systems, which later became known as IntegraSoft.

As the company's new VP of Strategy, Hanna had used the Q Model in another organization and understood its power to accelerate change. He stepped into the role of *executive champion* for the company's breakthrough project, which included the introduction of the Q Model. While he had a *strong vision* for the success of the transformation project, most of the 60 other people in the company had *no vision* of success. The CEO himself was skeptical but had grudgingly agreed to invest the necessary time and resources.

Brian had convinced the CEO of the opportunity for a Software as a Service (SaaS) cloud-based transformation, and we developed an ambitious 90-day plan to kick-off the transformation. Although the skepticism of the CEO and the company's employees was an obstacle, Tech Systems itself had many business strengths. Over the past 20 years, they had developed a small business focused Enterprise Resource Planning (ERP) online service which had a loyal customer base. Most of their clients had locked their data and business to their service and were generally satisfied.

We-R-Stuck: Unfortunately, the software the company utilized for the online service was an ancient codebase written mostly in Cobol, a computer language left over from the 1960s. This old software made it difficult to scale up their servers, so there was little point in expanding the business. We were also working with an older, lower energy team largely made up of people who had worked for Tech Systems for over twenty years, and they consistently ranked low in customer support. On top of all this, customer software customization projects often took twice as long as promised.

You can't teach an old dog new tricks: The *real* challenge was that, having gone through generations of failed initiatives, most of the staff and leaders didn't actually believe that *any* change was possible. The company was stuck in a cycle of resource scarcity which triggered poor customer results which triggered more resource scarcity. In short, they had a classic model of low-performance leadership.

Never waste a good crisis: Of course, realistically it wasn't possible to complete an entire cloud migration of the legacy codebase in 90 days. The point of the deadline was to energize the transformation and move the company from a low-energy state into a high-energy state. We needed to demonstrate that speed was possible and to simply get the transformation started.

We followed a very standard Q Model business transformation process. First we ran a series of intake meetings with team leaders to discuss the current state, then we identified challenges and defined a set of key breakthrough projects. The good thing about transformation programs with a smaller company is that you can get all the stakeholders in one room and hash out all the issues at once.

Team Blue Eagle: Breaking the entire staff up into multi-silo workgroups, over a weekend we ran an intensive two-day program. We facilitated each team to tackle one of the company breakthrough projects using the standard Q Model and qTeam (see Chapter 14) processes as outlined. These sessions included lots of brainstorming, whiteboarding, and strategic planning, and in the end, each team gave themselves crazy names like Blue Eagle and 007 Cloud. The point was to get everyone in the company to own the strategy and step into their shared future. While our professional team facilitated the weekend intensive, our real goal was to empower the leaders to run the Q Model independently. We also assigned unique roles for skeptics to contribute critical feedback.

At the end of the second day, the multi-silo teams reassembled into a single group with the entire company. Together we hashed out a two-year vision of success with key metrics and milestones. Nine leaders emerged, each of whom were particularly active and energized by this vision of success, and these people became our project champions. In the end all the staff committed to the transformation plan, including the skeptics who were still a little confused. The end of day two ushered in a moment of company transformation, but it was also the beginning of the real work. Many of the employees were still looking around and asking, "Is this real?"

Multi-Silo Issues: After the intensive program, we ran a series of project focused qTeam sessions with the key working teams. Here the rubber met the road, and the main players had to deal with the real issues and challenges. Projects like streamlining the entire client customization process required difficult multi-silo negotiations. Getting better customer satisfaction from the support team required building a workload estimation system to accurately predict when projects would be completed and technical issues would get resolved. Through this process, we kept challenging the support team to report any difficulties and keep defining the new process and systems. After a few rounds, some of the champions started to model us and take on the Q Model approach independently.

Everything is Connected: These projects contained many problems nested in complex dependencies. Streamlining software customization required fixing parts of the code base, which took developers away from the customization projects, causing further delays. All of this broke many established protocols, which in turn disrupted the day to day operations; it was all one big confusing mess of limited resources and conflicting interconnected priorities. These are the kinds of complex technical project challenges that can only be sorted out by an empowered multi-silo team.

The Big Bang: To re-engineer so many long-established business systems all at once required each team to build a visual model of the priorities and to whiteboard a detailed implementation map. They also had to build a structure of accountability to track the conflicts and project breakdowns that would inevitably occur. We transitioned management of the projects to the internal group of champions, and from that point on, monitoring key milestones became critical. At the end of the 90-day program, the senior team agreed to change the company's name to IntegraSoft, signaling to its customers the transformation that had occurred via a shiny new website front-end.

One year later, IntegraSoft was starting to look like a lean Silicon Valley start-up. Although the cloud migration was still underway, revenue and customer satisfaction had dramatically increased. The key champion team had internalized the Q Model approach, and it was now simply "the way we do things here."

- Visioning

See the Result: People need to see the result they want to achieve. Visioning is the process of getting people to clearly see that result, in their mind, and on paper. Humans do this regularly throughout their day. Think about what you want to eat for dinner tonight: does a picture of the prepared meal flash into your mind for a split second? Visioning is so automatic that most people are not aware that they are constantly doing it.

See Future Success: With Visioning, we want to go a step beyond seeing just any image, as people see many random pictures in their mind's eye throughout the day. Visioning specifically refers to seeing a clear picture in your mind of a future in which your project is successful.

Often business leaders get confused by the idea of vision. A statement like "You need to be a visionary leader" is one of the best ways to bewilder an overwhelmed executive. In reality, vision is simple: It is when you see a picture in your mind of your ideal future.

Think about a fundamental business function like planning. No human would ever bother to plan anything if they didn't already have some vision of success — a plan is built on top of a vision. People may see many images of future success as they think about each stage of a project's implementation from many angles. All these images can coalesce into a final image of success that represents one big vision.

Strong Vision: Specific questions drive the visioning process. The more you ask visioning questions the stronger the vision becomes, which provides a more personal connection to the desired state. A strong vision is essential to achieving a breakthrough result.

Executives Like Visioning: Many people are embarrassed to ask visioning questions. They think they will appear unprofessional or flaky if they enter the realm of imagination. However, contrary to popular belief, executives love visioning. Provided you have a foundation of trust, senior leaders are eager to get into the details of the success of their projects. CEOs will even pay top dollar to have a professional coach assist them to build their vision of success.

Task versus Vision: If you have a job that requires *action without thinking* there is a good chance a robot will soon replace you. There are many types of work that don't require much vision. But if you are a manager or information worker, you probably have to deliver complex results using unstructured time. Most modern jobs require visual thinking, and if you are delivering complex results you probably get paid more.

Vision Drives Alignment: When people see the future they want clearly, their thinking and actions begin to shift into alignment with that future. They also report that they have more energy and enthusiasm, as feedback from thousands of Q Model conversations demonstrates. For more controlled research on this topic, spend some time looking through the sport psychology literature on visual rehearsal.[2-1] The ability to vision effectively is the on-ramp to high alignment and one of the key predictors of project success.

Visual Barriers: There are several big challenges when it comes to vision. First off, many people are not very good at visioning. Images will certainly pass through the mind throughout the day, but the process often seems passive; many people *get* images but rarely *make* them. Most people are not consciously aware that they are Visioning throughout the day. If you ask them what they are doing, they will say they're "just thinking."

Second, most people are not very practiced at *intentionally* using their visioning system. To build a vision effectively, you need to hold it in your mind, adding details that paint a picture of the future with many dimensions. Active visioning is not unlike a focused meditation, which takes a surprising amount of energy. Even the most dedicated of breakthrough teams are exhausted by the end of a day of visioning.

A third obstacle is that many people do not understand the value of visual thinking. There is a pervasive judgment that tells them, "If you can't touch it, it's not real." Associating the idea of vision with day-dreaming or fantasy, many people do not permit themselves to develop their visioning abilities.

What Would Success Look Like? Vision questions are a powerful tool for creating a small shift or a big breakthrough. By exploring a future success scenario with your team, you can assist them in building a solid plan supported by a set of positive visualizations. Visioning is an excellent way to develop more capacity for problem-solving.

Think Visual: Our visual system is unique to humans, and making internal pictures seems to be a uniquely human function. You simply can't think of the future or the past without creating an image. Invariably, you will already have some basic skills for using your visual system. However, by focusing on the past or on problems, you will not tap into the real power of the visioning system.

> "Life cannot just be about solving one miserable problem after another. There needs to be things that inspire you, that make you glad to wake up in the morning and be part of humanity." **- Elon Musk**

More Visioning questions:

What would success look like?
It is 30 days from today. You produced this result. What's it like now?
Just suppose that you have completed this project successfully.
Take a moment and stand in this future. What do you see?
How did you produce this result? What made the most difference?

Visual Brain: The internal visualization function is not well understood by contemporary neuroscientists. Although there is a visual cortex area in the brain, visualization certainly involves the entire cerebral cortex and is also associated with the visual-spatial brain area. Neuroscientist John Ratey states, "The visual pathway is not a one-way street. Higher areas of the brain can also send visual input back to neurons in lower areas of the visual cortex."[12-1] This suggests that our internal visualization function mirrors the brain process used for interpreting external visual images.

Surprisingly, the visualization function does not seem to be well-integrated with the rest of the brain. Whereas emotion and reaction are clearly linked, visual attention seems to be a very separate thing. If you observe people playing video games, you will see that as visual attention takes over, people dissociate from their emotions. This is why humans love TV, movies, and visual-spatial phone games. In the Q Model context, we often see a group of executives who are frustrated because a project is blocked. As we get into the visual modeling process, they all relax and dissociate from the negative emotions. This kind of visual modeling appears to engage the entire cerebral cortex.[12-2]

Visual Rehearsal: It is no secret that making a picture of how you want things to go is a great way to improve performance. Top athletes have been using *visual rehearsal* for many years as a strategy to win gold medals and championships. From a cognitive point of view, the Q Model owes a debt to the field of sport psychology. In the 1980s, a significant body of research demonstrated the link between high performance and a detailed visual rehearsal process. For elite-level athletes, this can add up to 30% in performance improvement. [2-1]

Inspired Passion: When you create a picture of what you want and commit to a future that inspires you, something unique occurs. You engage the positive visual system that unlocks the unique capacity that is responsible for all of humanity's greatest achievements.

Opportunities multiply as they are seized - Sun Tzu, The Art of War

Simple Mind: Power comes from simplicity. To cut through the noise and distraction of everyday life and drive breakthrough results, you need to reduce complex things into simple ideas. Simplicity is the art of finding the critical breakthrough ideas, representing them with a single keyword, and putting those keywords into a visual map.

See it three times: Another key point is that most people need to see an internal picture at least three times before it becomes persistent. Given that images flash in our minds all day long, how does the brain know which pictures are important and worthy of long-term memory storage? As you may know, the human mind is a pattern recognition machine. When we repeatedly think of an image that is closely linked to our positive emotions and value of getting *what we want*, the brain cannot help but recognize it as a pattern that is important to us, and consequently it takes steps to ensure that we do not forget it. When we commit to take action, we are promising to take that vision out of our internal imagination and bring it into existence in the real world. This is the final signal to the brain that this vision is of critical importance.

- Representational Map

Theorists have long presented a strong link between visual processing and general self-awareness.[12-3] Because we see ourselves in the center of our field of visual awareness, *who we are* is the person in the middle of *where we are*. Despite this, it is difficult to observe our processes of cognition and self-awareness in action since we are right in the middle of it all the time. This is akin to trying to look at yourself without a mirror. However, one easy way to observe the self is to examine our representational map of how we create meaning in our life and our world.

External Vision: The visual system expends tremendous brain processing power to convert the tiny blobs of light coming into our eyes into a three-dimensional model of the world. On top of this basic spatial awareness, we add many layers, such as language, relevance, and meaning. From these, we construct our representational map of the world, which we constantly update.

You don't see with your eyes, your eyes create the world." **- Alan Watts**

About the Tree: If you look at a tree out in the world, you see a basic image of the tree with your eyes, including parts of it such as the trunk, branches, and leaves. If you were to describe the tree, you might notice that you are automatically adding language on top of the image.

You could zoom in and get into the details of the colors or textures of the tree. Likewise, you could zoom out and notice the overall size or shape of the tree. Notice that all this seems completely natural and automatic. This is how we experience and make sense of the external world.

However, notice that this tree is not merely an object in the external world. It is also something you are creating with your mind right now. You are currently adding "seeing a tree in my mind" to your representational map of the world. You will probably forget this tree immediately because you have looked at so many trees, and there is not much information here that isn't already in your map. Besides, you have limited time, so you want to keep moving to the next point of interest.

Focused Attention: Attention is the brain's scarcest resource. With *relaxed* attention, we let our mind wander between whatever ideas or objects drift through our conscious experience. With *focused* attention, we try to keep our mind directed toward a single topic or result. Because our minds are constantly inundated with sensory input and information, focused attention takes a lot more energy and cognitive resources. The executive function of the brain must determine what is important and what requires focused attention. Everything else gets discarded.

By now the tree you were looking at or imagining a few moments ago has probably already dropped out of your current focus. This is because it is no longer relevant and you already know how trees fit into your life; there is no need to re-examine this category of experience right now. Indeed, the brain can only retain information that is extremely new, unique, and compelling — 99.9% of all sensory input must be discarded. This point is of critical importance in building *sticky* high-impact breakthrough results, which we will learn more about in Chapter 20.

The Map: We live in our representational experience of the world. From our point of view, the external world is always solid and consistent. However, there is a vast layer of subjective interpretation that we usually filter out, and this becomes our internal "map" of reality. Of course, we constantly update this map, based on our objective experience of what is happening *out in the world.* We also make social agreements about *what is real*, based on a common understanding. But we tend not to notice that much of this map is built from our own subjective interpretation. Humans have a strong implicit bias to ignore our own perceptual filters:

We cannot see the map because we are the map.

This layer of interpretation is of particular importance when we are dealing with the past or the future. From a physics point of view, the past and the future do not really exist. They're more like a beautiful work of *art* or *fiction* that we build individually and socially. For the past, you could ask "What happened in World War II?" and you would get many perspectives. For the future, you could ask "Is climate change real?" and many people would agree or disagree. These are negotiations over the social maps of the past and future. This may seem like an overly philosophical point, but this discussion is essential when building a breakthrough project or company transformation.

"As if" the Future is Real: Our interpretation is a fundamental issue of perception. When we envision the past or future internally, we make use of the same visual processing systems we use for interpreting the external world in the present moment. In other words, we use the same brain systems for processing both internal and external visual images.[12-1] We tend to operate as if the past and future are just as real as the present objective world that we can see and touch, easily forgetting that one is subject to interpretation and the other has not happened yet.

Be Here Now: It is easy to get stuck in a negative story or *blame-frame* about the past. Our interpretation of the past fundamentally affects how we see the present. This is why the Q Model emphasizes building trust with an open dialogue about the current state. When we gently question the current state, we begin to open up our interpretation of "the way things are" and this creates space for many new ideas. Remember the golden rule of trust:

Rule 1 Again: Trust comes from an open dialogue about the current state.

As people engage in that discussion, they start to move beyond their interpretation of the past and examine the current state as a direct experience that is shared by everyone in the present moment. People begin to respect each other's interpretation or points of view and agree on a common understanding of "where we are, right now." This is the foundation of trust.

Predictive Function: Humans operate with a set of expectations of what will happen in the future, and predicting threats is of vital importance. Although logically we know the future is fluid and changeable, we don't tend to operate this way. Instead, our repetitive routines of work and personal life settle us into a predictable understanding of our future expectations, which we base on the map we have created from our past experiences. This need for predictability means that most people tend to equate change as a sudden threat, and this triggers reaction.

Change the Map, Change the Future: How do we change our map of the future without triggering a negative reaction? The easy way is to have an active role in building our new future map. To alter the future, we not only need to imagine a new possibility, but we must also have a realistic plan for achieving it. Otherwise, our future map will be rejected as a fantasy or an unfounded dream.

Engage in building the vision. Own the plan. Alignment will be automatic.

Fundamentally, what we are talking about here is vision, which is a specific Q Model function. Vision is the moment when you create a clear picture in your mind of a desired future state. Once this vision is well-established, everything changes. The core transformation tool of the Q Model, vision redefines our perception of the future and makes lasting change possible.

You have to trust that the dots will somehow connect in your future. **- Steve Jobs**

- Is it possible?

Once a future is seen as possible, it gets included in the map of potential future scenarios, moving from the category of unknown *threat* to potential *opportunity*. As more details are added to the plan, we may link more value to the scenario or even commit to the first steps. All of this can transform your outlook of the future, turning a potential threat into a probable opportunity.

Could this work?
Could this strategy be effective?
Is it possible that this breakthrough approach could be successful?
Is it possible that this scenario could work?

When a team is engaged in a challenging project, they must be able to say yes to one of the above questions to move forward. Notice that these are closed questions and that the "yes" in response is like switching on a light switch that initiates the visioning process. We are not asking the team to believe in a crazy idea or fantasy. Instead, this is about developing the plan to the point where it seems possible and realistic. Once the team declares that success is possible, the strategic thinking process tends to speed up.

"Why, sometimes I've believed as many as six impossible things before breakfast." – **Alice, Through the Looking-Glass**

Risk Versus Vision: Risk must be managed, but too much *risk management* can kill growth. Humans spend vast amounts of energy trying to anticipate what is going to happen next. We are hard-wired to make assumptions about how things are going to go and repeatedly run scenarios in our mind about how we might respond to them. Any time you discuss risk, you must build a negative visualization, which reduces engagement. All this attention to risk comes at a high cost — if a team puts too much mental and physical energy into reducing risk, it displaces their ability to see a positive future, and this caps their potential to produce breakthrough results.

Containment Zone: In every large company transformation project there is almost always a conservative CFO type threatening to shut the whole program down at any moment. Of course, getting a solid buy-in from these people is a critical step — we need to honor the skeptics. But give them exclusive ownership of the future and nothing will change. This is why we design breakthrough projects, which act as a container to isolate projects from the skeptics until they get traction.

Vision before Risk: First, find a supportive team, define a breakthrough project, and build a vision of success. In the early stages, pushing back on the need to manage risk while still respecting the things that could go wrong is a critical skill. In the Q Model process, there is a specific place for risk assessment. In general, avoid assessing risk until after a vision of success is well established. At this point, usually just before a team is ready to commit to action and implementation, assessing the risk will often increase the level of commitment.

"If you were to do a risk-adjusted rate-of-return estimate on various industry opportunities, I would put building rockets and [electric] cars pretty much at the bottom of the list." **- Elon Musk**

Paradoxically and to our benefit, addressing risk marks a key junction point that can expand vision. As you become more comfortable using the Q Model to deliver results, naturally you will begin to scale up your ability to see further into the future. And as the range of what is possible expands, your capacity to create more success scenarios and become a visionary leader grows with it.

Focus on the Foundation: Sometimes managers using the Q Model struggle to create a vision with their team and the process gets stuck. A lack of vision is often the product of a weak foundation, meaning that the hard work of building trust has not been done. To earn trust, you must have authentic conversations with your team, asking questions and listening to their answers as you explore the current state, strategic opportunities, and the challenges you face.

Realistic: Only when the plan seems realistic and the breakthrough seems possible will you engage the visioning system in your team. At this point, you can ask a few simple vision questions to get things going. Team alignment will become natural and automatic, and the transformation will take on a life of its own. If this is not happening, something is missing. You may have to go back and loop through the process again. This loop is normal, and it is best to conduct project conversations as an iterative process that unfolds in stages. It is rarely possible to build a strong vision for a successful company transformation in a one-hour conversation. Typically you need a series of discussions, in which you address related areas and hammer out an overall strategy. As you build the big plan, the vision of success naturally forms along with it.

Q&A: Here are the top five visioning questions. These are questions that business leaders ask over and over again.

Question 1: How do you make someone "see" a vision?

Unfortunately, another person's vision is not within your span of control. Your job is to ask questions that engage the visioning system. Asking good visioning questions coupled with some whiteboarding or visual planning will often naturally engage your team's visioning system, but not always.

Question 2: How do you test if the visioning system is engaged?

Testing for vision is quite easy. When an individual or team starts to see a clear vision of success, there is almost always a sudden increase in their energy or excitement. Watch for a jump from low engagement to high engagement quite suddenly. Once you think they might have a vision, you can ask them questions like "What would project success look like?" or "How could we measure that result?" They will answer in detail, and their vision will become even stronger. As people and teams establish a vision of success, they will often get excited and tell you about it.

Question 3: What is the difference between a plan and a vision?

The difference is your level of emotional engagement. Often a plan seems external. It is something you "have to do," like a task or a to-do list. Although plans can be loaded with details, it is impossible to fully engage and own them until you can see an outcome that is possible and meaningful to you. Once you begin to think through the plan *as if* you are going to make it happen, you will naturally start to engage the visioning system. And when you do this, an external plan quickly becomes your internal vision of success.

Question 4: What is the difference between a fantasy and a vision?

It comes down to your internal point of view. While a fantasy is something you know is impossible or completely unrealistic, a vision is something that seems possible or achievable to you. You invest time to explore and develop a strategy or plan and the associated vision of success expands. At this point you might switch roles and assess your vision critically, either abandoning it or committing to the actions required to move it forward. Ultimately, committing to the first action step makes all the difference.

Question 5: What if my direct report's vision is entirely unrealistic?

There is no rule in the Q Model that says you must support every vision. A lot depends on the context. Many start-up entrepreneurs have presented crazy ideas to me, and later they went on to develop very successful companies; one early-stage company I dismissed as a lost cause now has a valuation of $2b. However, as a manager, you must choose your role. In your boss role, you would typically shut down ideas that don't make sense to you. As a Q Model leader, you may decide to ask some clarifying questions to help your people make their plans more realistic. By asking questions, your direct reports begin to engage and own the results independently. You have to decide if this is worth the effort.

- Visioning and Design Thinking:

So far we have presented the topic of visioning by focusing on one specific type of vision based on the successful completion of a project. This is simply one of many visioning systems. Recall that the cerebral cortex and visual-spatial area of the brain have a huge range of thinking capabilities. Using these resources, you can view the external world in *minute detail* or as an *expansive whole*. You can remember an image from the past or imagine a scene from the future. You can also imagine seeing through the eyes of another human being, or from the perspective of a bird looking down upon you from thousands of feet above. These last two cases are examples of *point-of-view transformation*, a potent tool for producing positive and lasting change.

Customer Empathy: Design Thinking is a mature discipline that you can explore in many books or web articles, and so for this discussion, we will only focus on its Customer Empathy tools in the context of point-of-view transformation. While product managers and marketing people might envision a target customer and make assumptions about the needs of this hypothetical person, by default most employees adopt a point of view that values the needs of the company above all else. Organizational groupthink tends to lock in this corporate point of view, which results in flawed products and failed launches.

Flexible Mindset: The first stage of any Design Thinking process is to empathize with the customer and try to experience your potential product through their eyes. The goal of this exercise is to upend the corporate mindset and take a more *human-centered* approach to design. However, many companies have dumbed-down Design Thinking to a simplistic exercise in User Interface (UX) design or the 'unboxing' experience of customers over the actual use of the product. They have missed the point that Design Thinking is a complete identity transformation system and one of the most potent tools for moving from a *fixed* to a *flexible* mindset.

Point of View Transformation: When I first studied NLP in the 1980s, this entire domain was known as a *point of view shift* and was well understood as one of the most effective change tools. A great example would be conflict. If you find yourself in an argument with someone, you can only remain in that argument by refusing to see the other side of things; a conflict can only take place from within the confines of your own point of view. By envisioning yourself and your position through the eyes and ears of the person with whom you are arguing, your ability to maintain the state of conflict simply disappears. Test this on yourself the next time you and a colleague (or anyone else for that matter) and find yourselves at loggerheads.

It is important to note that point-of-view transformation is embedded throughout Q Model:

> When you build a vision of success, you imagine looking through the eyes of your future self, who has become the person capable of producing the results you seek.

> As you build a team identity, you naturally start to see things through the collective eyes of the team. See Chapter 14, 'Missioning Team Identity'.

> As you develop multi-silo solutions to complex organizational challenges, you naturally assimilate perspectives and potential solutions from other areas of the company. See Chapter 19, 'The Company as a System'.

> As you engage in missioning, you naturally look through the eyes of your stakeholders and customers and imagine amplifying the value they receive. See Chapter 17, 'How do you do Missioning?'.

> As you engage in systems thinking or whiteboarding, you naturally take a top-down view of potential solutions. This dissociated perspective from above allows you to step into an imagined thinking space where solutions can be seen in a clear and neutral way. See Chapter 13, 'Whiteboarding'.

All of the above tools are identity transformation systems. As soon as you and your team engage in these activities, you begin to transition from a fixed mindset to a more flexible way of approaching people and solutions.

Gretzky's Secret: Here is a story that will illustrate the performance potential of visioning and point-of-view transformation. Being Canadian I am unsurprisingly a hockey fan, and like most people consider Wayne Gretzky to be the greatest player to ever lace up a pair of skates. Everyone knows that he scored more goals and accumulated more assists than any other player in NHL history, and this was largely due to his uncanny ability to anticipate where the puck was going to be in advance of anyone else on the ice. What most people don't know is that Gretzky had a secret weapon: he would imagine what the rink looked like from above, and would visualize the shifting locations of his opponents and teammates in real-time. He would then speed his visualization up and run it three seconds into the future. Gretzky describes how he began practicing this technique at the age of 12, and how long before he turned professional at 17 it had become entirely automatic.[12-4] With practice, even the most unconventional of techniques become second nature. Using this system Gretzky became unstoppable, shattering endless records and winning four Stanley Cup Championships over the course of his 20-year career. And it all began with a simple shift in his point of view.

Chapter 13 - Whiteboarding

What is Innovation? How does a company like Apple consistently deliver industry-changing products while other companies with the same resources fall behind? Where do you get all those game-changing creative ideas? How can you boost your team's ability to generate solutions? Innovation is what gives a company its competitive edge, providing fresh solutions and the ability to create new products or services for changing markets.

How is Innovation Generated? What precedes the "A-ha" moment? How do teams move from *problem state* to *brilliant solution*? While creativity and innovation are commonly thought of as individual personality traits, current research demonstrates that creative solutions are highly contextual or situational.[13-1] When individuals encounter the right context or situation, they become innovative. To trigger this ability, all that is required is the right environment, context, and process.

External Visioning: Visioning can take place internally in the mind and externally in a visual thinking space. To build strength, your team needs to see a plan for success in many different ways, and whiteboarding a visual model of a plan or solution is a simple and effective process to drive innovation, strategy, and implementation.

What is Whiteboarding? Whiteboarding is any process where you create or utilize a visual thinking space to represent the desired state and the means of achieving it. Ideal for developing innovative thinking and fresh ideas in team conversations, whiteboarding is an indispensable tool to wield whenever a project requires a complex solution.

History of Whiteboarding: Many of the concepts of whiteboarding were first developed by Marilyn Atkinson in 2003. In 2006, Atkinson and I were developing team coaching systems and jointly coined the term "whiteboarding."[13-2] Of course, all of this might seem like another version of *Ideation* or *Design Thinking*, which have been around for some time. However, whiteboarding goes much deeper by turning visual-spatial thinking into a team-alignment system.

Visual-Spatial Thinking Games: If you have ever played chess, you will fully understand how visual-spatial intelligence works. To play chess, you have to use visual thinking. A chess piece like the knight moves in an L-shaped pattern, and you can visualize where your knight could be in a few moves by connecting a sequence of these L-shaped patterns in your mind. To be good at chess, you have to rotate and connect many possible patterns of different shapes. You could compare this to rotating the falling shapes in the classic video game Tetris.

Relax Reaction: If you take a commuter bus or train, you will see most people are looking at their phones. While some people are browsing the web, texting, or engaging on social media, many are playing games. These kinds of popular mobile games are designed to engage the visual-spatial system. They involve movement, color, and pattern recognition in a visual thinking space. Humans love to play these games because they bring us into a relaxed, high-performance state, drawing our attention away from our negative reactive system. This gives us a much-needed break from the harsh internal dialogue that often dominates our thoughts.

Why Build a Visual Model? Intelligence is highly contextual. Consider that there are many kinds of intelligence, which are created on the spot to solve an urgent issue. Necessity being the mother of invention, positioning your team in a carefully designed environment with a real business challenge, and giving them team thinking tools is an ideal way to trigger team intelligence. As we explore the subject of visioning, note how *emergent team intelligence* is much more sustainable than *individual intelligence.*

If you didn't make it, you can't own it: If people cannot see the strategy, they cannot engage with it. Whiteboarding is a visual thinking process where the team collectively generates ideas, moves Post-it notes around, and creates visual models, all in an effort to develop a high-level cognitive model of a workable solution. The visual modeling process in particular drives engagement and ownership of the solution, allowing the team to *self-identify* with that solution because they had a hand in building it.

Harness Visual Intelligence: The ability to engage a team in a visual thinking process — specifically one that models operational implementation of a solution to a complex problem — is a core competency for leaders and managers, and a crucial component in the innovation equation. We used to say that 60% of people have a habitual preference for visual thinking,[13-3] but in the modern world, this has become a ubiquitous skill that anyone can develop further.

- Think Visual

Howard Gardner's *multiple intelligence* research draws a link between visual thinking habits and people with strong problem-solving capacity. [13-1] Although the literature on it is complex, visual thinking is a natural skill that anyone can learn quickly, and it won't be long before you and your team discover that the whiteboarding process is both easy and indispensable for delivering results.

Bypass Conflict: Visually modeling a complex business process allows a team to discuss challenges without defensiveness or conflicting personalities, and it is particularly useful for people with a technical, scientific, or engineering background. It is a simple and effective way to develop problem-solving and strategic thinking skills in your team and radically increase their engagement. With practice, managers and team leaders will begin to naturally model visual solutions to challenges.

Turn on Vision: There are two primary ways to turn on the visioning system:

> **1 – Visioning:** Imagining an image of success
> **2 – Whiteboarding:** Outlining a visual map of that success

CoLab-or-8: Conflict in teams is a big challenge, to which whiteboarding is an ideal solution, creating team alignment and driving collaboration as it takes the best results of a brainstorming session and integrates them into an emergent visual model of a team-developed solution. This naturally energizes results and unlocks team thinking, which is a force of nature.

Abstract vs Detail: At the root of many team conflicts is an age-old war between *big picture* and *detail-focused* thinking styles. But these conflicts simply disappear when a team uses whiteboarding to scale *up* and *down* between the big picture and the detailed parts of a project solution. This ability is a critical component in the MetaQ model for Agile intelligence, which is presented in Chapter 21.

What is the basic whiteboarding idea? Here are six steps that outline the whiteboarding process.

1 - Keywords: Keywords are powerful. The logical mind is quickly overwhelmed by too many ideas. When you establish keywords, you condense many ideas together, boiling them down to their essence until they are reduced to a single word. This streamlines thinking and allows team conversations to move much faster.

2 - Drawing: You don't have to be an artist to master whiteboarding. No matter how imperfect and inelegant, if you can draw an oval or a square you already have the necessary skills. It may not seem like much, but drawing a shape around a keyword sets the stage for a tiny but powerful shift. Because we use language to process ideas our logic system tends to dominate, but the moment we put a keyword into a shape, the visual thinking system starts to engage.

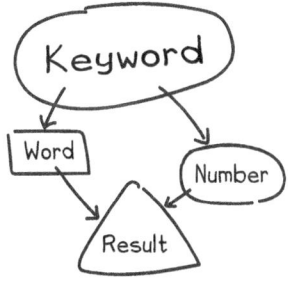

3 - Post-it Notes: These are ideas that can fly. Write a keyword on paper or a whiteboard and it is stuck there. But scrawl it on a Post-it and you give it wings. Imagine what this potential for movement means for the visual-spatial mind: anything becomes possible, it is simply a question of the proper arrangement of ideas. Keep in mind that the perfectly square outline of the Post-it note automatically puts ideas into a shape. The bright neon colors of the Post-its coupled with their movement also works to entice visual thinking in the minds of your team members.

4 - Movement of Ideas: Movement adds meaning. The more people play around and experiment with the placement of the Post-it notes, the more they engage with the ideas and create visual-spatial relationships between them. One of the most simple but transformational questions is "Where should we put this idea?" Being able to rearrange things in an open dialogue also sparks further discussion and a sense of freedom. The more a team can move, touch, or discuss the placement of the Post-it notes, the more flexible thinking becomes.

5 - Visual-Spatial Thinking: Think of three large rocks placed at random on the raked gravel of a Japanese garden. Imagine the scene and notice how your mind automatically creates a spatial relationship between the three rocks. This is analogous to placing several critical ideas in an empty white space, since we cannot help but notice a visual relationship between the concepts. Arrows and lines between these ideas formalize these connections. You might ask, "How does this part relate to that part?" as you connect them with a line. The more we build a spatial relationship between ideas, the more we add meaning to the representational map we are creating.

6 - Visual Modeling: Arranging critical ideas into a visual model is a core transformational tool of the Q Model. There are many ways to do this: you can organize keywords into a model using a blank flip chart page or place Post-it notes into an empty shape you have already drawn. Different models produce unique meanings and thinking results. For example, placing ideas into a *hierarchy of importance*, a *process flowchart,* or an *implementation timeline* will all trigger three very different thinking styles.

Brainstorm then Model: A typical format is to begin with a *brainstorm* and then move into a *visual model* as you build momentum. You can think of whiteboarding as the missing second part of any brainstorming session.

Here are some general pointers for the process: Whiteboarding can include any form of external visioning or planning process that engages visual-spatial thinking.

Whiteboarding:

- Design visual thinking systems
- Use visual modeling
- Use logical thinking habits to drive the creative process
- Trigger fresh thinking with process, system, and model discussions
- Bring a team into a fresh thinking space

Innovative Thinking:

- Expect to get messy with the team thinking process
- Bring real projects and work with serious challenges
- Step into a space of true inquiry with your team
- Relax into a hands-on experiential discussion process. Get into the tools
- Know that each whiteboarding tool is backed by deep Q Model principles
- Use debrief discussions to integrate a broad understanding

Whiteboard Keywords:

- Stop writing down all the words. Focus on keywords
- Always listen and track for the main concepts or keywords
- Take that keyword or key idea and re-confirm it
- Try to label complex ideas with a one-word placeholder
- Always capture or write down the keywords somewhere
- Capture ideas by getting them out of the mind and into physical existence on paper
- Leave white space around main ideas or keywords
- Circle or draw a shape around key concepts
- Leave white space around main ideas to add focus and clarity
- Add more related ideas or sub-elements around the core ideas
- Look for a relationship between ideas
- Ask questions to confirm the links between ideas
- Draw lines or arrows connecting the key ideas

Flowchart:

- Draw a box or shape around each idea
- Notice the systemic relationship

- Connect the ideas with arrows
- Build the flow chart into a system or process
- Step back and view it from a distance
- Look for an overall path or flow through the system
- Add system-level tools, such as a critical junction or a process control

Mind Map:

- Start with a central idea
- Branch out related ideas
- Create sub-branches
- Balance the overall system
- Transition into general whiteboarding

Draw a map of the solution:

- If you are facilitating, draw with your team
- If you are using a notebook, show them the page while you draw
- Include the key elements of the conversation
- Circle keywords. Link ideas with an arrow. Draw a flowchart
- Highlight the value of the solution and link value words
- Draw the solution with them. Get them drawing
- Recap key elements. Show them the picture
- Ask "What do you notice about this...?" and discuss main elements

Draw a Map: Help your team members build a map of their projects. Mapping is especially important when the project requires a complex solution.

- A good map includes all the critical elements of the conversation
- Include key components and features of the conversation
- Shift attention towards a larger project goal or challenge
- Focus on what is most important to success
- Track project risks and include them in a special section of the map
- Draw the solution with them (good) or get *them* to draw it (better)
- Summarize the key elements to build a narrative or story
- Test the map with the team as you draw it: "Did we get this part right?"
- Test whether the completed map seems right. Ask, "Does this seem right?"

When the process is finished, give the map to the project owner or team. It belongs to them. Ask them to post it in a visible location and discuss it again in the near future.

- Visual Modeling

What is Visual Modeling? We will now bring everything we have discussed so far together in a process we call *visual modeling*. This is the process of getting a team to collaboratively build a series of models that represent a strategy or solution. It is important to emphasize that they must build a series of models because, if the process is well orchestrated, somewhere between the second and third model a fundamental shift in collaboration and team thinking occurs.

Set-up: We will assume you are working with a team on a project and you have already completed a brainstorm and collected 20–50 ideas on Post-it notes that relate to a project solution.

Transfer the Post-it notes: The act of collectively moving the Post-it notes is profoundly transformational. The team is fully engaging their visual-spatial thinking systems to develop a strategy and implement it.

Where should we put this? The magic question is "Where does this idea go?" In the beginning, the model has not formed so the team will need to engage in friendly debate. Make sure everyone is involved, and get them to rearrange the Post-its with their own hands. Team thinking is an emergent quality, which means that the team intelligence emerges *in parallel* with the formation of the model and the development of a workable solution.

Cluster: Simply clustering similar ideas is a good first step. With this approach, you start with a blank flip chart page and without further instructions simply ask the team to place similar ideas together. Some groups do this at random and create odd shapes. Other groups put the Post-its into lines or grids. The most critical step is to *name* each cluster, which creates a category or meta-idea that defines each area of the solution. We are working with the keyword principle, so the name of the cluster becomes another keyword that represents all the ideas within it.

Start positioning the Post-it notes on the page. Keep repeating the key questions: "Where should we put this?" or "Where does this fit?" The process design naturally creates a flow of dialogue. Patterns will emerge at some point, and you will notice clusters or shapes forming. These might relate to key areas of leverage or points of challenge.

Shapes: Placing the Post-it notes into an existing form is another secret weapon. Simply pick a shape and draw it out on a large flip chart. Sometimes you might show the team a set of shapes and ask them to pick one randomly. Other times the team will discuss the shape in advance and make a logical or emotional decision. Either approach will work.

Transfer the Post-it notes into the areas defined by the shape. This process is radically simple but truly transformational — the act of moving the Post-it notes around and the tiny discussions about where each idea fits in the model creates team alignment and a holistic overview of the project. The most common shapes fall into one of three categories:

Geometric   **Scientific**   **Metaphoric**

Geometric: The human mind likes symmetry, so the very basic shapes you learned in geometry class are a good place to start.

Scientific: With an XY grid, we place a specific meaning onto the X and Y axis, so this is a direct path to visual-spatial thinking. There are many other ways to approach this, and we will explore them in the next section.

Metaphoric: A mountain or flower shape is rich in metaphorical meaning. A tree is the most common shape that groups select and it is one of the most flexible metaphorical shapes for visual modeling.

Something Clicks: As the process develops, the *random* shape somehow becomes the *perfect* shape in the team's eyes. This experience is triggered by the brain's innate function to recognize patterns and add meaning to that pattern. As the team aligns around it, watch how the visual model becomes an operational metaphor for the team or project success.

Develop the Model: This metaphoric team transformation might not happen on the first try, so it is often necessary to further develop the visual model. Ask the team to rebuild the model without the Post-it notes, or build an entirely new model from scratch, using fresh sheets of flip chart paper to get them drawing. It's not unusual for a team transformation to occur somewhere between the second or third attempt to build a model, so don't settle for the first version unless your team has strongly rallied around it.

In the next chapter, we will present the visual modeling process again in the context of a high-energy team transformation.

- System, Process, and Model

Team transformation often takes place in the *magical* domain of system, process, and model thinking. System, process, and model seem like three different styles of thinking, but we cluster them into one domain because these thinking styles always interlink. By way of a set of questions that develop into a higher-level organizational framework, you can give your team a holistic understanding of the overall solution in this domain. Often this comes at the end of the process and refines all the previous ideas into a single map.

Systemic Whiteboarding Models:

There are many ways to add meaning to your whiteboarding shapes and models. Each of the following shapes is a container influencing the nature of the ideas that emerge in the whiteboarding process.

X/Y Graph:

Remember these from science class? Just take two variables and place them on either side. A classic example of two variables would be *timeline* and *priority*. This approach creates a discussion of *when things happen* and *how important* they are. We will discuss this in greater depth in Chapter 18, when we get into the nitty-gritty of implementation.

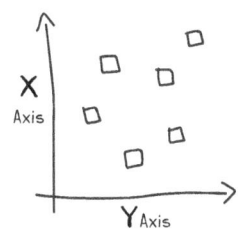

Cartesian Coordinates:

First developed by Descartes in 1637 and designed as a mathematical thinking system, the Cartesian coordinate system later proved instrumental in Newton's development of calculus. Elegant in its simplicity, it can be utilized to face just about any challenge. All you have to do is place two opposing ideas into a 2x2 grid. A simple exam-

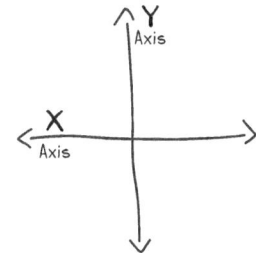

ple would be Covey's *Urgent vs. Important* graph, which fills in the two empty areas with *Not Urgent* and *Not Important*. Most people already know about Urgent vs. Important, so it is important to understand that you can take any two opposing ideas and run them through this process. The key step is to spatially position the Post-it notes into the right areas and ask questions about their placement. As you do this and engage in a discussion with a team, the thinking shifts and conversations are taken to a higher level.

4 Quadrant Thinking: The four-quadrant whiteboarding process was first developed by Marilyn Atkinson in 2002.[13-4] Shown here in generic form, it is a powerful thinking system that can include:

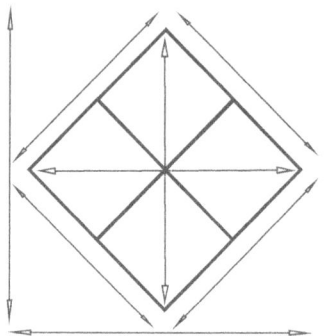

A four-quadrant diamond with four key ideas.

A vertical and horizontal dimension.

Arrows on the outer edges of the box.

Up to 10 lines of axes for discussion

We may define all the axis lines in advance, but most often we place ideas into the shape and see what happens, establishing definitions as we proceed. As we develop ideas a robust, four-quadrant thinking space emerges:

Deeper thinking takes place

Dialogue becomes richer

Teams become aligned

Intuitive harmony naturally emerges

Chapter 14 - Team = Energy

Never underestimate the power of a great team. The ultimate secret weapon, the ability to generate and harness the team energy needed to create alignment is a core transformational leadership skill.

So-called "team-building" activities don't do much. Taking people rock climbing or to a social event is only a baby step in the process of developing a great team. In the last chapter we presented the *visual modeling* process, a key element of the Q Model team development system we will explore here. Ultimately, the only formula for building a great team is tackling *real projects* and working through *adversity* until everyone collectively achieves success.

Team = Energy: The qTeam process is not about having a "happy" team, nor is it just about coming up with the best strategy or implementing the project. These things are products of energy rather than its origin, and it is the strength of the team itself that is the primary energy source for company transformation. The team *powers* the transformation by generating confidence, commitment, and momentum.

qTeam Process: qTeam is an energetic process for driving collaborative relationships with teams by giving them a shared mission. This approach takes the most effective elements of a brainstorming session and combines them into a visual model that unlocks the atomic force of intuitive team thinking.

Wisdom of Crowds: We say team intelligence is greater than expert intelligence. By designing the right context and environment, a team can generate an elite level of strategy and implementation. However, it is important to focus on the *quality* of team discussion while the team solves problems, implements solutions, and makes decisions. In the end, a true team requires some level of *collective decision making* to maintain its existence.

> Open team dialogue is the key to high-quality decision making.

Multi-silo Collaboration: Big companies move slowly because individual business units and departments have different interests and value different things. They get stuck into a fixed *silo* point of view that creates conflict between departments and stifles progress. In Agile we often talk about multi-discipline teams. Likewise, many companies use cross-functional teams. Like these, qTeam is a multi-silo collaboration system, where the goal is to get a diverse group of people to work collaboratively. Many companies do this, but what's missing is the team alignment process. If you simply put opposing groups in a room, they may perpetuate existing conflicts and even further entrench their positions. The qTeam process fosters team thinking and a high-alignment end result.

If you didn't make it, you can't own it: The team needs to get their hands on the creation of the plan. Even if you think you already have the perfect plan, turn it into a set of questions and send it back to the team. This hands-on participation is the key to project engagement and ownership.

Real Team Alignment: Ask a leader if they are in alignment with their team and they will say yes. However, in most company cultures you must be perceived as a team player, so this comes back to Rule 1 of Low Performance: *always say yes.* Fake alignment destroys trust. Actual alignment can only be achieved by facing the challenge and developing an effective strategy to which everyone can commit.

Team Ownership: Turning to face the challenge takes courage. People will only have that courage if they feel they own the project. Ownership is an identity-level transformation where a leader or team member *becomes* someone who steps into a state of high performance and becomes 100% committed to a breakthrough in the project.

- Team Thinking:

What makes a company great? Why are some executive teams completely aligned and committed, while others get stuck in endless conflict over strategy and resources? Where do industry-changing strategic ideas come from?

Creativity is a team activity: Creativity, strategy, and innovation are fundamental to the intellectual capital that gives a company its competitive edge. But innovation doesn't happen in isolation. It takes a team to create a strategic transformation, and enterprise transformation, in particular, requires the ability to generate fresh solutions to challenges and changing markets. Even for the smartest people, it takes the right tools and environment to bring out the best ideas.

What is Team Intelligence? The "wisdom of crowds" theory presents that collective team intelligence will often exceed the highest individual IQ.[10-4] Team thinking is the key to boosting performance and innovation, so how do we turn on the *team brain* and transform it into a multiprocessing supercomputer? Fickle by nature, the ability to think as a team can be disabled by one negative comment. An effective team thinking framework is built on trust, shared vision, and a strong set of supportive agreements.[14-1]

What is qTeam? qTeam is a set of tools, ideas, and agreements for bringing out the best in a team. Beginning with good questions and the relaxed style of a great brainstorming session, the qTeam environment facilitates the high-alignment thinking needed to iron out a strong set of agreements. This warm-up process lays the foundation for the required level of team trust.

Business Runs on Teams: Although many businesses still pigeonhole their people in static roles, more and more companies are moving toward project-based business models. This shift means that a manager or subject matter expert might engage in many projects, wearing many hats while still retaining their core role. As project cycles get shorter, project teams must get up to speed even faster. Having virtual teams that are spread around the globe is now common in many multinational companies. It is also normal to see multi-stakeholder teams include suppliers and customers in their discussions.

Building team thinking and high-alignment is *the* core transformational leadership skill. Surprisingly, it does not take years to become a great collaborative team leader. Because the qTeam mindset is so simple to acquire, achieving team alignment is a skill you can learn quickly. You can start practicing by turning a regular meeting into a qTeam session. At first, it may seem awkward, but rapidly your leadership skills will emerge and team alignment will soon follow.

Collaborative Leadership: qTeam is a collaborative leadership style. While there are many useful approaches to collaborative leadership, the qTeam process is one of the most effective. We will approach this by presenting a model for self-directed teams, which are the direct path to team thinking.

Appreciative Enquiry: A great team is a magical combination of talented people and an inspiring project that bonds them together. Everyone has had some experience of being on a great team. Think of a time when you were and ask yourself, "What was your shining moment?" and "What was the quality of the team that made you proud?" These *appreciative inquiry* questions are some of the best ways to evoke the quality of a high-alignment team in a group of strangers.

Missioning: The qTeam process interlinks with missioning, which we have touched upon and will explore thoroughly in Chapter 17. Missioning is the process of linking a project goal to an inspiring higher purpose. Rather than scaling up to an organizational mission, a small team can apply that same energy and passion to a specific project or product. Embedding a project mission into a team's planning process is one of the most effective ways to drive passion and commitment.

Strategy without implementation = Zero: Keep digging into the current state of the implementation process. The qTeam is ideal for engaging in discussions that address the challenges of implementation.

Question: I tried to introduce the Q Model to my team, but no one seems interested.

In the beginning, don't focus explicitly on the Q Model. Start with a real project that is important to your team. Select a few people who already have a good working relationship with you. Ask permission to lead a short conversation and use the Q Model to work on a project breakthrough. Once they get some fresh ideas from the conversations, introduce the Q Model and explain the questions. They will get curious. This approach is an excellent way to build your first Q Model team.

- Start with Trust:

Fake Team Engagement is Destructive: Traditional leaders want everyone to be a *team player,* a polite term for "Do what I tell you and pretend to be happy." If there are "always say yes" team players in your midst, be aware they may have a secret agreement to ignore critical issues and obvious truths. This agreement will have killed team engagement and trust, and to regain them you must address the *elephant in the room.* There is no engagement and no trust without the freedom to openly discuss *all elements* of the current state.

First Rule of Trust: Developing a project breakthrough is an inherently messy process, so managers often avoid discussion about problems and solutions. This may keep things neat and tidy, but it discourages the open dialogue that leads to team engagement and trust. If you are facing conflict, you may need to go back to Chapter 8 and assess the current state. Time and time again, bosses push for results without first building trust, and this makes a weak team even weaker.

Rule 1 Again: Trust comes from an open dialogue of the current state

If you didn't make it, you can't own it: Your team needs to get their hands on the creation of the plan. Even if you already have the perfect plan, turn it into a set of questions and send it back to the team. Never waste a crisis. When you encounter a project challenge, use it as an excuse to review the strategy and re-engage the team in the solution building process.

- Team = Energy:

A highly engaged team is the ultimate source of energy. Business leaders inherently understand this, but the majority do not have the skills nor the systems in place to move a team into a sustainable high-energy state.

The primary difference between one-on-one conversations and team conversations is the level of energy. One-on-one conversations tend to be more internally focused and intimate, whereas team conversations are about unlocking and sustaining energy. The purpose of the qTeam system is to create high-energy engagement and align team thinking. Team conversations are the secret weapon for becoming a transformational leader who achieves breakthrough results.

qTeam Roles: There are three ways to use the qTeam system:

1 - qTeam Facilitative Leader

Facilitate: From the Latin root *facile*, to make easy.
A facilitator is someone who makes achieving breakthrough business results easy.

The job of a great facilitative leader or external professional facilitator is to get fired quickly. Getting "fired" is a code word for replicating your skills in the team, so they don't need you and can maintain their high-alignment state independently, even when presented with new challenges.

Adopting a facilitative leadership style is one of the most powerful ways to transform the energy of a team and drive business results. Know when to use the directive and facilitative style of leadership, moving from a *tell* to an *ask* style as needed, and you will become a formidable qTeam Facilitative Leader.

2 - Self-Directed Team

The difference between a group of bored mid-career information workers and a team of "change the world" start-up entrepreneurs, self-directed teams are the essence of what it means to be in high alignment.

Self-directed teams have become a hot topic, and an army of elite external professionals is ready to *tell* your team how to become self-directed. However, self-direction can only emerge from within the team. Agreements to align must be natural and made internally, otherwise they will not be maintained by the team.

Self-Directed Means

- Each team member is equal
- We value the contribution of each person
- The group shares all ideas
- There is no idea ownership
  (Rule 23: never say "my idea" again for the rest of your life)
- Keywords: fair, balanced, shared, collaborate, solidarity, equality
- Self-directed team leadership can be balanced with a facilitative leadership style

3 - qTeam Professional Facilitator:

There are many external professional coaches, trainers, and consultants who also function as facilitators. But even if you are an internal manager, leader, or team member, you can still benefit from the mindset of an elite facilitator who can transform any company or executive team.

An elite facilitator can quickly take any team or project from a state of *slow* or *stuck* into a high-energy state where everyone is 100% committed to a breakthrough plan. After integrating qTeam skills, elite facilitators can transform executive teams and even entire companies.

Elite facilitators call to mind the metaphor of a team of *transformation commandos*: dressed in tactical gear, we repel from a helicopter onto the roof of a large corporation's headquarters. Wasting no time, we burst into the board room and transform the company in *three chess moves or less*, then we move on to the next enterprise and do it again. Unfortunately, the reality is not quite so exciting, with many days of behind the scenes preparation leading up to a few *tactical* events.

Don't Facilitate, Transform: Managers can become facilitators, who then become enterprise transformation experts. If you are an external professional, remember that the more you create client value, the more you can charge higher fees. But take to heart that a great facilitator wants to get *fired* as soon as possible by creating so much *client value* so fast that they can quickly move on to the next project. This kind of speed is what makes you an elite enterprise transformation expert.

Team Coaching Style: qTeam is similar to team coaching, but there are differences:

- qTeam can be more *directive* than team coaching
- qTeam seamlessly integrates with regular *business* conversations
- qTeam can be self-directed, where no single person takes the leader role

Collaborative Leadership: qTeam is the ultimate collaborative leadership style. Designing qTeam sessions with leaders from multiple departments or business areas is an ideal way to *de-silo* an organization. A multi-silo team that co-designs a project breakthrough spreads the ownership of the project out to a larger network.

Why Team Thinking? The market has become saturated with brainstorming tools and processes, but qTeam offers unique and singularly effective ways to generate team thinking. For example, Design Thinking is all about brainstorming and whiteboarding from the *end user's* point of view. While powerful, Design Thinking is only one small expression of the power of team thinking, whiteboarding, and *point-of-view* transformation.

Team thinking goes far beyond simple brainstorming tools. A specific and measurable state, people deep in the team thinking process report that it seems as if they are thinking with a single collective brain. When a team is in this state and presented with a challenge, they can often output a fully integrated solution and implementation plan within 30 minutes.

Team Brain: When a team achieves a team thinking state, they operate with a *team brain* that persists as they go about their regular work. Have you ever had the experience of working in a strongly aligned team, where it suddenly seems as if everyone is on the same page? When this happens, people get the same ideas at the same moment, and they finish each other's sentences. The concept of a team brain is not yet something that can be proven externally, but rather a shared collective experience that most people recognize, even if they can't articulate how or why it transpired.

Press the Button: When the team agrees on a unique or sticky team or project name, it marks a critical turning point. Simply mentioning this code name can *trigger* the team thinking state because it is linked to their metaphoric identity of success. People are not robots, so you must do this with humor and respect. You could say something like, "Hey team, how is the *Blue Monkey* project coming along?" This question will bring your team back to the high-alignment state they were in when they first named their breakthrough team or project.

The Collaborative Team:

- Engage Trust: dissolve creative blocks
- Drive team engagement and ownership
- Team Thinking: engage your team Supercomputer

The Q Model empowers managers to think like a consultant. Empowering this new strategic capacity, flexibility in thinking, and culture of collaborative solutions it creates encourages people and teams to own the solutions they develop. This ownership gives them the strength to deal with the many challenges they will encounter in the project implementation.

Disperse Group Think: Open team thinking is the opposite of closed herd mentality. When people work together, they tend to agree. Over time, people in a corporate department will almost always herd themselves into a closed *group-think* mentality. The magic of collective thinking only works if you have many independent viewpoints: a diversity of opinions is what makes multi-silo breakthrough project collaborations such an effective force.

- How do you do qTeam?

Team Conversations: The qTeam process uses the same one-on-one conversational elements as the Q Model. You may wish to first practice a conversation with a trusted associate to build your basic skills since one-on-one conversations are more linear and easier to manage. Conversely, team conversations are a lot more like *herding cats,* where ideas and attention wander off in random directions.

Herding Cats: Feed the goats and they will follow you everywhere, but cats are independent and will go where they wish. If you are working with a group that is not aligned, there will always be people who head off in a random direction. Many facilitators will talk about *forming, storming,* and *norming,* as they are important stages in a team's evolution that cannot be managed too tightly; try to be OK with the beautiful *messiness* of the qTeam process.

Facilitated Discussion: The main approach to the qTeam process is a free form conversation with one person in a facilitator role. In this context, you might simply go through the Q Model questions in a formal or organic manner and engage the team in a healthy discussion. Ideally, you do this while standing in front of a flip chart and conduct the basic whiteboarding process, as outlined in Chapter 13: capturing keywords, you draw shapes around them and connect key ideas with lines or arrows. Even in a self-directed team, members can take turns acting in the facilitator role to maintain the balance of team equality. A good approach is beginning and ending with a facilitated discussion while using the qTeam tools to build momentum in the middle.

Tools are Critical: Conversational tools like brainstorming, whiteboarding, missioning, and team identity formation makes all the difference. If you only ask Q Model questions, the process can sometimes stall or lead into a dead-end. Adding in some group tools, such as the visual modeling process outlined below and in Chapter 13, is an ideal way to warm up the group and build momentum.

Get the Real Issue: Most teams are not teams, they are groups of people who have somehow been placed together. It takes time, energy, and commitment to create a real team: trust is earned and builds up in a series of stages as the team collectively agrees on solutions or strategies. Getting these critical challenges into an open discussion is the direct path to building a real team.

Real projects: No one wants to do *fake* team building or endlessly discuss the *dysfunction* of a team, so focus on real projects and critical challenges instead. Get this right and your team will fully engage. Get it wrong and you will have another *boring meeting* on your hands. Remember, achieving your team KPI number is often the best breakthrough project to start with.

Use the Q Project Definition Model: Find the critical goal and turn it into a project. Find the key challenge on that project and turn it into the focus of the team conversation. Identify any points of conflict in advance.

Luck is Planning: Invest in project definition and current state analysis before you begin. As external professional team facilitators, the qDrive staff generally spends about three days of planning and preparation for each day of executive-level facilitation in a business transformation project. There is a large amount of behind the scenes preparation required to make these executive sessions "magically" work. Do your homework and find out what is going on before you jump in.

Paradox: You can't find the real issue until you engage the team. You can't engage the team until you find the real issue.

This is a nested problem that you have to work through. Ask people individually what the real challenge is and you will get many different ideas or potential solutions in response. Start with a small issue or complaint that gets everyone engaged. Generally speaking, executives and senior managers are more *out of touch* with the real front line issues and challenges than they are willing to admit. In practice, it is only when the front-line teams engage that the real challenges and issues emerge.

How to do qTeam in five steps: You might be an internal functional leader or an external professional. In either case, you can start with these five steps:

Step 1: You introduce the *company breakthrough* concept and invite selected executives or business leaders to attend. You can also start with a functional team lower in the organization.

Step 2: You start the project definition process. Look for the top strategic goals, existing initiatives, or areas for revenue growth. Look for critical challenges that may block business results. Begin to define several key breakthrough projects. Identifying the challenges is the key to achieving high-impact qTeam results.

Step 3: You carefully select the other key leaders, managers, or technical experts who are involved in or are relevant to this project area. Getting the right people at the table is essential. They should care about this project area and be interested in a breakthrough.

Step 4: You and your team run the qTeam session. Warm up the team with the process below. Introduce the tools and the new mindset. Get fully engaged in working with your team on your project breakthrough. Go through the three stages of the qTeam process:

    1 - Brainstorm
    2 - Visual Model
    3 - Missioning Team Identity

Step 5: After the first session, work to maintain the momentum of your project execution. As you continue, your team will naturally become engaged and begin to master the Q Model tools. Keep going — real breakthrough project results are just around the corner.

- Warm-Up:

Start with Trust: A team will not instantly jump into a high-alignment collaborative state. It takes a solid foundation of trust and careful framing of the discussion topics to build engagement. In the initial state, before the warm-up process, a team will always be lacking in trust. People know that the other team members are judging them, and will naturally hold back.

Ideal Team Size: There is no hard rule on this, but the ideal team size is around 5–7 people. With three people, there will not be enough diversity of thinking to build momentum. With eight people, some will hold back and observe, and the team may end up being a mix of leaders and followers. Large teams are more difficult to manage and align: break a team of ten people into two groups of five and have them work on different parts of the project.

Start with the Basics: Identify the project or challenge and turn it into a question. Ask soft questions three different ways to warm up the brain. Remember the basics of asking them:

I am curious…?
Can we explore…?
What are some ways to begin to…?
What are some small first steps…?

Question Design is Critical: Turn the project or challenge into a general open-ended question to set the frame for the entire conversation. You may have to ask it several times to warm up the team. From this first question, you can begin to ask more detailed questions about subtopics. You will never get the perfect question in the beginning, so ask questions until something sticks and you start to gain traction.

Current State Wheel: Once you have agreed on the main topic for discussion, invite the team to spend ten minutes discussing the current state of the project. Simply draw a large circle on a flip chart page and divide the circle into eight pie slices. Ask, "What are the main issues or challenges for this project?" and try to get them to fill in all eight segments of the wheel, with one issue per segment. Try to fill all of them, but make sure to have a 1–2-minute discussion on each segment you get. In the end, try to agree as a team on one or two of the most challenging issues.

What are the main issues or challenges for this project?
What are the most significant issues we are facing?
What is the current state of this challenge?
Where precisely are *we at now* on this issue?
What is the most challenging area?

The Current State Wheel will get your team to focus on the issues and engage with the challenges. Remember to be non-judgmental, never delving too far into the past or assigning blame. Keep digging on the current state of each area, trying to get everyone to add to the discussion.

1 - Brainstorm

Yielding new ideas and original solutions, brainstorming is the most effective way to unfreeze the team brain. Consider it the ultimate warm-up tool.

Brain Freeze: HBR's survey data suggests that 87% of all managers operate in a state of *brain freeze*.[1-1] If you take a group of stuck managers and ask for a breakthrough solution, they will probably not respond. Don't expect the first brainstorming question to do anything. Instead, use the following brainstorming approach to unfreeze almost any stuck team.

Evil Brainstorm: We have all been through one of these. Your boss is conducting a brainstorm and asks for a new approach. You suggest the first thing that pops into your mind and there is a moment of silence — the tension builds. Suddenly, the boss explodes! He rants about how terrible your stupid idea is and embarrasses you in front of the entire team. Eventually, still feeling like a fool, you realize it was all an evil trick. We will now take the opposite approach.

Every idea belongs to the group: Ideas cannot be *owned*, so ban the concept of idea ownership in your team. If you wish to be successful in life, never say "my idea..." again for the rest of your life. The moment you propose an idea or place a Post-it note on a whiteboard, that idea belongs to the group.

Every idea is equal: Honor and respect all ideas, no matter how bad. The one rule is that everyone must agree that all ideas are equal. There is no place for idea judgment. Enforce this as a rule.

Post-it Notes: Only one person can write on a flip chart, but anyone can write on Post-it notes and place them on the board. Using Post-its naturally builds momentum in any brainstorm.

Post-its are Physical Objects: Ideas are just random thoughts. We don't think of them as real. Writing an idea on a Post-it note gives it a physical form. When we place it on the whiteboard, we surrender control of the concept and physically give it to the group.

Numbers: While facilitating for IBM in 1993, Marilyn Atkinson developed the *numbering* brainstorm principle: if you fill a flip chart page or whiteboard with numbers from 1 to 40 and ask the team to come up with 40 new ideas, approaches, or solutions, *they will do it*. Provided they can place a few ideas on the board and get going, the team will somehow presuppose that there are 40 solutions or ideas; keep adding numbers and they'll keep going. You can go to 100 if needed.

Eggplant: What can I say, people give me eggplants. Yes, as I travel around the world, people from every country will hand them to me. It is extraordinary when someone hands you anything, let alone a purple vegetable. I have now received eggplants from my students in Europe, Asia, and the USA. Use the power of eggplant.

What is Eggplant? An eggplant is a purple vegetable that thinks it is a fruit. It is also a random, silly, or downright crazy idea that we *intentionally* introduce into the brainstorm. Remember, everyone has already agreed that all ideas are equal. When you introduce an idea like "Get a breakthrough in technical quality by giving *free beer* to all staff," everyone laughs.

Honor the Eggplants: Ham it up with low-grade humor. "Free beer! What a great idea, I wish I thought of that." Enjoy acting a little stupid, being embarrassed, and losing face. Breaking the box of "looking professional" is the direct path to a leadership breakthrough.

Hide your Eggplants: After you have presented a few terrible eggplant ideas, offer a few *possible* eggplants. The tricky part is that people will not know if you are being serious or silly, and the ensuing *cognitive dissonance* will confound the judgmental part of their minds. As the *judgment brain* relaxes, the ideas flow quickly.

High Quantity – Low Quality: If you put the numbers, Post-it notes, and eggplants all together into a system, you will get a high volume of *low-quality* ideas. Remember, the point of the exercise is not to come up with a brilliant solution. It is to warm up and energize the team thinking system. If you do this right, you will get popcorn.

Make Popcorn: If you have ever made popcorn in a pot, popcorn maker, or even a microwave, you will know how this works. First, you turn on the heat and awkwardly wait as nothing happens for a while. Then a few *leader* kernels pop, perhaps as many as four or five. Suddenly all the kernels pop all at once, and just when you're really starting to enjoy yourself, the whole show is over — save for a few stragglers that will never pop. Ignore them.

Having conducted the qTeam brainstorm process more than 300 times in companies around the world, I can say that the popcorn analogy is 100% accurate. It doesn't matter if you are using an old-fashioned pot on the stove or some newfangled popcorn maker: just set it up right and be patient. It always works.

Setup:

- Set the contract as an open-ended question
- Use the Q Model. First build Contract, Rapport, and Outcome
- Use Post-it notes for each idea. Slap them on with a bang!
- List 40 numbers with blank spaces for ideas
- Get the group standing up to increase energy
- Switch the team facilitator every five minutes to disrupt any leaders

Foundation:

- Frame effective Opened-Ended Questions.
- Use Plurals: "What are some of the *ways*…?"
- Be OK with silence. A good question takes time to sink in.
- Repeat the question. Teams won't engage until they hear it three times.
- Begin softly, slowly building energy and momentum.
- Include everyone: If one person dominates, agree to equal participation.
- No judgment of ideas: All ideas are equally valid. Write them all down
- Go for quantity, not quality: the more ideas, the better.
- All ideas belong to the group. Don't attribute ideas to any one participant.

Build Energy:

- Increase your energy, Increase the pace
- Have people declare their idea as they post it
- Have them slap the ideas on the board with a loud sound
- Add more numbers. Always have ten more blank spaces to keep ideas flowing
- Encourage loose, wild ideas
- Build up to a climax and move into the visual model
- Appreciate the group. Thank them for getting such a high number

2 - Visual Modeling

The Visual Model: Once your team has finished the brainstorm and generated 40+ ideas or solutions on Post-it notes, they are ready to move into the visual model. We already went through visual modeling in Chapter 13, but here is a quick summary of the process:

Pick a shape: Draw it on a flip chart

Key ideas: Bring in some of the key concepts from the brainstorm session.

Ask: "How can we fit these ideas into this model?"

>Start to fill in the ideas
>Notice where they fit
>Be curious. See where it leads

Start to build the model:

- Look for patterns
- Notice any symmetry or asymmetry
- Watch for emergent models begin to form
- Add arrows, movement, flow-chart sequences
- Use many different-colored markers for maximum impact

Pick a visual model shape from below or make your own:

3 - Missioning Team Identity

The process of missioning a team identity can begin as a silly game but will evolve into a serious declaration as the vision and mission of your team becomes real. The following presents the process in a lighthearted way useful for teams having difficulties, but you can find a more formal scenario for missioning team identity in Chapter 17. This process works best if you have multiple teams, but it can also work well with a single team.

Mission: Once the team has built several versions of a visual model, get them to explain the value of the mission. Ask them, "How will this project help everyone in: your city, your country, the Earth?"

Pause the process and announce:

> The top news outlet in your country (CNN News in the US) has a broadcast crew arriving in ten minutes.

> Tell them they must deliver a two-minute presentation on their project to the camera. The best presentation will be broadcast nation-wide.

> They need to build a presentation and explain why their project is vital to everyone in the county.

Brand: Ask the team to pick a crazy team or project name. Ask them to create a logo for the project. Pick an animal, color, and metaphor to represent your project.

Present & Declare: Ask the team to present the plan together to a live audience. They must include graphics or visuals to tell their story. Use a countdown clock to increase pressure and team energy.

> If you have multiple teams ask, "Which team is going to *win*?
> With a single team ask, "Are you going to *win*?
> To win you need the *best*: story, graphics, song, dance, music, costume
> You have ten minutes… GO!

> Use a countdown clock to increase energy as you approach the ten-minute deadline. Have the team or each group present their project and declare their team identity.

Why go Crazy? If the crazy game show version of this qTeam process is too much for you, you can, of course, conduct it in a serious manner. However, breaking through the *threshold of embarrassment* is a key tool in getting past the *business as usual* mindset. Wanting to look good, people like to play it cool, especially in group settings. The crazy game show format pushes everyone on the team past the threshold of embarrassment, to the point where you can't keep playing cool unless you play along. Once everyone sees that everyone else is on board and equally embarrassed, they will drop their business as usual mindset and be unable to resist the force of team integration.

Peak Moment: Teams need to be consciously aware that they have gone through a peak moment of transformation, and the declaration at the end of the qTeam process is that moment. From here on out, the team is in a *transformed* state, and now has the team momentum needed to take on any challenge.

Chapter 15 - Transformation

Transformation is:

A shift in self-perception
A shift in the way you see yourself
A shift in the way you see your team, project, or products
A shift in the way you see the business opportunities
A shift in the way your staff, stakeholders, or customers see the company

- Stiefel – Acquisition Identity

The VP said, "We don't want to be part of that company. They do things differently than us." We had a 2.9 billion dollar problem.

Stiefel, a pharmaceutical skincare company, was acquired by GlaxoSmithKline in 2009, in a $2.9 billion transaction. Fiercely proud of their 165-year history, Stiefel's independent management style became an operational challenge over the next 18 months, as successive merger integration programs encountered internal resistance. Some GSK executives began to call the value of the acquisition into question.

Compliance: In 2011 the entire management team, including the former CEO, participated in a strategic session facilitated by myself, Paul Gossen. This short program focused on the implementation of industry ethics and regulatory compliance. At the time, GSK was facing related lawsuits of $3.7 billion, so this was a critical issue. On the first day, the executive team began a rigorous discussion of how to shift their business practices. Inevitably, the discussion of compliance led to much more significant issues, such as their lack of faith in the GSK leadership. We began to build trust through the conversational process, but as we proceeded the executives began to push back on the entire idea of adopting GSK's regulatory policies. We had to address the hard questions, such as "What do we want from GSK?" and "How will we fit into GSK?"

Become GSK? These difficult questions revealed the inevitable identity-level conflict faced by every acquisition management team: how do we fit our current business identity into this larger enterprise? Every acquisition company goes through some kind of accounting integration to harmonize reporting. However, most acquisition companies never address the much more important identity-level questions that are always on everyone's mind during mergers, such as "How do we fit our old company self-identity and mission into this new larger enterprise?

For the Stiefel team, this was disrupting their ability to engage in the new enterprise. The former CEO had retired but was still around, keeping one foot in the door. The team was not fully able to step up to the new opportunity because they had not built a new vision of success in GSK. This discussion required carefully facilitated exploration. The team had to negotiate some fundamental trust and alignment issues to even engage in this conversation.

Vision for Integration: We worked through their objections one by one. Finally, they all reached a point where they could begin to develop a vision of success within GSK. We asked them to commit to this vision, as part of the new compliance integration program. They created a 60-day integration project that they would manage themselves, calling it "We are GSK."

Over the next two months, the leadership group created actions and accountability for the integration compliance program. However, the main project focus became continuing the integration of their new team identity with the rest of the 75 staff. They maintained their independent leadership style but shifted to a more active partnership with the parent company. They continued the discussions and reported a fundamental shift at the end of the two months. This new point of view had generalized to become the new normal.

- What is Transformation?

Breakthrough Results are Not an Accident: As a manager or business leader, you must generate a real breakthrough in business results. The only reason you would not invest your precious time in a breakthrough result is that you cannot see a path to get there. If your team could have generated this breakthrough result on their own, they would have already done that. This is where the Q Model comes in.

Transformation is a shift in how people see themselves, which fundamentally alters their mindset and behaviors. However, they will not believe the shift is real unless they see evidence that includes taking the first action steps and producing some actual business results. Unless people physically act in alignment with the vision, the transformation will rapidly disappear. With seven days of inaction, the breakthrough will turn into another good idea that didn't happen.

Transformation is Easy: Transformation can take place in a single conversation. But getting to that point of transformation can be an intricate process. Working through all of the trust and current state issues and strategic possibilities to align on a single vision can take many focused conversations. However, when you achieve alignment, the actual transformation part is easy. It can take place in a single moment.

Resistance is Futile - You will be Assimilated: Even in a large company, real transformation can spread very quickly, if it is already *wanted* and *needed*. It is difficult to paddle a boat upstream. It is much easier to go in the same direction as the current of the river. The key is to get the transformation into alignment with the existing organizational needs, culture, and values.

There are five key systems to transform a project or team:

1 - **Visioning:** A clear picture in your mind, in which you see a future where you get what you want.

2 - **Whiteboarding:** Any kind of drawing that shows the process of seeing *what you want* in a visual model.

3 - **Team:** Developing a team of people who are firmly committed and engaged in a breakthrough process.

4 - **Value:** Humans only do things that create value. Building a clear value chain that links project success to the shared values of a team will create a strong internal structure of motivation.

5 - Missioning: Continuously amplifying the potential scope and impact of company success, so that the mission expands, is another engine of transformation.

All five of these conversational systems can be interlinked to create a high-alignment state in a person, project, or team. You can't make people transform, but you can assist them to transform themselves. As you guide the team through a series of transformational questions and conversations, a shift or transformation will inevitably occur.

Small Shift: People love fireworks. Looking for a big bang explosion with lots of colors to dazzle the eye during a transformation, they miss the small shift that has already happened. A big transformation is made up of many small shifts in thinking or perception. Transformation is often an incremental process that builds momentum. In the end, when seen from the outside, it looks like a big transformation. Internally it was step by step. Remember to appreciate the small shift.

Secret Code Name: This high-alignment state can not only be held in place but can transition into a persistent long-term motivational system by using a project code name, which serves as a metaphoric team identity.

- Transform Identity:

To understand identity transformation in a business, you need to separate the *what* from the *who*.

"What" Transformation: Leaders in every industry are talking about transformation. Many transformation projects focus on a new strategy, business model, market, or technology. However, the majority of them are "what" transformations focused on content and strategy. Leaders are so focused on these surface-level issues that they miss the underlying structure of real transformation, which is all about a shift in how people or companies see themselves. Here are some "what" questions:

> What is the new strategy?
> What is the better business model?
> What is the new technology?
> What is the new product or market focus?

With a "what" focus, leaders are fundamentally missing the real power of business transformation. A team can alter focus, strategy, and implementation, but if they do not fundamentally alter identity, it is not a transformation.

"Who" Transformation: Real transformation always comes from a "who" question:

> Who am I? Who am I becoming?
> Who are we? Who are we becoming?
> Who will we become when our project is successful?
> Who will we become when the company transformation is successful?

These kinds of "who" questions are difficult to answer. This is not something that gets sorted out in a single one-hour conversation, but rather a series of identity-building touch points that take place over many discussions and ramp up momentum.

Identity - You are soaking in it: Any new project or business initiative naturally begins an identity-level shift. As we create a vision of success, we naturally see ourselves *becoming* the person who has the ability to achieve our goals. We automatically form a metaphoric identity around this new possible vision of ourselves, and this new identity gets stronger. As we take action in alignment with this vision, the identity becomes stronger still, to the point where it is undeniably real. This natural identity process can be enhanced with any of the following tools:

- A strong vision of success
- A strong link to the value of the success
- A strong link to the value words associated with the vision of success
- Any kind of Missioning (see Chapter 17)
- A team name or secret code name for the project
- A brand, logo, or mascot that represents success
- Links to themes or metaphors that underscore a unique quality of the team

Here are a few more ideas that define the "who" of identity:

- Identity is contextual – It is ever-changing with your role
- Identity is who you think you are, in the moment and over the long term
- Identity drives Vision. Keywords are: be, being, become
- An identity-level shift is the essence of transformation

Here are a few key identity Questions:

- Individual future or success-based identity: Who are you becoming?
- Team identity question: Who are we becoming?
- Missioning identity question: How will our success help others?

- Who am I?

Some people view the word "identity" with suspicion or view the very topic of identity as inherently manipulative. When we refer to establishing a new success-based identity, some people even think of *brainwashing*. In truth, adding in some new element in your self-identity is quite the opposite. People only build a new vision of themselves if they *want it* and it seems *aligned*. Teams will only step into a success-based team identity if they collectively agree and align as a team. A shift in identity is all about *internal alignment*. However, it is still best to approach the subject of individual identity with the utmost of respect.

> A system will reject any change that is out of alignment with the whole. **- Milton Erickson**

Ask yourself and your team:

> Who do I want to be when I achieve my career breakthrough?
> Who do we want to become when our project is successful?
> Who are we becoming as we transform our company?

Core Identity: In a normal social context, it is almost impossible for anyone to manipulate an individual's core identity unless that person willingly agrees. By *normal social context*, we do not mean Nazi Germany, where people were put under extreme social pressure, by the threat of death. By normal social context, we mean a job where someone can always quit as a last defense. This *walk-away* defense sits above a lower-level protection which comes from your intuition or right-brain processing patterns. A person's core intuitive system is a built-in, top-level identity management system. If a new self-conception comes along which doesn't seem aligned with your current self-identity, it gets rejected. Alignment is an efficient self-correcting mechanism that governs identity.

Alignment: If a change seems wrong, you won't be able to *see* it as yourself.

Below are two playful thought experiments you can try with your own identity to demonstrate this concept. They prove that any identity shift has to fit and link to the real world to make it stick. An identity-level shift is not magic. It is an iterative process of self or team alignment.

Test 1: Say out loud, "I am a frog."

Are you a frog? No, you are not a frog — proof being that frogs cannot read this text. To shift to a frog identity, you would have to declare to yourself and the world that you are a frog every single moment of every day. Your mind would have to commit to becoming a frog. Finally, you would have to take physical and mental action every day to become a frog. As you build concrete evidence over time that you are becoming a frog, this new identity would get stronger. Clearly, this is not going to happen, and before any of it possibly could, you would reject the entire process as ridiculous — unless, of course, you had some serious mental health issues, or were already a frog to begin with.

Test 2: Say out loud, "I am a parent."

There are three categories of people who could be making this statement. For any of you who are parents, this would fit with *who you know yourself to be*, and the statement would reaffirm your existing identity. For any of you who *are not* parents, this statement would seem strange, and your *intuitive mind* would probably ignore it. However, there is a third category: what if you are thinking about becoming a parent? This third category will begin to demonstrate the real power of an identity level shift — the one you are creating here with your declaration.

Future Parents: If you are thinking about becoming a parent, how would the phrase, "I am a parent" impact you? What if you were actively trying to have children? What would be the effect of the statement in this case? What if you were expecting a baby soon? This statement might be exciting and support you in becoming prepared for this key shift in your self-identity. The moment you had that new child, you would again declare, "I am a parent." The evidence of seeing your new child would complete this shift in who you know yourself to be. While this shift would be complete the moment you saw your new child, it would have *begun* the moment you initially declared it.

Brainwashing 2.0: By now you have started to realize that identity transformation *is* brainwashing. Fortunately, it is not the kind of brainwashing we see in 007 spy films. Instead, it is a normal and self-directed process that people naturally go through as they develop in life. Typically, an Olympic athlete must visualize and meditate upon becoming a gold medal champion hundreds of times to get a performance boost. But a Q Model leader can accelerate this process by asking a few good questions to enhance internal integration and alignment.

- Success Based Identity:

Steps to Building a Success-Based Identity: As we use the Q Model to build a *success-based* identity, our vision, commitment, and actions will provide the context our intuitive system needs to make the changes stick. We will build this identity one step at a time using the following formula:

1 - Declare your vision
2 - Commit to it
3 - Take action
4 - Build evidence

1 - Make a Declaration:

- Declare your vision out loud and in writing, with intention and intensity
- Work with your team to build a team vision of success
- Repeat this declaration out loud to your team.

No Affirmations: If you are familiar with positive psychology, this declaration may sound like an *affirmation*. But a declaration is not an affirmation — those are feel-good phrases you say over and over again, such as "excellence is our core strength." Affirmations are ineffective because, at some level in your gut, you know the statement is not true. And the more you say it, the stronger your lack of belief in it becomes. This happens because the affirmation lacks commitment, action, and evidence. By contrast, a declaration is founded in 100% commitment and realized with action and evidence.

2 - Make a Formal and Public Commitment:

- Commit to beginning your first project steps in the next seven days
- Commit to building the first project *win* in the next 30 days
- Share your commitment with people you respect and trust
- Make your commitment in writing and out loud with your team
- Set a timeline of 30 days or less for achieving some critical first step.

3 - Take Action:

Take the action steps you promised for the next seven and 30 days. Our intuitive system knows that sometimes we say things but don't do them. Likewise, it knows that action takes place in the real world, not in words or intentions. You cannot lie to yourself about this stuff.

If we do what we said we would do, we know the declaration was real. The new identity will begin to influence our thoughts and decisions throughout our day-to-day experience, provided we continue to take action. If we don't take action, we know the declaration was false. Consequently, our new success-based identity gets discarded and disappears, and our previous identity takes over again. For example, you may have an "'I like business as usual" identity or something else linked to comfort or routine. To achieve long-term results, your success identity must be stronger than your business as usual identity.

You must perform the actions required to make the new identity stick. Even if the action is small, any real progress made on your breakthrough project will start to make the new identity stick. This way, you will be working directly on building the new identity and achieving project success at the same time.

4 - Build Evidence:

1 - Do The Work: You must take action on the key steps even if it is just planning the breakthrough project.

2 - Collect Evidence That You Are Making Progress: Take a little time each week to recognize that you are achieving results. This evidence shows that your new success identity is getting stronger. Build your evidence further by tracking your success.

3 - Actively Appreciate Your Progress: You have to be systematic in how you measure and declare your progress to yourself and your team. The evidence won't stick unless we speak to people about our progress. If you are working with a team, make sure to spend a little time sharing success stories each week.

- 3 Containers of Identity:

Here are three more ways to make your transformation identity stronger:

Personal   **Team**   **Metaphoric**

Identity building always links with high-alignment. People reach their peak of performance by exploring the areas of life where they have the most passion. You can express this in a personal, team, or metaphoric way.

Personal Identity: This is your core personality, values, and the intimate thoughts you might share with close family or friends. Your personal identity is "who you are" most of the time. You are always in control. You are in the driver's seat, behind the wheel of this new way of viewing yourself.

Your present personal identity is focused on "who am I now," which includes your interests and experience. Your future personal identity is focused on "who am I becoming," which is an expression of your future goals, vision, and values in life. As you develop and express your vision and values, you get more energy and become more engaged, which further entrenches your new success-based personal identity.

Ask yourself, "What kind of person do I want to become?" A clear image of this *future you* is the foundation of any personal shift. All other facets of self-identity are built on that solid base. As such, the question "What do I want?" is a good place to start. As you envision getting what you want and collect corresponding value words, your success-based personal identity gets stronger.

In life, we all maintain a close inner circle of people. As you declare your new success-based personal identity to those people in your life whom you trust the most, your commitment gets stronger. You can't let down your closest confidants, so you must remain strong and committed. This step takes courage. Begin slowly. As you build evidence, it will get easier.

Public Image: Beyond your trusted circle of family, friends, and close associates there is a larger circle that encompasses your professional identity. This includes anything to do with how you wish to be perceived in public, at work, or as a professional. You can think of this as anything you might post on your LinkedIn page. Playing around with your public identity is not the same as transforming your personal identity. Most people understand that their public image is not closely linked to their authentic personal identity. Because of this, the former will have less identity-transforming impact. If you are courageous, go ahead and express your vision publicly or post it on your social media page, but understand the limits of your public image.

Team Identity: Team identity[15-1] is the collective self-identity that emerges in a committed team, and it is one of the most powerful concepts in the entire Q Model. This team identity will form around any shared vision of success that a team builds. As a Q Model leader, you can develop your team's identity by asking good questions. This is embedded throughout the qTeam process we discussed in Chapter 14.

A team identity is an ideal source of energy. As you collectively develop a vision for a project breakthrough with your team, *"who we are"* as a successful team naturally gathers momentum. As the team builds a vision for breakthrough project results, they naturally begin to express their success-based team identity. You can take this even further by *Missioning* the team identity, as you'll see in Chapter 17.

Metaphoric Identity: This is about comparing yourself to, or imagining yourself as someone or something that expresses a metaphoric *quality* you wish to possess. [15-2] Humans constantly use metaphors to express themselves. This expression is the core foundation of a metaphoric self-identity.

Animal Metaphoric Identity Exercise:

What animal most represents your success?
(An eagle, lion, dolphin, butterfly, or something else…?)
Why did you choose that particular animal? What quality does this animal have that you feel most represents your success?

Heroic Metaphoric Identity Exercise:

Think about some successful people you admire.
(Steve Jobs, Bill Gates, Oprah Winfrey, or someone else…?)

What great historical figures inspire you?
(Gandhi, Einstein, Abe Lincoln, Mandela, or someone else…?)

What fictional characters inspire you?
(Jame Bond, Gandalf, Spiderman, Harry Potter, or someone else…?)

Look through all the possibilities and pick your top three.
Ask yourself, what are the qualities you admire in these people?

Imagine you are one of these people, possessing their qualities. You admire someone when you can imagine being or becoming that person. Identify the quality you admire and turn it into a value word. Practice linking these value words to the success of your projects.

You have just touched upon some elements of your metaphoric identity. While you can do these two exercises individually, they are most often integrated into the team development process to build a powerful team identity. At the end of the Visual Modeling process in Chapter 13, we also included a team color, icon, logo, or brand names, and a team cheer to further reinforce team identity.

Crazy Code Name: A metaphoric team identity is one of the most effective ways to create an unstoppable team. Making a secret code name for the team or project is the easiest way to do this. It is important to have a discussion and reach a consensus on the best name. This should take place after the team has a strong vision of success-and it should be reaffirmed just before the team makes a final commitment to the project breakthrough. First touched upon in Chapter 14, here is a little secret of the Q Model:

- A silly or crazy team name is your secret weapon
- A crazy project code name is the simplest way to maintain alignment
- A crazy team or project name is the *container* of a team identity

As we have previously mentioned, a crazy team or project name breaks through the *threshold of embarrassment* and the business as usual mindset, because it links project success with team identity. The most embarrassing part is usually the team cheer, which does most of the break through the threshold of embarrassment After this, the code name itself becomes a trigger you can use any time to regenerate a high-alignment state in the team.

Declare Team identity: As a team aligns around a plan project success, a team identity forms naturally. The practice of declaring team identity is a direct path to a team 100% committed to project success. The team starts by declaring the team identity to themselves. As they build confidence, they expand by declaring to trusted supporters.

Viral Transmission: When the project has sufficient traction and momentum, team identity should be declared to everyone who will listen. You don't have to ask anyone to do this. Your team will simply be proud of their results to want everyone to know of their success. This is the magic *buzz* that accelerates the very idea of breakthrough results. They will introduce the unstoppable Q Model *virus*, which will begin to spread transformation throughout the company.

Chapter 16 – Value Transformation

Key Value Questions:

Why is this important?
How can we measure this result?
How will this help the company?
How can this result help our customers?
What is the impact on the bottom line?
Why is producing this result important?
Why is this meaningful for the team?
How will dealing with this challenge make a difference?

- Golder: Value Driven Transformation

The global CEO came to Gordon with an impossible task: to fundamentally alter the mindset and behavior of 6000 stubborn engineers in less than 12 months. "You are the only person in the company who can fix this," he said.

In 2009, Golder Associates faced a client revolt over poor customer service. One of the top global environmental engineering firms, Golder's annual revenue exceeds $1 billion. Specializing in testing and cleaning up large industrial sites, the firm's clients were consistently complaining of cost overruns and project delays. Internal surveys reported that the engineers were more focused on project quality than customer satisfaction. In addition to keeping the customers happy, these engineers had to also comply with government regulations and ethical standards intended to protect the environment. Low quality project delivery could expose the company to liabilities. For example, in an acid leach site used for metal excitation, the clean-up and soil remediation costs can easily exceed the entire set-up and operational budget if the project is poorly executed. The stakes were high.

Late and Over Budget: A critical internal measurement was project cancellations, or "kills." The number of project kills was increasing each quarter, posing a grave threat to the long-term future of the company. Client surveys would come back with feedback such as: "They do a good job, but they don't really care about your project," or "If you want it late and over budget, send it to Golder."

The company was owned and run by a group of about 300 senior partners. These were elite engineers, who had worked their way up to managing vertical business units and technical teams of specialists. Most of these partners would *passively agree* that client satisfaction was an important issue. There was a core executive leadership team of about 15 directors who were acutely concerned with the problem. Naturally, they told everyone to improve their customer service, but nothing seemed to change. Over the next year, they introduced new process management systems, operating guidelines, rules, punishments, customer service training, and project management training. However, the rate of project kills kept increasing. They could not seem to get at the root cause.

Technical Excellence: Already an influential executive and champion of the Q Model, in 2010 Gordon was appointed Golder's VP of Client Satisfaction. We began to work together to analyze the current state, and after dozens of interviews and conversations, we found that the senior partners were driven by technical excellence and project quality instead of customer satisfaction. It became clear that the words *technical, excellence,* and *quality* were the implicit core value words of the organization.

It's much easier to ride a horse in the direction it's going: The challenge of enterprise transformation is to use the existing force and direction of the company. If you fight against the direction that everyone is already going in, you will quickly run out of energy. You have to find the existing momentum of the people or culture and use that to take them where they need to go. For Golder's senior partners, this existing momentum was their passion for technical excellence and project quality. In any project, you can always add *more* of these things. But how do you know when to stop? As with all core values, these three words were the company's source of strength, but also its Achilles' heel.

Know yourself and you will win all battles. - **Sun Tzu, The Art of War**

The challenge was to get the partners to link client satisfaction with their core values for technical excellence and project quality. If you work in support or sales this link might seem obvious, but many engineers, scientists, and technical experts see customer service as an annoying external thing. The Golder engineers were resisting this mindset shift, and we needed them to see customer satisfaction as a *critical component* of technical excellence and project quality. The partners would often fight over who would get to lead a project. For partners, leading a project was about the power and prestige of telling the staff what to do, not keeping the clients happy. They also did not have the interest or skills to track a project's estimated-to-actual project delivery timelines.

The company had an effective ERP system for tracking project budgets. However, it did not track the ongoing rate of project delivery; unless the project became a *kill*, project risk was invisible. The only early warning system might be a phone call from the client, threatening to cancel the project. While this threat might reach the senior partner managing the project, they would not usually share a *project at-risk* status in the ERP system. Only after a project cancellation would it show up in accounting, and only then would anyone other than the project owner discover the risk. At this point, it would be too late for any intervention.

How do you change an engineer? Ask them to solve a problem: We piloted a program that eventually rolled out across the company. At round table events with teams of senior partners and their top project engineers, we presented them with raw customer feedback data. Playing dumb, we did not attempt to frame the problem or explain what was going on, but merely presented each team with the raw data and asked open-ended questions, like "What's going on here?" If they asked questions back, the event organizers would pretend to be confused and bounce the questions back to the engineers.

Engineers love to solve problems. Give them a technical challenge and they get right to work. Once they got into analyzing the data, we asked them to use their insights to frame questions like "How might we improve our tracking of *at-risk* projects?"

Not offering any advice, we asked them to suggest ideas and potential solutions. In the afternoon sessions, we would ask more structured questions and assign each table to work on a specific customer satisfaction project area.

Ask Core Value Questions: When discussing client satisfaction, we would ask very simple questions like, "Why is this important?" Every time a group proposed a solution, we would ask them to name it with a single keyword. At the end of each day, each group would have to present three keywords that represented client satisfaction. These core value words were the key to getting the managers to own client satisfaction. We would then ask questions to link these client satisfaction keywords back to the same three core value words: *technical*, *excellence,* and *quality*. The goal was for leaders to see *customer satisfaction* as a fundamental tenet of *technical excellence*.

Too Many Leaders, not Enough Managers: This project did not go as planned. There was a small segment of senior partners who pushed back and had little interest in the change. They saw managing day-to-day *estimated to actual* budgets and timelines as beneath them. We designed a new role for Manager of Project Budgets and Delivery, coming up with the most "unsexy" name we could think of so that senior partners would not interfere. These new managers would move between teams, collecting ongoing budget and progress data so that *at-risk* projects could be flagged into the ERP tracking system.

The Client's Point of View: The real breakthrough came from the layer below the senior partners. These were the younger, technical project managers who were much quicker to develop the new mindset of "budget and delivery equals client satisfaction." We kept working to influence these younger engineers to link client satisfaction with their core values of technical excellence. Besides their natural ability to see that customer satisfaction was a critical element of technical excellence, they were also in a position to influence the senior partners on a day-to-day basis and could thus advocate the client's point of view when it was time to make difficult decisions on *delivery time* versus *technical quality.*

The one-day event became a series of events, as it took longer than expected for the change to proliferate. But we persisted, and within a year *project kill* numbers were significantly reduced.

- Why Values?

Why do some business leaders have a seemingly innate ability to attract respect and trust? Are great leaders born or made? Ask any great leader how they became successful and they will almost always talk about their values. Values express an idealized state of being. Values are the internal structure of motivation and commitment. Values define leadership.

- What are values and how do you use them in business?
- How do values unlock energy and engagement?
- How can you use value words to drive motivation and commitment?

Values Theory of Everything: There are lots of good theories of everything that try to reduce the entire universe into a single formula or model. The most famous would be Einstein's *Unified Field Theory*, in which he attempted to reconcile high-energy physics with the quantum universe. He spent most of his life working on this and never found the magic formula. However, his unsuccessful quest paved the way for modern theoretical physics.

In our Values Theory of Everything, we will make a lot of blanket statements, such as "Values are the structure of *all* human motivation." It is important to state that the Q Values Model and philosophy are *not proven* in the scientific sense. Values are based on your individual subjective experience of the world. They are a structure through which we organize and make meaning of the world in which we live.

Value versus Values: In the next few sections we will explore both *value* and *values*. Value is any kind of economic benefit that can be measured externally. Values are the structure of emotional motivation that makes things important or meaningful. We will also refer to *value words*, which are a discrete expression of emotional values, and do not directly link to economic value.

Values versus Ethics: When people think of values they often interlink them with ethics, which are principles that tend to be external. Linking to morality, ethics form a set of external rules that govern behavior, where people who behave within certain constraints could be judged to be good or better than other people who don't. From an external point of view, developing strong ethics is essential. However, the power of Q Model values is based on a *relative* internal experience of values that drives motivation and commitment in people, teams, and projects.

Relative Values: With the Q Model, we work with values or value words in a particular way, taking a bottom-up approach of listening to and respecting people's individual experience of their values. We call these *relative values* because they are entirely subjective to the point of view of their owner. The fundamental skill of a Q Leader is to listen for *other* people's value words.

High-Energy State of Being: In his Special Theory of Relativity, Einstein declared that as you approach *high-energy* states such as the speed of light, time becomes a localized phenomenon based on your point of view. This local point of view is a good metaphor for the role of values in leadership. As people commit to a result and approach a *high-energy* state, such as committing to deliver a challenging business result, their commitment ultimately rests upon their *relationship* with a set of core value words. If they have a *strong* relationship with these words, their commitment will be strong. If they have a *weak* or *fuzzy* relationship with them, their commitment will be weak. We will test this idea further, as we explore the Q Values approach to motivation and commitment.

What are Values? Values are words linked to the positive emotions that give us energy and motivation. Since positive emotional energy is hard to define and manage, it is only natural to give it a label or name. This label is what we call a *value word*. The more we use this word in life, the more we define it as an idealized state of being.

Value Words: There are many books and theories about values. However, in the Q Model, we are deconstructing values, motivation, and commitment into a single sub-atomic particle, which is a *value word*. Here is a basic definition of a value word:

1 – Single: Value words are always single words
2 – Positive: Value words represent a positive emotion
3 – Energy: Value words give people energy and motivation
4 – Ideal: Value words represent an idealized state of being

What is important? When you ask people, "What is important?" or "Why is this important?" they will answer in a myriad of ways, but those answers will always contain their value words.

Question: What is the difference between a value word and a keyword?

Keywords can represent anything important. This can include goals, challenges, and SMART results. Keywords are all about taking many ideas and representing them with a single word, one that can be positive, negative, or neutral. Value words are a subset of keywords and are always positive. Values create energy and motivation. Values can fuse and transform into other values.

Tabletop Fusion: Values are like hydrogen in the sun fusing to form helium and then continuing on to form other elements. These elements are constantly in fusion, merging into other elements, and releasing energy. Elements in a fusion chain always reach a final state, which is Iron-56, at which point fusion is no longer possible. You can think of Iron-56 as a core value. A core value has reached its highest form and can no longer fuse with other values. This continuous fusion of values releases tremendous energy, which can be channeled into breakthrough results. Core values are the ultimate elixir of transformation.

- The Science of Values:

What is the brain science of values? Neuroscientists see values as mental states that combine cognition and emotion. Values seem to be neural patterns that link cognitive representations of results to positive motivational emotions.

The Reward System: In a Q Model conversation, your visual thinking system makes a series of pictures or movies about your interpretation of a desired future. If you are discussing a positive future, the reward system naturally gets energized as you repeat the process.

Test Your Reward System: Think of your favorite food. Perhaps you like chocolate or a freshly baked pastry? When did you last eat it? Make a close-up, colorful picture of the experience in your mind's eye; can you see it? Ok, now imagine how this food smells. Is your mouth watering? If it is, you are using your reward system.

As we link our reward system to what is important to us, our emotional system starts to engage with positive emotions. We begin to *want* this future, linking the reward to the steps required to get there. Articulating these links is how a team becomes aligned with a promise.

Dopamine – Reward-Driven Results: Neuroscience correlates the concept of creative problem solving with a healthy addiction to dopamine.[16-3] Dopamine is a neurotransmitter and hormone that functions by sending signals to other nerve cells. The release of dopamine is associated with motivation, concentration, and learning. Every time an activity releases a jolt of dopamine, you connect that activity with a rewarding feeling, which motivates you to engage even more.

- Corporate Value:

Before we can proceed with emotional values, we need to talk about economic value and address some common corporate myths and practices that can be destructive.

Money ≠ Motivation: The prevailing view is that pay, incentives, and bonuses determine motivation. However, in the 1962 Candle experiment, Glucksberg found that adding a monetary reward caused stress for the participants and seemed to shut down their creative thinking and problem-solving abilities.[16-2]

In 2009, researchers at the London School of Economics looked at pay for performance schemes and found that financial incentives can result in a negative impact on overall performance. They concluded that too much external motivation can crowd out internal motivation.[16-3]

> "For challenging problems, higher incentives often lead
> to lower performance." **- Daniel Pink, Drive**

External Corporate Value: External value is anything that can be measured. This basic idea is the heart of traditional business management. As Bob Nardel, former CEO of Home Depot says, "If it can't be measured, it didn't happen."

External value measurements can range from finishing your day-to-day business tasks all the way up to the macro-economic value of the global gross domestic product of all humans on earth. However, no matter how you measure external value, you will always miss the other 50% of the equation. This is the internal emotional value, which is not so easy to measure.

Shareholder Value: In the ever-changing sea of leadership models, the concept of creating shareholder value endures. You could ask, "How does our small project create value for the shareholders of the entire company?" This question might expand the thinking of a team, but its scope is narrow in terms of potential value creation. Building an innovative product has a deeper structure of meaning that extends far beyond its simple economic value to the shareholders.

Profit is a Weak Motivator: Humans have a basic need to seek and find meaning in things. Unfortunately, creating shareholder value does not provide much in terms of meaningful experiences. If a company's only purpose for existence is creating shareholder value, only the shareholders will care. Unless employees can relate to some structure of higher meaning, they will default to a lower state of performance. In essence, they will only be in the company to exchange their time for money. Too much focus on profit is a great way to entrench low performance.

- Create Value:

Value is Created: Humans exist to create value. If you need proof, look at the developed world around you. If humans *took more* value than they created, we would live in a wasteland of destruction. Instead, people *create more* value than they take, so a civilization gets built. Look at the development of science, medicine, and education over the past 1000 years, or the physical construction of cities including their infrastructure of buildings, roads, power, and water supply. This is all a net result of each human adding a little more value than they take away. Julius Caesar may have accidentally burned the great library of Alexandria, but fortunately, the Persian's kept a backup copy of all human knowledge, which allowed European science to flourish during the Renaissance. Caesar did establish the modern calendar, which comes in handy for planning things, so on the whole, we could say that he did create more value than he took away.

Companies Create Value: Companies exist to create value. Companies take resources or inputs and assemble them into a new form that has a higher value. This is Michael Porter's classic definition of the business value chain that every MBA student learns.[16-4] However, some companies are *much better* at creating value than others. The point of the entire Q Model is to accelerate that value creation process.

Value is Divided: You could reverse this statement and say *value is divided*, which is the essence of Marxism. Karl Marx did not recognize the idea that value is created. He viewed the industrial age as static and unchanging, focusing on how to divide economic value in a *fair* or *equal* way. As such, even a perfect expression of communism would result in a fixed or static society.

Value is Created Faster: In the new digital economy, one of the primary resource inputs for creating value is ideas. Intellectual capital drives value creation in the world of accelerating competition, and the disruption of static industries is driven by breakthrough ideas. Entrepreneurs who create value faster than others can disrupt industries and *eat them for lunch.*

Why Create Value? Why do humans work so hard to create all this value? What is the structure of motivation that propels each of us forward? It seems like it's all just survival, but surely there is something more to life than just getting our next meal; is the purpose of life shopping?!? Are we using our lives to chisel a stone block or build a great cathedral? We propose that how each of us creates our *context of meaning* in life is governed by a specific set of "why" relationships that are largely unseen.

- Get the WHY:

In traditional business leadership, an executive might first ask, "What do we want to achieve?" and come up with a goal or strategy. That taken care of, they would then ask, "How will we achieve that result?" and come up with a plan or implementation process. This *What/How* mindset is the standard approach to business leadership and management. You can display this in a simple flow chart:

What do we want to achieve?

- Goals, Results
- Strategic Result
- Metrics, KPI, Measurement
- Projects, Milestones

How will we get that?

- Planning, Implementation
- Execution
- Tracking, Accountability
- Project Management

What is the default mindset of many business leaders? It is summed up in the phrase: "Just do it." The problem is that "it's your job, just do it" is a low-performance mindset. This default approach cannot deal with the accelerating nature of complexity in the business world today. It fails to recognize the inevitable barriers that any significant business project will face. To address these challenges, we can update the model like this:

What are the challenges?

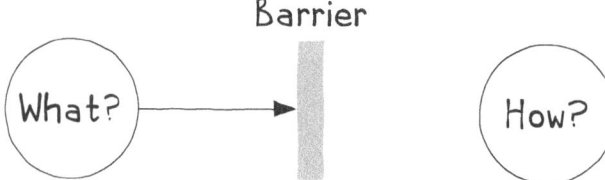

How will we deal with...
- Problems, issues, complexity
- Lack of time, people, talent, resources
- Conflicting priorities, internal conflict, politics
- Competition, markets, rate of external change
- Resistance to change, complacency

In truth, many strategic projects fail when they hit one of these barriers. The more insidious problem is that strategic projects simply get stuck — people look busy, and it seems like the project is moving forward, but the significant milestones keep slipping by and remain unfulfilled. Projects get stuck because the business mindset and approach are missing the key ingredient, which is *motivation*.

Task = Stuck: For many traditional leaders, it seems counter-intuitive that they must first build motivation. The *task* mentality of "it's your job, just do it" pervades many traditional business leadership systems. However, to go from *task* thinking to *result* thinking, you must first build a *why*.

"*Why*" Takes You Over the Barrier: Unless you build a strong *why*, trust, vision, alignment, motivation, and commitment will always be brittle and easy to break. When you develop a strong *why* people and teams become resilient. You can throw bigger and bigger challenges at them and they will respond by getting stronger and stronger.

Significant strategic projects require a stable structure of motivation. An engineer designs the structure of a bridge to exceed the traffic load. Likewise, a manager or business leader must develop the *why*, or structure of motivation, to exceed the challenges and complexity of a project. Engineers also build in a safety factor. For example, a safety factor of 2 means a structure can handle twice the expected load. Learning to think this way is easy for managers, provided they begin by appreciating the very idea of a *structure of motivation*.

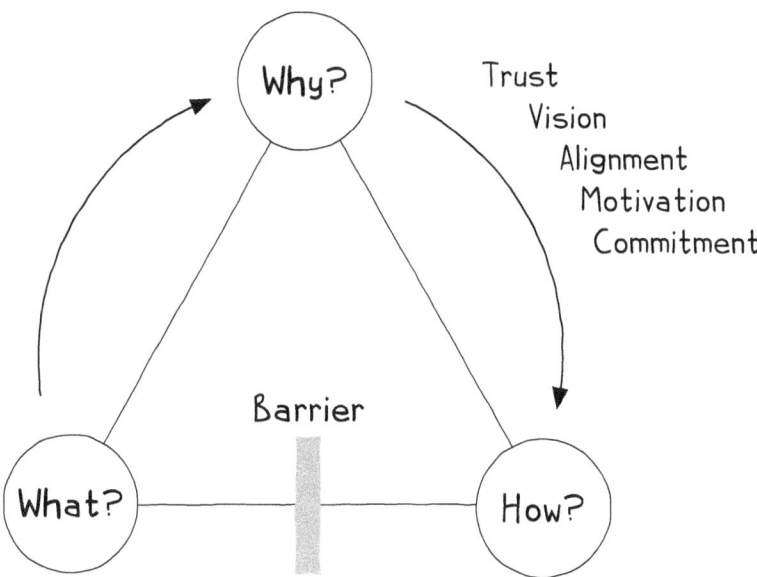

Trust: Trust yourself. Build authentic confidence. Create trust in your team. Build confidence that the project will succeed.

Vision: Develop a clear idea of the desired goal. Co-develop the plan with the team. Build a visual model of success.

Alignment: Develop a shared set of team agreements. Work through the most challenging issues. Build internal congruity.

Motivation: Understand and communicate *why* it is important to achieve this goal. Listen and ask questions about the *why*. Build internal drive.

Commitment: Strongly support the team to commit fully.

Scale the Why: Getting the why is the essence of the Q Model approach to values. We are exploring a complete system for building motivation from the inside to the outside. You can work with individual managers and leaders, or you can help a group of executives to align into a motivated team. You can quickly apply this to value in breakthrough projects, and you can even scale the *why* up to an entire enterprise. But you must first begin with your own *why* at the individual level. You won't really understand values until you know them from the inside out.

- Individual Values:

Take a moment to reflect on the Ancient Greek maxim *Know Thyself*, which is an earlier version of the core question of human existence, "Who am I?" Attempting to answer this question begins one of the most difficult journeys we can take, and often people freeze and ignore it altogether. But it doesn't have to be *so* hard: values are a simple doorway to begin exploring identity and finding inner strength.

Corporate Constructivism: Jean Piaget was the father of constructivism, upon which the field of developmental psychology was built.[16-5] In essence, he validated through research that children assembled their experience into games that serve as cognitive maps or models for forming a more complete understanding of the world. We propose that the core particles of these cognitive models are value words.

Evolve the Model: Based on my experience of working with hundreds of companies, I can state with certainty that the constructivist approach is a perfect fit for managers, teams, and projects. When you work with your team to develop a solution to any sort of challenge, you naturally move through a series of approaches, testing your solutions and updating your model as you get feedback or results. In the Visual Modeling process, we explicitly ask teams to develop and evolve a series of models. However, it is important to notice that the underlying structure of motivation in the model is built from keywords and values words.

Cognitive Models: The idea that business teams build a series of cognitive models and then *transform* them is a central tenet of the Q Model. These are not just business models but cognitive models that fundamentally define a team's perception and behavior. Any view of the world or thinking model that you are operating with will always have inherent limitations. If you wish to have *more* power and freedom, you must first recognize the model you are operating within before you can transform it.

Value Map: Just as an atom is made of subatomic parts, we are breaking down the structure that humans use to build their maps of the world. We are proposing that *value words* are the fundamental particles that humans use to create and then transform these maps. A cognitive model is something that forms or evolves in the mind of an individual or team, but with a little work, we can get this structure of motivation out in the open where we can work with it. We call this a value map.

What is this thing you call "Happy?" We always use a bottom-up approach of listening *for* and respecting people's individual experience of their value words. We need to reiterate that value words are relative to the subjective experience of the speaker. As a listener, assume that you will never be able to understand the speaker's true experience of their value words.

Mouth Sounds: The best approach is to pretend that you are an alien visiting Earth and one of the humans you encounter is making a strange sound with their mouth. You have no prior context to conceptualize what this "Ha-Pee" sound could mean to them. However, you are very curious to find out, because it seems important to this person or team.

We call these *relative values* because they are entirely subjective to the individual's experience of the world. Each of us lives our entire life on the island of self. You have no idea if anyone else sees the same color "blue" that you see. If you take this approach, you will always respect each person's individual value words as completely unique to them. This is the foundation of respect.

What happened at the Age of 2: Before the age of 1, all of us lived in a prelinguistic state of direct experience. Around the age of 12–24 months, we began to develop language. This usually begins by naming external objects, quickly develops into more complex communication, and at some point, babies start to develop self-awareness. The Mirror Test is a simple way to assess self-awareness and has been formally tested on many animals.[16-6] Elephants can recognize themselves in a mirror, but dogs cannot. Around the age of 20–24 months, most humans achieve this capability.

We don't learn language, we *become* language

What happened at the Age of 5: From the age of 2 to 5, humans experience a profound language transformation. You can say that humans learn a language, but perhaps it is more accurate to say the human mind forms *in language* and therefore a human *becomes* their language. However, not all words in our language are equal. Value words are the most important elements in the structure of our mental map because they define the structure of meaning around which we build the mind. From the age of 5 onward, our mind forms *around* our value words.

In the beginning was the Word... - **John 1:1, King James Bible**

Baked in Values: Value words are baked into the structure of language. A sentence must contain a subject and a predicate, or in more common parlance a noun and a verb. Similarly, human communication always links to values. Every communication includes an implied motivation, which must link to some kind of value word.

Why is this important? Remember that children are always asking "Why?" Why is the sky blue? Why must I brush my teeth? As parents, teachers, and peers respond to these queries, they automatically embed values. Children are naturally trying to organize meaning and make sense of the world.

What is most important in life? These value words are presented hundreds of times, as children are evolving into language. These value words form a structure of meaning for what is most important in life. For example, it is critical for children to be *safe*. Being a *helpful* person is also important. How many times did someone tell you to be a *good* person before the age of five? Safe, helpful, and good are some of the most common core value words in many cultures. In Chinese, the word *hao* (good) is so common that you will often hear it several times per minute in casual conversation.

Hierarchy of Values: Values are all about what is important. Because some things are more important than other things, a hierarchy naturally forms. Value words are intrinsically hierarchical. You can think of them as a pyramid, with many less important value words at the bottom and a few self-defining core value words at the top.

Value words are an invisible matrix that formats our perception of reality

Water Unto a Fish: A fish is swimming in water. The fish cannot see the water, because the water is everywhere. You are swimming in the air. You do not think about the air, because the air is always there. Hold your breath for just a few seconds and you will remember how much you like air. The *air* is not the point — *values* are the point. You are swimming in values. You cannot *see* them, because you are *in* them.

Wake up Neo. The Matrix has you. **- The Matrix, 1999**

You are soaking in them: Consider that you live in a world governed by your values. You cannot see them because they are everywhere. Values form a matrix of importance, through which you see the world. However, you cannot see the matrix, because you are looking through it all the time.

Bringing core value words into our conscious
awareness begins a fundamental transformation

Harvest Value Words: How do you pull out value words? The simplest way is to ask "Why is this important?" This will begin a value conversation. There are many other questions and approaches that also work; all roads lead to Rome. All conversations are potential value conversations. Here is an easy way to begin to identify some of your core value words.

Try this on yourself: This is a simple formula that will bring out your core value words. It works with the idea of procrastination, which results from an unresolved argument between our internal *intention* and our external *action*. We will distinguish the core value word by flipping between positive and negative motivation.

Pick Something Important: Think of something important to do, that you have been procrastinating about. Write it down, then answer the following three questions with a little detail.

Why is this important?
Why do you have to do it?
Why do you care?

What is the strongest positive motivation? Try to pull 2–3 value words from your answer to each question. It is OK if you get the same value words. Write them down. Now flip to the negative questions:

Why don't you "not" do this?
Why do you hate doing this?
What is the opposite of the proceeding negative word?
What would you rather do instead? Why is *that* thing important?
Why not forget about that first thing you were procrastinating about altogether?

What is the strongest negative motivation? Try to flip the negative words into positive words. For example, "What is the opposite of *annoying*?" Pull out three more positive value words from your responses.

Now, look at all the value words you have written down. Which ones seem strongest? Which words seemed to get repeated? At this point, most people will begin to get a sense of a few value words that define their internal motivation.

Way too Easy: Perhaps it all seems too simple? Remember, in the Q Model we consider value words to be the elemental particles of transformation. Some people will be very clear on their core value words, while others may be confused about them. Value words are contextual. When you present people with new projects or challenges they have to develop new skills and a fresh mindset. This means they must work with a new set of value words, integrating them with their old core value words to form fresh relationships. How successful they are in this process defines their ability to deal with change and complexity.

Common Value Words: When you ask people what is most important to them, they will likely use many of these common value words:

Good	Nice	Family	Responsible
Right	Caring	Growth	Adventure
Love	Helpful	Creativity	Professional
Joy	Accepted	Happiness	Learning
Fun	Respect	Honesty	Security

From the list above, pick the three words that seem to govern your life the most. Circle them or write them down somewhere. Perhaps a word is jumping out at you that is not on this list. Feel free to write that one down instead. When you have three words, ask yourself:

> Why did I choose those words over other words?
> Which of these words is strongest?
> Why is that word important to me?
> How do I use that word to sort out what is important?
> How do I use that word to make decisions or set priorities?
> Where else in my life does that word show up?

The words you choose might seem deeply familiar, or they might seem quite alien. Don't worry either way and keep exploring the questions. This is an ideal exercise for one page of journaling. Start with a blank page and write down a few core value words. Try to answer the six questions above for each value word. Try to keep writing and fill the whole page with notes. The process requires some intense self-reflection, but it will give you powerful and lasting insights by the time you put down your pen.

- Motivation:

As you explore the world of values, you might discover that for the most part, *you are* a set of core value words. Over the past 15 years, we have gathered feedback from our programs and hundreds of businesspeople have reported that this one process was the key that allowed them to unlock inspiration, motivation, and a deep personal commitment to what they wanted most from life.

Motivation: Q leaders must also be accountable for generating a structure of motivation. Remember, you cannot tell someone to be motivated. You have to ask questions that assist them in discovering their own inner motivation.

Rule 22: Action without motivation will always yield low performance

Structure of Motivation: A motivation structure is not complicated to build. If you explore the question "Why is this important?" you will get lots of keywords. When you put these keywords on paper in a visual map, you will see your structure of motivation as a physical object in the world.

Vision and Values: It is important to note that values and motivation are almost always interlinked with a vision of success. When you imagine completing a project successfully, you automatically interlink the project into your existing structure of motivation. This builds a set of emotional drivers that propels you toward project success. It also helps you form a *success-based* identity, where you imagine yourself *becoming* the person who has successfully completed the project. This self-image naturally interlinks with your values and motivational structure to build a broad matrix of inner strength.

The Power of Motivation: Strong internal motivation provides the energy and focus needed to deal with complicated business challenges. It also helps you:

- Begin your journey toward becoming a value-based leader
- Discover the power of visually displaying your value map
- Build a value-based management and leadership style
- Fluidly shift between an *action/results* management style and a *values-based* leadership style
- Shift between business, technical, and people-focused value words
- Understand value-based leadership as a comprehensive model

Growth at the Individual Level:

- Experience your values in language
- Become clear on *who you are* as a leader by mapping your value words
- Become effective working at any value level from *technical* to *inspirational*
- Differentiate the short term vs. long term fulfillment of values

If you wish to understand yourself you must look for the source of your motivation, which you will find in value words that fundamentally influence your thoughts and actions.

- Value Agreements:

External Agreement: Humans are constantly making tiny agreements about what is important. Remember, value exploration is not just about your own internal journey of discovery. As we go through life we encounter ongoing narratives about what is most important. We inherit our value words first from parents, teachers, and friends when we are younger, and then our boss, significant other, and society at large when we are adults. There is a natural relationship between external agreement and internal motivation, and our individual value words form in tandem with our understanding of the external agreements about what is most important.

Cultural Value Words: We also live inside a matrix of social agreements. The culture we operate within influences and defines our core value words.[16-7] Likewise, we are attracted to ideas, movements, and sub-cultures that align with these words.

It is very important to note that most of this is unseen; the value word relationships that define our culture simply appear to be "the way things are."

What Makes you Proud? As I traveled around the world over the past 15 years, I developed a program for testing core value words in cultures and companies. Working with a group of 20–40 people, I would ask a series of simple questions to find their core value words, like "Why are you proud to work at Alibaba?" or "What makes you proud to be Russian?"

Everyone Agrees: After creating a list of the group's responses, I would then ask "Which word is strongest?" We would have a short dialogue and the group would always agree on a set of 4–5 core value words. We would then rank the words to find the most important cultural value word. What is most amazing about this process is that everyone would always agree — there was never any counter argument or mismatch. At the RMCP, over 180 people agreed that doing the *right* thing (or being *right*) was the most important thing for a police officer. At American Express, I worked with 74 managers who all agreed that being *responsible* was the most important thing at Amex.

Values are an Implicit Bias: It is important to note that this value elicitation process is not a double-blind clinical study. In fact, the process of establishing value words is inherently based on implicit bias. In the process outlined above, individuals would propose cultural value words and then collectively align around them. With this process, we were not seeking to prove that all these people were already aligned on these internal values in advance. What is definitive about this process was that each test group would always agree on what value words were most important to them. In this process, they were collectively *establishing* cultural value words.

The Muslim World: If you ask an American, "What is the core value of the Muslim world?" you might get some very strange responses. Some people have even answered *terrorism* to this question, which indicates that they have almost no understanding of the mindset of 24% of the population of the Earth. As I traveled between Muslim countries running programs, I would always run the same value word experiment outlined above. I tested this in (and with people from) Turkey, Oman, Saudi Arabia, Lebanon, Jordan, Pakistan, Malaysia, and Indonesia. There were many different words that scored in second or third place in these countries, such as family, faith, culture, or heritage. But the top value word was always the same: ***respect.*** It is remarkable to have this level of alignment across 11 time zones.

We are Family: If there was a single core value word for the human race, it would most certainly be *family*. Throughout the developing world, the word family always appears in the top three value words. In Western culture, it is usually among the top five responses. Here are some of the top value words by culture:

America:	Freedom, Happiness, Success
China:	Success, Peace, Harmony
Asia	Family, Education
Europe	Solidarity, Autonomy, Equality
Global	Family, good, right
Universal	Peace, love, joy

Value Wars: The world looks very different when you see it through the lens of core value words. If you dig deeper into the underlying motivation of the 9/11 attack on the Twin Towers and the subsequent wars in Iraq and Afghanistan, you might arrive at a cultural value war between the word *freedom* and the word *respect*. If you look at the Brexit movement in the UK and the fight between the UK and the EU, you might see a conflict between the words *sovereignty* and *solidarity*.

How to do Conflict: If you wish to create conflict, it is easy to say that those other people are not like us. In the conflict game, value words are powerful tools. You simply say those other people do not respect our fundamental value for *X*, so they are not like us and cannot be trusted. This is the way that many companies end up with toxic silos of people who don't trust anyone who is not from *their* group. However, this approach violates a core premise of Q Model leadership, which is listening for and respecting other peoples' value words.

How to do Respect: Value words can only be positive so it is actually impossible to ever have a so-called value conflict. You could say that "I don't like my boss because she doesn't value integrity," but this would be your external judgment. Your external judgment of others has nothing to do with their internal experience of the world and their relationship with their value words.

Value Leadership: If you wish to be a Q Model leader, you must build enough trust so that other people will share their values with you. You entrench that trust by listening for their value words and respecting them. However, this can be hard to do because we get so wrapped up in our relationship with our own value words. Most people will react emotionally when people don't seem to be respecting their value words. To have power in all this, you must be able to distinguish your own emotional value chain.

- Emotional Value Chain:

Value Takes Two Forms: External and Internal. Anything that creates external value can be quantitatively measured. The results of your measurements can represent value that has already been created in the past or value that will be created in the future.

Internal Value: While we are creating or measuring this *external* value, there will be a corresponding *internal* value. External results will always be linked to internal motivation through a value word. The radical idea is that a company's *emotional* value chain is just as important as its *business* value chain. This is essentially what management pioneer Peter Drucker means when he says "Culture eats strategy for breakfast." The emotional value chain is the structure upon which a company's culture is built.

Bridge of Meaning: For any project, a team will always have a set of value words that are somehow linked to an external result. If they don't have this, they will have no interest in the project or result.

Rule 18: A value word always links internal motivation to external results

In the thesis of Value Transformation, we propose that the relationship between external results and internal value words defines the structure of *all* human motivation. Value words link to a higher purpose or meaning that underpins motivation. In a business team, the linkage between project results and the elements of the value map can have a *strong* or a *weak* connection. A weak or fuzzy connection between the value map and the project result is the main cause of low-performance or low engagement. A leader can quickly learn to target these weak value links and help strengthen a team's inner motivation. A self-directed team can also learn to do this on their own. This simple conversational activity is one of the main ways to move a project from a *low* energy state to a *high* energy state, the latter being a high level of motivation and commitment. Here are some key elements on the journey to a high-energy team:

- What is the value of project success or the value of the vision?
- How does project success link to internal emotion or value words
- How does project success link to motivation? Why do we care?
- Listen for value words that trigger engagement and ownership
- What is the connection?
    Project Value (external) = Values (internal emotion) = Value Words
- Listen for, respect, and confirm value words
- Move between project value and value words to build motivation
- Begin to own the motivation of yourself and your team

Internal motivation: In order to do things, humans need motivation. To create this motivation humans create an internal representation of a task's value in their mind. Assisting people to be clear on this internal representation of value is the key to long-term sustainable motivation, energy, and commitment. You can link individual, team, and organizational values to any project or business result in a company.

All roads lead to Rome: External and internal motivation will always link with a value word. Building a conscious awareness of this connection is the key to unlocking inner strength. Just as every sentence must have a subject and a predicate, every conversation must have a value element, otherwise, you would not bother having that conversation. This means every conversation is a value conversation, whether you realize it or not.

- Values in Your Work:

Real Company Values: All companies have an *existing* set of core value words that drive corporate culture and harmonize day-to-day actions. If you start to explore motivation across an organization, the same value words will come up again and again. Just as people and teams need strong motivation, companies also need a structure of motivation that drives their purpose. Always look for the value words that are already present in day-to-day discussions, rather than the corporate values posted in the lobby.

Values at the Organizational Level: Challenge yourself to understand the real power of organizational values. Companies always have a set of value words that people use for internal motivation and decision making. Often the fundamental role of these words is unseen or unexpressed. Authentic company value words always emerge from the ground up, so start by listening for and respecting those words that are woven into the fabric of the company. This must never revert to the fake telling of values, as exemplified by the poster in the boss's office featuring a photo of a man standing on a mountain peak with the word "achievement" under it.

Team Value Words: When people work in healthy teams, they naturally start to align on a background structure of importance. Over time, these shared interests will naturally align into a set of core value words. Identifying shared values is one of the most effective ways to build solution-focused teams that are well-integrated and sustainable.

Customer Value Words: Establishing customer values is an ideal path to energizing customer satisfaction. This is especially effective in sales and support roles, where you can have direct one-on-one discussions with your customers. It is important to *aggregate* these individual customer value words into a central pool, as this is some of the best information about *what matters most* to your customers.

Authentic Marketing: Combining the words *authentic* and *marketing* might define the word oxymoron, but value words can be an ideal way to transcend fake brand communications. First, find the authentic value words that are already being used by the team or organization. Then begin including those values in internal messaging communications. You then must go back and test alignment by asking if they think those words actually represent *who we are?*

Like everything else, it is almost always more effective to *ask* rather than *tell* when it comes to values. It is very easy to mess this up and lose the authentic voice by putting a *marketing style* human in charge who prefers making the company look good rather than telling the truth about who you all are and what you truly stand for. When you are ready, extend beyond the internal team by having real conversations with your customers, suppliers, and stakeholders. Ask for and then listen for the value words they associate with your business relationship. With any internal or external broadcast of corporate values you have to *tell* your values, so be careful to avoid the trap of a *prescriptive* "You should be X" communication. First, do the hard foundational work of asking and listening to build a broad consensus so the messaging gets accepted as authentic.

Values at the Project Level: Ask value questions to align project goals with project values. Use value words to align project stakeholders. Understand the power of these project-based value words to build an empowering project context.

Commit to Mastering the World of Values:

- Learn to listen for value words in every conversation every day.
- Listen for employee, team, and project value words
- Master the simple art of confirming value words
- Understand the nature of long-term commitment and motivation
- Learn when, where, and how to have value-based conversations
- Practice naturally weaving values into your management style
- Trigger: Values are a trigger or button that fires a positive state

- Understand the value-based communication model
- Learn how to respectfully assist people to establish their values
- Drive trust: Learn to respect, honor, and express values

- How to Work with Values:

The critical skill is *listening for* value words. Work with the project owner and assist them to identify the personal, team, and project values that link to their future success. Working with their values requires the highest level of care and respect in the conversation; recognizing and respecting the values of another person is the most effective way to build trust.

Working with value words establishes the domain of higher purpose, meaning, and the sense of accomplishment that we all seek. The key question is "Why is this important to you?" Another way to bring forth values is by asking *quality* questions. "If you produced that result, what *quality* would that bring to your project?" The following questions will bring out values:

Why is this (project/result/solution) important to you?
If you produced this, what difference would it make?
What *quality* would success in that area bring?

Higher Purpose: Value Words are the keywords that people use to internally represent the value of a solution to themselves. As you listen for, recap, and clarify your conversation partner's value words, their energy and engagement in the process will become stronger.

How to Establish Value Words: Here are ten critical stages in the development of your relationship with your value words. You can use these stages on yourself or use them to assist an individual or team to become more integrated with their values.

1 - Listen: The fundamental skill of a Q Leader is to listen for other peoples' value words to find out what is motivating them. Respectfully ask "Why is that important to you?" and listen carefully. Pick out the keywords as best you can.

2 - Respect: Never tell people what their value words should be. Be curious and use a light tone of voice as you ask them about their values. Respecting people's value words is the fastest way to build trust. Telling people what they should value is the fastest way to destroy trust.

3 - Confirm: You can ask a closed question, like "So let me confirm, *trust* is important to you, correct?" Likewise, you can simply say the word "trust?" with a slight uplift in your voice to make it a question. They might say yes, or they pause for a moment of reflection, which usually indicates a confirmation.

4 - Capture: Write down value words to show respect. Use a notepad or flip chart, and make sure they can see you write the word. When they see their value word written down externally, it becomes a physical thing. See their value word on paper can be another small transformation

5 - Test: Often you may get a bunch of value words. Ask "Which one is most important?" and get them to choose one or two. Each time you do this, it makes their relationship with those words a little stronger. The more you confirm a value word, the stronger that value word becomes.

6 - Reconfirm: The most direct approach is to draw an oval or box around the value word. As you draw the shape, you can say the word out loud one more time to reinforce its importance.

7 - Awareness: People are not always conscious of their inner motivation. As we work with their value words, the structure of inner motivation "pops" into their awareness. Value words are hard to touch and fade very quickly if they are not displayed externally. The more you discuss and ask questions about value words, the more they stay in your conversation partner's long-term awareness.

8 - Display: Putting value words into a visual shape and adding bright colors makes them stick in the mind. Integrating value words into a strategic map, visual model, or a business system brings them to life. Try this: find one of your core value words and write it on a brightly colored Post-it note. Put it up on the edge of your computer monitor. Leave it up for one week and see what happens.

9 - Honor: Ask yourself, "How can I honor this core value every day?" Honoring your value words is about creating *internal* respect for who you are. The more you do this, the more you will authentically respect yourself and give yourself permission to be *who you are*, which is the formula for confidence in life.

10 - Express: Ask yourself, "How can I express my core values every day?" Expressing your value words is about creating *external* respect for who you are. Think of a real action, declaration, or activity that you can use to express your value words. The more you can do this, the clearer and stronger you will become. You will begin to know *who you are* out in the world and *what is most meaningful* to you in life.

Circle Between Value and Values: Remember, economic value and internal values are always linked. For example, let's say you have an important project and you wish to build more motivation for success:

1 - You need to satisfy the needs of the *logical* mind with a clear plan, numbers, and results.

2 - You also need to satisfy the *emotional* mind by agreeing on why this result is important and representing that with a few of your value words.

3 - Finally you need to agree on a *clear link* between the logic and the emotion. Ask questions to establish how getting this *logical thing* will give us this other *emotional thing*. This is a good place to whiteboard or flow chart the key elements into a value map.

You will have to go through these three steps many times. Repeatedly connecting value words to project implementation results is the key to building a long-term motivation structure. It may seem repetitive, but the opposite is true — each time we loop around we dive deeper into the spiral of values.

Value Transformation: The transformative power of values cannot be overstated. In the human condition, having a conscious awareness of the value map that defines our motivation, is intrinsically transformational. As you become more aware of the value words that define your motivation, the effectiveness of your decision making increases. The challenge is that we are always reacting to unseen emotional drivers.

If you *can* see your value map,
you will make decisions based on your values.

If you *cannot* see your value map,
your *emotions* will make decisions for you.

- Core Values

Value words are naturally hierarchical. If you ask people, "What is more important, *joy* or *happiness*?" they will usually tell you. In any project, if you keep asking, "What is most important?" and keep exploring you will get to core value words. In 1988, I worked with Connirae Andreas, who later published *Core Transformation*.[16-8] This work introduced me to the idea of a hierarchy of values that leads to transformation. Marilyn Atkinson also influenced this process, spending many years focusing on the transformative power of working with vision and values. But it was not until 2004 that I began to formulate the theory that humans have a set of core value words that govern motivation.

One *thing* is always more important than some other *thing*. This importance forms a hierarchy of value words or a value chain leading up to the core value words. These words are like prime numbers — they can only be divided by themselves. When we use the core values approach to coach leaders and teams, we find that most people have a set of about four to six core value words. Vocabulary-wise, these are usually words a five-year-old could understand; kids don't want to be *professional* or *efficient* — they want to be *happy* or *nice*.

I have personally conducted more than 3000 coaching conversations, interviews, or exercises to help people determine their set of core values. As a coach, I would follow this value chain with my executive clients to find out what was most important to them. At some point, the chain would stop on one word and the conversation would inevitably loop around it. This was an indication that we had reached a core value word.

Working with a client to develop a more developed relationship with that word would always yield insight and growth, and I quickly realized that a person's relationship with their core value words was a fundamental particle of transformation.

Eventually, you and your conversation partner will keep looping back to the same value words. The project owner might say:

"The purpose of *trust* is... *trust*." or
"If I had a life of *happiness*, I would be... *happy*."

It may seem strange, but these looping declarations signify a moment of transformation. This loop is the exact spot where people and teams declare true inner leadership, and these core value declarations create the resilience required to overcome adversity.

 **Uroboros:** An apt metaphoric example of this loop is Uroboros, the Ancient Egyptian symbol of the dragon eating its tail, which in many cultures represents the creation of the world. On a personal level, we could say that we *create* our world by looping through our core values and we can *transform* our world by noticing the loop.

Relative Values: Let's delve a little deeper into the idea of relative core values. In a postmodern sense, we could say that everyone has their own subjective experience of the world. As if you were trapped in a Philip K. Dick story or The Matrix, you can never really know that the color *blue* that you see is the same color blue that everyone else sees. This becomes especially important as we approach the world of core values.

More Mouth Sounds: We might all agree that being a *good* person is important. However, we all might have a very different subjective experience of what being *good* means. To create a higher level of respect, you must appreciate other people's internal experience of their values words as being completely relative to their point of view. You can take this to an extreme level and consider that the word *good* is just a sound someone makes with their mouth. You can't ever really know what *good* means to another person, and you have to learn to ignore all of the additional meaning you are creating as a listener.

- Unexpressed Values:

Insight Driven: Most people quickly understand the idea that value words are the source of positive motivation. But paradoxically, value words can also be our greatest weakness. While we love our values because they define our *strengths*, to explore them as a potential *weakness* is intrinsically insulting, so handle discussions of unexpressed values with care.

Anytime you identify a strong core value, there will also be an unexpressed element. The magic question for recognizing an unexpressed core value is:

How do I use (*core value word*) to get into trouble?

To make this work you could first identify and then insert your core value word into the phrase. However, one easier way to approach unexpressed values is with the word *perfect.* You could say:

How do I use being *perfect* to get into trouble?

Being Perfect: Ever fall into the trap of trying to make something perfect and waste a lot of time getting stuck in the details? Under normal circumstances, this can be healthy and balanced, but our love for idealized *states of being* can quickly get out of hand and get us into trouble. You might remember the stress of trying to make the perfect presentation to your boss or orchestrating a perfect Christmas holiday with your family. If the word perfect doesn't fit, try replacing the keyword in the statement above with a related word like *best, ideal,* or *excellence.* It is our love of this idealized *state of being* that is getting us into trouble.

> This is the very ecstasy of love, whose violent property fordoes itself
> And leads the will to desperate undertakings **- Shakespeare, Hamlet**

Being Responsible: Unexpressed core values have a *must be* or *have to* feel to them. As adults, most of us can relate to the idea that there are times when we *have to* be responsible. The question is, how do you use *being responsible* to rob yourself of joy, freedom, or happiness in life? You can try this question again with some other words and see what fits for you:

How do I use "being a *good* person" to rob myself of happiness?
How do I use "being a *successful* person" to miss out on joy in life?
You can keep going by trying to substitute your own core value words into the above statements.

Capture and Display: If you recognize yourself in any of the above statements, immediately capture the value word on a Post-it note and display it in your workspace area. This will keep your new relationship with this word in your awareness over a longer period of time.

Negative Impact: When you stumble upon an unexpressed core value word, it is important to gently explore the negative impact it has on your life. The more you can work through *exactly how* you use this word to get in trouble and block yourself from getting what you want in life, the more things will start to shift.

A Sick Feeling: These questions may make you feel slightly uneasy or annoyed. When you find core value words, they tend to be deeply familiar. However, when you notice the unexpressed part, it's natural to feel a little ill. If you don't feel sick, then *keep exploring* until you do feel sick.

Common Value Words: Now look at the same list of common value words and try to identify the three words that seem to get you into trouble.

Good	Nice	Family	Responsible
Right	Caring	Growth	Adventure
Love	Helpful	Creativity	Professional
Joy	Accepted	Happiness	Learning
Fun	Respect	Honesty	Security

Think of three ways your overexpression of those three words causes problems in your life or work. Also, try to find the negative impact or *cost* this has on your vitality. Capture these thoughts immediately by giving them a physical existence on paper or in a journal.

Welcome to the Machine: Unexpressed core values make us aware of any habitual binds we have unconsciously trapped ourselves in. We use these value words to make tiny value-based decisions throughout our day, but over time these decisions become deeply embedded into thinking habits. We think we are making these decisions thoughtfully, but we are really just replaying a well-worn groove on the record.

> Working with core values was amazing. I have been a coach for 20 years, and I thought I'd explored everything about myself. Paul asked me three core value questions and I realized I had a complete blind spot in one area of my life.
> **- Rosemary Davies-Janes, 10x Business Growth Expert**

Water unto a Fish: It is painful to see that the *thing we love* is the problem. For this reason, it is difficult to maintain awareness of our unexpressed core value words over extended periods of time. By default, all our thinking patterns are correlated with *my strength is what makes me strong.* Seeing the weakness in your strength is a mastery mindset, allowing you to *pop* into a new level of self-awareness in an instant. But remember, a fish cannot see the water it is swimming in. A few minutes later, you will find yourself back in your old thinking habits. It takes a strong commitment and a *physical display* of your positive and negative value map to remain mindful of our unexpressed values. When we say physical display, we mean posting your unexpressed value words in a place where you will see them every day and taking a moment to reflect their cost. This is challenging to maintain but the high returns are worth the effort.

Unexpressed Cultural Values: Every team and company will also have a set of unexpressed cultural core value words. When a group makes a promise to keep the negative impact of these words at the forefront of their attention, everything changes. This is a direct path to a team transformation. For example, at American Express I worked with a team of 47 managers and leaders. They identified being *responsible* as their core strength, but they also identified how they could get wrapped up in details and busyness by trying to be too responsible. I assisted them in creating a 60-day program to manage their *need* to be responsible, and channel that need toward producing the most value for the company and its customers. We had short team coaching conversations every week to celebrate success stories and deal with challenges, and upon completion of the project, the VP in charge reported that many of his staff went from junior managers to potential executive leaders in those 60 days.

Being Right: We all know that sometimes there is a *right* way to do things. If there is a right way, there must also be a wrong way. Earlier, we were talking about the leadership culture at Golder and the need for *technical excellence.* Can you see that as an engineer, you have a professional duty to *fall in love* with the *right* way to do things or the *right* way to build things?

Professional Layers: Trying to look professional, it is easy to keep adding layers of value words until you're practically buried in them. Engineers talk about *high-quality, efficiency,* or *technical excellence,* and large organizations will always naturally harmonize on a set of value words that expresses their cultural agreement on some idealized state of being. But these added layers of value words can get people, teams, and the companies they serve into trouble.

Extreme Positive Stress: Under normal conditions, our structure of motivation operates normally. However, when you expose any structure to extreme stress, things can destabilize. Remember, stress can take two forms: positive or negative.

A deadline can introduce fear of loss. Likewise, a new opportunity or an interesting project can introduce *excitement* for a reward. Chasing *my great idea* can be just as destructive as *the big deadline*. The real danger is our love for a fixed value word.

> Some Cupid kills with arrows, some with traps.
> **- Shakespeare, Much Ado About Nothing**

The Dark Side: Where you are strong also determines where you are weak. When you are only looking at the *positive* motivational side of your values, you won't see much of anything else. It is when you become aware of the destructive *negative* side of your values that you experience profound insights into your inner nature.

Value Transformation: Where you are *strong* determines where you are *weak*.

The Tao of Values: Learning your strengths to know your weaknesses also applies to the MetaQ system (Chapter 21), which is a system for navigating between the six common extremes of polarized thinking. For example, *big picture* thinking and *detailed* thinking are diametrically opposed ways to see the world, but both perspectives are necessary to get things done. The Yin and Yang symbol is a visual expression of this same idea, whereby we polarize into one extreme or the other and get stuck there. Only by seeing things from both extremes can we pry ourselves loose.

This is the essence of the Tao, as expressed by Lao Tzu: First, we are stressed but we cannot see the source of our stress. Then we realize we are stuck in a battle between two opposites. In the journey to wisdom, we somehow find a way to create harmony between these extremes. This is the path to value transformation. It is also the path to an organizational breakthrough leading to a business culture of alignment.

> He who controls others may be powerful,
> but he who has mastered himself is mightier still. **- Lao Tzu**

Chapter 17 - Missioning

- Missioning at Alibaba

Xu Ming suddenly discovered his purpose. He knew that each member of his team would be proud to stand with him. Together they would help thousands of people in China to live a better life

Jack Ma, the CEO of Alibaba, is a hero in the world of the top-down corporate mission. He consistently demonstrates an innate ability to create a higher purpose for his senior leaders. This higher purpose translated into a $29 billion IPO, the largest in global history. However, on the ground, the Alibaba middle managers had challenges translating the big picture mission and strategy into real-world projects that managers could implement. The company's rate of annual employee growth exceeded 30%, which meant that new staff could not assimilate into the Alibaba mindset quickly enough to maintain the company's extreme performance culture.

We introduced the missioning process at Alibaba in 2016, working with the entire organizational development team and key HR staff to identify the challenges and train them in the missioning approach. After this, we conducted a series of round-table events with the technical managers and project managers and found that the challenges were much more acute. But by asking them a series of simple missioning questions in a two-hour open workshop environment, the managers were able to fully integrate the missioning approach.

Before the missioning process was implemented we asked Xu Ming, a project lead who managed about 30 developers, to describe his team's current state at Alibaba. His response was typical:

> **Xu Ming:** We are dealing with extreme deadlines. We lost several key technical people. My team is now working very long hours because we are missing the critical talent we need. My team is stressed.

Here are the responses of Xu Ming at the end of the process, after he had worked through all the Missioning questions with a group of peers:

What are you building? We are developing an automated e-commerce store-building system.

What is your team mission? To have a simple process so that building an online store is fast and easy for uneducated people.

How does this help your customers? If we can assist people to quickly build an online store, they can transition from a small retail shop to an e-commerce store that can reach everyone in China. They can earn a lot more money.

Why is this important? An online business can help people to have a good life. It brings success to their family.

How does this help the world? If we can help thousands of people to set up small online stores, it will transform the economy of China. We can help everyone in the world to get things they want and enjoy their life.

Why is this result important to your team? We are proud to be part of such an important project. It is an honor to be building a great product that can help so many people.

He went back and put the same questions to his top technical staff. When we checked in later, he told us his staff gave similar answers and began to cascade the questions out to their own teams. This story is an example of how quickly the missioning process can transform the mindset of a team and create a state of high-alignment.

- What is Missioning?

Missioning is the continuous process of linking small goals for projects, teams, or products to the benefits of success. By turning a static company mission into a dynamic set of daily questions and conversations that drive team passion, missioning creates a high-energy state of alignment that fosters a shared vision of future success.

We can paraphrase Einstein and say that many organizational challenges cannot be solved at the same level upon which they were created. Yes, you can run programs and train all the managers on employee orientation, engagement, talent development, and employee retention. But none of that will do much, because you would only be addressing the lower-level symptoms of the problem. By working at the higher level of mission and purpose, your team can self-generate a transformation that will spread virally throughout the entire organization.

If you are not bringing a little missioning to at least one conversation every day, you are missing out on a powerful source of business energy. To develop a truly engaged workforce, people need to link their individual career mission directly to their project and team mission. With this approach, people can quickly engage in the ongoing process of developing tiny team and project missions that align upward toward larger strategic goals and outcomes.

Start missioning your personal vision for career and life, then align that with a simple mission for your projects. Ask questions to assist your team to integrate everything into a single project mission and collaboration will become automatic. Missioning is both a philosophy and a comprehensive management system, one where you weave the missioning process into your every action and communication. As the process advances, an organizational mission that is fully aligned at all levels of the enterprise will emerge naturally.

Test: How do you Know if your Mission is Alive? If you wake up each day and jump out of bed inspired by your mission, your mission is alive. If you don't jump out of bed inspired by your mission, you probably have a dead mission. Most people have a dead mission: once it was alive and now it is dead, but we still pretend it is alive. Likewise, many people have no mission, living or dead. They simply have a blank space where a mission might go, accompanied by a feeling of emptiness. Lastly, some people are trapped in someone else's mission. They inherited a mission they never wanted and are living out a dream that is not their own. In any case, you can quickly build a *vibrant living* mission that is tailor-made for you and deeply meaningful. But first, you must *tell the truth* about the state of your current mission, and declare it D.O.A. if necessary.

- Dead Mission:

How to Create a Zombie Army: Most companies have a dead mission. Tell the truth: if your company's mission does not inspire you to action on a daily basis, it probably died a long time ago. A dead mission reduces engagement and creates a culture of low-energy compliance.

Dead Mission: Most leaders use the corporate mission the wrong way. The boss *tells* the mission to the staff, who then agree to *pretend* to be inspired by the mission. Conjuring this kind of fake mission is the most efficient way to mass-produce disillusioned staff. In reality, most corporate mission statements gather dust and attract the dead energy typical of a top-down tell.

Missioning is the reverse process, where each person in the company is asked to continuously link their personal goals in life with the highest intention for the success of the *customer.* Missioning is the ultimate skill of a great leader.

Why Mission is Killing Engagement: Most people are skeptical of the idea of a mission or big dream to help everyone. Most corporate mission statements are so out of alignment with the day-to-day experience of employees that few people buy into them. In general, trust in the *big dream* that we are helping everyone is low. The first part of missioning is a strong anti-mission declaration — everything about a traditional mission is *wrong* because it is a top-down tell that breaks trust and further embeds a culture of low performance. Missioning is the opposite of the *top-down* tell. It is a *bottom-up* ask.

The negative mission message is the key. Don't trust your company's mission. Be skeptical. It is not real. It is dead, a zombie mission that anyone who still has half a brain left will want no part of, lest they lose that half and become a member of the undead horde. But almost everyone has been forced to accept a dead mission. We know it is dead, but we go through the motions of pretending it is alive. This fake acceptance creates *compliance* instead of *engagement* and spreads cynicism instead of trust.

Try Missioning Your Life: Start with yourself. Begin with a little missioning of your life and your career.

- Ask yourself sincerely, "What do I really want from life?"
- Write out one page of possible ideas of things you want from life
- Give yourself permission to scale up success and look further into the future
- Ask yourself, "Who else benefits from my success?"
- Look beyond your life and think of who else could benefit from your success

Take a moment to reflect and appreciate what you wrote. Your authentic engagement is the foundation of the missioning process.

Once you build some personal missioning strength, move up to the level of your team. Ask them, "What do we want? How can we extend our team vision further into the future?" It may take a few months to build a powerful team mission, but the first step is to build credibility by talking about the evil zombie mission.

Missioning History: The basics of missioning were first developed by Marilyn Atkinson in 2002, and formally introduced in her *9 Point Map of the Future* and the *Stakeholders* process.[22-4] In 2006 I began to develop the current missioning process as part of the Leader as Coach workshop, which has been delivered around the globe.

While the missioning concept might seem like a catchy marketing slogan intended to entice brand loyalty, the thinking behind these simple tools goes much deeper. Missioning is about how to unlock the higher purpose that resides within each one of us. It might seem a lofty subject, but we will bring it down to earth via simple concepts and questions you might ask in an everyday conversation.

Define Missioning

Classical definitions: *Verb.* 1. Christians proselytizing their religion in distant lands. 2. The active process of creating a mission.

Dead mission definition: *Noun.* A directive statement of a company's long-term goals, revenue targets, or a shareholder value goal.

Our Fresh Missioning Definition:

- A continuous process for creating a higher goal or purpose
- Creating a small project-based mission that can scale up with success
- Expanding the vision and value of a project
- The process of scaling up a small mission that can range from short-term, personal, career, team, project, product, company, or customer goals up to large long-term goals that help everyone on Earth
- Creating a high-alignment state for people and teams by linking to a bigger picture of success
- Scaling out further in time and expanding the range of what is possible for the success of a project
- Expanding the "Who else benefits?" of a project to amplify energy
- Expanding the frame of success so a goal serves more stakeholders
- Including all levels of a team or company in the process of creating a vision of success and committing to that future
- A continuous success-visioning process that can be embedded in every business conversation

Apple: 40 years of Missioning

Urging us to "think different," and use their "insanely great" products, you'd be hard-pressed to find a human being whose life has not been touched in some way by the mission of Apple Inc. While the brand slogans may seem familiar to the point of nostalgia, consider the deep purpose and culture that underlies the success of products like the iPhone, iMac, and iPad.

I got my first Apple product in 1981. It was an Apple IIe computer with 16KB RAM and one 140 KB floppy drive. Even as a 13-year-old I had a sense of the Apple mission, and might have said it was to create a future where everyone uses wonderful technology. It's clear to me now, looking back on my childhood, that the continuous missioning process of the Apple we know today is not a new phenomenon — fast-forward about 35 years and nothing has changed in the Apple culture and community. They still have the same mission. The only difference is the amount of evidence that proves the mission is real.

"Rally your troops with flags and drums." **- Sun Tzu, The Art of War.**

Insanely Great, Think different: Two of Apple's more famous marketing slogans, *Insanely Great* and *Think Different*, speak directly to the missioning process. Like flags to rally the loyal troops, ask any passionate Apple user what these statements mean to them and you will get a lot of very heartfelt answers. But while these answers will be similar in spirit and equally robust, each person will have their own unique understanding of what these words mean to them. Missioning is an internal, bottom-up process that combines individual and collective community interpretations to create a wholly original experience for everyone involved. Apple understands this better than any other company. Or at least, they used to.

Here is Apple's Official Mission Statement, circa 2019:

> Apple designs Macs, the best personal computers in the world, along with OS X, iLife, iWork, and professional software. Apple leads the digital music revolution with its iPods and iTunes online store. Apple has reinvented the mobile phone with its revolutionary iPhone and App Store, and is defining the future of mobile media and computing devices with iPad.

Was this written by someone in the accounting department? The Apple mission is nothing more than a list of products. Perhaps everyone on the mission statement committee had to agree on every word, so eventually, the words became meaningless. Apple's mission statement is a classic example of a *dead* mission. No one reads it and no one cares.

Compare the official Apple mission statement with the magic of *Insanely Great* and *Think Different*. Can you sense the difference between a living mission and a dead one? A living mission is something you find by talking with people out in the world who care passionately about the future of the company. By contrast, a dead mission is some text posted in the lobby of the head office with a mandate to gather dust.

Humans Seek Meaning: No matter how unclear the ideal outcome may seem, humans always work toward a higher purpose. Whether we're seeking improved health, stronger family ties, or more professional growth, what we want most is the *meaning* and *purpose* these future states bring us. In the beginning, our picture of this future may be in *low resolution*, but as we add details and align ourselves around this higher purpose, the picture is remastered into *high def.*

We have already discussed the power of value words. Missioning builds on the inner meaning and higher purpose of these words, assisting people to be clear on their meaning so that they are focused and empowered enough to incorporate them into their daily actions.

Missioning can take place at many levels:

Personal	Career	Team	Project
Product	Company	Customer	World

- How do you do Missioning?

Missioning takes place in everyday conversation. It is the art of bringing to life a team's higher purpose or potential in even the most casual of settings. Consider the possibility that every person on earth craves a higher purpose in life, above all else.

Humans have been missioning for thousands of years and every great leader does it. The problem is that somewhere along the way, the process got overly formalized into a very dull mission statement. Missioning is about getting back to the very basics of motivation and passion.

Key Missioning Questions

What would a long-term future success look like?
What would this look like if we were even more successful?
How will this success help your career? Team? Project?
How does this benefit our customers?
How can our project success benefit even more people?
How can we scale up success even further?
If we were exceptionally successful, what would we achieve in three years?

Missioning Step One: Once again, missioning is the continuous process of building a small ongoing mission for a project, team, or product. If you are not bringing a little missioning to at least one conversation every day, you are missing out on a lot of untapped potential energy in your team.

Here are eight steps to begin Missioning:

1 - Define a project with a clear outcome
2 - Build a vision of success or a visual model of what success could look like
3 - Amplify possibility: create a scenario in which more success happens
4 - Amplify success through time: go further into the future to expand success
5 - Add more people. Ask who else benefits
6 - Name the mission to keep it in existence.

A crazy secret project name will create a mission identity that sticks.

7 - Take the small steps needed to make the mission real

8 - Loop: Repeat the process once every 14–30 days to further amplify

Project Missioning: In the Q Model we see business transformation as a series of challenging breakthrough projects. Missioning a project builds the strength needed to deal with the challenges you will encounter.

Team Missioning: Team missioning is one of the most useful tools that any business leader can employ. The simple idea that you can transform the effectiveness of a team in a two-hour conversation may seem outlandish, but this is something I have personally done at least 600 times in the past 15 years. I have also taught hundreds of business leaders how to conduct these simple missioning conversations themselves. Once you get the basic idea and personally experience the results, you can begin to conduct these conversations successfully in a short amount of time.

In your journey to mastery, team missioning is one of the best places to begin. Missioning is all about creating a breakthrough in energy and engagement that directly translates to business results. The very best place to do this is in a small team of 5–8 people who are working on a shared project. Team missioning is where you will see the most results within the least amount of time.

Product Missioning: Building a product mission is another simple way to energize a product development process. The critical question is: "How will this product serve our customers?" You need to see the successful product through the consumer's eyes, so focus on developing the parts of the product that make the most difference from their point of view. Product Missioning is highly aligned with the Agile mindset and Design Thinking, both of which empower the customer's point of view.

- Amplify Time & Success:

How to Scale a Mission: The primary reason leaders have a *dead* mission is that they don't really understand how to build a *living* one. They hire an external consultant to tell them their mission, then they relay this outsider's opinion to their staff. All this telling creates a cycle of disengagement because missioning should begin with questions instead of answers.

Amplify Mission: Missioning is a step-by-step process of expanding the time frame of a project or product further into the future and amplifying the vision for possible success.

Missioning requires two functions:

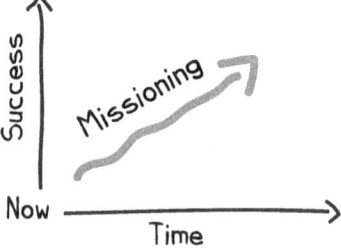

X-Axis - Scale-up Success
Y-Axis - Scale-out Time

Scale-up Success: Begin by gently introducing the possibility of more project success. The problem with scaling up possibility is that it requires people to step into the world of abstract or big picture thinking. As we'll learn in Chapter 21 when we examine MetaQ, the opposite of big picture thinking is detailed and measurable down-to-earth thinking. People tend to have strong habitual preferences for either big picture thinking or detailed thinking. Those who are detail-oriented may object because we don't yet have a detailed plan for how to deliver that success. You may need to develop a contract or agreement to *explore* a possible scenario to get them engaged.

Another MetaQ pattern that will get in the way is *possibility* versus *process*. Some people are initially uncomfortable with missioning because they have a preference for processes that have clear procedural steps. While you may have to explain the benefits and build a clear contract before beginning, rest assured that anyone can get comfortable with missioning and quickly master the skills for scaling up what is possible.

Vision First: Missioning will only work once you have developed a functional vision of success. Even then, every organization has groups that focus on stability — not everyone is a budding start-up entrepreneur, so start slowly. Indeed, some groups may never *want* or *be ready* for missioning, so never force the process or you will end up with another dead mission.

Here are some basic questions to begin the missioning process:

Is it possible that this project can work?
What would success look like?
How can we scale up success?
How successful could our project be in two years?
What would even more success look like?

Scale-out Time: Humans are bad at looking into the future. Most people do not schedule anything past a few weeks. To work with missioning, you must become comfortable scaling out time.

Practice by looking out two, five, or even ten years into the future. When you first try to scale out time, you may not get much response. Come back to a comfortable timeframe and try scaling out in smaller stages, remembering that the process should run in parallel with your expanding vision of success.

Many Success Scenarios: Add too much success to your vision and some will call the missioning process an exercise in fantasy. However, if you do not plan for success, you will most certainly not achieve it. The best way to frame this is as a set of many success scenarios. When you only have one vision or a *single scenario* for success, it is easy to fall in love with that future and hope it comes true, which distorts your thinking. Many people inherently recognize this and so avoid any kind of visioning. As soon as you create *multiple scenarios* the process becomes much more objective and detached. This allows the team to fill in the details of the scenario to the point where they might have several robust outlines of future success. In the end, your team may align on a single scenario as the main goal, but the point is that multiple scenarios give your team permission to push their visioning capability to its limits.

Realistic Plan: Many people are uncomfortable with looking too far into the future or imagining too much success. To maintain credibility, missioning should be done in stages that include some practical planning that addresses implementation challenges. Always strike a balance between dealing with the challenges and expanding the frame of success.

- Contribution:

1x1=1: Individual wealth does not scale. Unless you are selling a get rich quick scheme, no one *other than you* cares how much money is in your bank account. Obviously, people need to know what's in it for them or they will have a hard time getting motivated.

Profit is Weak: Stating that a company's only purpose for existence is profit is another way to say 1x1=1. If a company's only purpose for existence is *shareholder value*, no one other than the shareholders will care. Oh, they will pretend to, but this response is nothing more than the culture of fake compliance in action. Of course, there is nothing wrong with profit, but we need to recognize that profit is a weak source of motivation. You can't build meaning or a higher purpose with profit alone.

Value is Created: In missioning, we always focus first on the customer: how do you create the *most* value for your customers? How will your company contribute to their lives? Profit is a net result of all that contribution. Focus on the contribution part instead of profit and profit will come along for the ride.

For more Energy, add more People: Focusing your team's attention on the success of the customer or end-user of the company's product serves two aims. It forces your team to build a *better product*, and it also gives them a *higher purpose* beyond the company's success. Ask, "How will our project success help our customers?"

To expand your missioning energy, add more people. Ask, "How will our project success help even more people?" You can express this idea using the following formula:

Energy = People²

This formula indicates that the energy or momentum of a company or product will always be the *square* of the number of people who benefit from that product. This formula creates an exponential relationship with the number of people who will benefit from your project success.

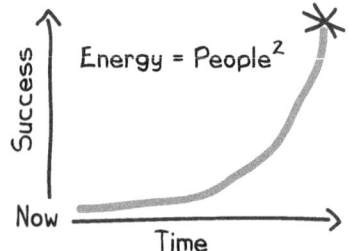

You can do the math like this: 2 people equals 4 energy, 3x3=9, 4x4=16. You can see that you will rapidly get large numbers. This is another way to explain the *network effect* or *platform model* that powers the growth of many tech giants.

Expand Stakeholders:

• Imagine a future success

- Amplify success by adding more value
- Bring in more stakeholders. Ask, "Who else benefits from our success?"
- Expand value by asking "How can this success contribute to more people?"
- Scale up by asking "How can our success help everyone on Earth?"
- Find the timeless quality of that value. Express it as a value word
- Include that value word as part your project missioning map
- Express that value word in a promise to take the first action

Humans Seek Meaning: A basic function of the human mind is to try to connect the dots of our past, our day-to-day work in the present, and our future success into an overarching narrative or story arc that gives us a greater sense of meaning and purpose in life. Consider that this narrative or story is a basic human need. Missioning is the process of asking questions that allow people to formulate their own meaning and higher purpose for the work they do. How we link this meaning into our vision of the future fundamentally defines our motivation. As we go through this process we naturally link value words and a metaphoric identity around the story arc.

All stories come back to a single root, in which the hero finds the courage to face a great challenge. This is the story you are building with your team as you engage with the missioning questions.

Mastery: Great masters of missioning from the past, such as Steve Jobs, found meaning in facing challenges. Today, masters like Jack Ma and Elon Musk carefully *weave* meaning and a higher purpose into their product design, integrating their vision of the future into their company, products, and customer psyches. They naturally message their vision and mission both internally and externally, intuitively expressing that mission into each of their products. As you fall in love with your iPhone or Tesla Model 3, you can't help but *become* an Apple or Tesla person.

Chapter 18 - Action

Key Action Questions:

What are some of the key actions to get this going?
What is the most important action to complete in the
next seven days?
What does the implementation plan look like?
What are the key steps and milestones?
How do we track results? How can we stay on track?
What might get in the way? How can we deal with the challenges?
Can we set up a series of check-in meetings?
Are you 100% committed to this result? Is this a promise?

- Vision Before Action

The habit of jumping into immediate action is pervasive in the world of business. If you are dealing with an emergency issue, this is an appropriate response. However, many so-called emergencies are not emergencies at all.

Resist the urge to go straight into action, and first ask some Q Model questions. Have you established a clear desired state and a strong vision of success? Most business leaders already have a very pervasive action mindset, but they approach action the wrong way. If you jump into action without first building a vision of success, you will end up with *task thinking* rather than *committed action*. The urge to jump into action can be hard to resist. To train yourself in this mindset, remember the following rule:

Rule 23: Vision Before Action.
Before jumping into action, build a clear picture of the desired state

Action Makes the Vision Real: When you are dealing with a complex issue, gauging the initial progress can be difficult. Sometimes, the most important task is keeping the vision of success alive. A freshly created vision is in a fragile state; if no action is taken within seven days it may become just another good idea that never happened. As long as we are taking steps and making progress, the vision will increase in strength.

- 1 Small Action:

The assumption that there is a universal shortage of time is the accepted business worldview, and our never-ending to-do lists certainly make it seem true. To effectively fight this feeling that we have too many things to do, we must build a strong vision of success and a structure of motivation. However, the first action we take must be carefully designed, and we need to ask the right questions to get things moving to the next stage.

What is the first step to get this going?
What is the most important next step to get this project back on track?

The First Step: When you are dealing with a complex or challenging issue, we hold it in our mind as a hazy cloud of uncertainty floating somewhere in our future. But as soon as we think through the first small steps and commit to doing them, our thinking process will start to get clearer.

Make the Key Action Small: Most people make their plan too big and then freeze in the implementation of it. When identifying the first action, it is critical to make that action small. Ask, "What part of this can you actually do in the next seven days?" This business of "the next seven days" is about scaling down the size of the action so that it becomes doable. As you engage in answering this question, the hazy cloud of uncertainty disappears.

The Next 7 Days: The next seven days is a critical time frame. Most people have a relatively detailed map of the next seven days in their mind or in their schedule. As soon as you place something into your seven-day timeframe it starts to seem real. The *next seven days* is a filter that forces you to discard anything that cannot be accomplished within it.

> What can you do in the next seven days?
> What is the most important first step we can take in the next seven days?
> What part of this can we actually complete in the next 7 days?

For example, if you are looking at a complex three-month project, a first step in the next seven days might be building a detailed plan for the project. Perhaps there is a key decision-maker who you need to talk to first to get a buy-in. Think about what is most important. Is it building the plan or getting the buy-in? If it is getting the buy-in, consider what is within your control. In the next seven days, can you actually have that buy-in conversation? Perhaps the realistic seven-day action is just to set up the buy-in meeting? Notice how we are making the action smaller and smaller.

Even the most resilient leader will make plans that are too big, and freeze when they try to implement them because they can't see the next step. To avoid this, scale the action down into one small step that can be accomplished in the next seven days.

Agile Time-Box: In the world of Agile, the next 7 or 14 days is an iteration cycle. The idea is to *time-box* your team's work so there is a built-in cycle. This keeps people thinking realistically about what can actually be done within the time-box or next 7-day sprint. Naturally, you want to schedule your next team conversation for the end of the *current* iteration, which is also the beginning of the *next* iteration. This is the perfect point to go back and ask "What is our current state?" and begin the Q Model conversation cycle again. Even if you are not working in an Agile framework, Q Model conversations are *naturally iterative* and bring with them all the benefits of the sprint or timebox approach.

Make the Action Small: The guiding principle here is straightforward: we need to get a complex project moving. If a project is frozen we need to get it moving again. To sum up the entire Q Model in six words we say:

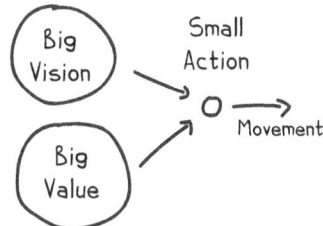

Rule 24: Big Vision, Big Value, Small Action

If you want speed, accelerate a small object with a large amount of energy. A rocket is essentially a *tower of power*, as it is nothing more than a giant fuel tank with a minute payload at the top. The smaller the action, the more acceleration. You will need a lot of speed if you wish to reach *escape velocity*, which is 42,270 Km per hour.

If you have a clear desired state, you know why the project is important, and there is one simple action step you can take to get it going, it is almost inevitable that you will complete that action. Once you do that, the vision will seem more real and down-to-earth. The project will naturally build momentum.

Commit to the First Action: The most critical step is to commit to the first action: We don't always need a complete detailed plan that shows every step required to produce the results. Detailed planning requires a very different mindset than commitment. Don't confuse the two functions. Committed action is about focusing on the one key action that will make the greatest difference. When you do this, life becomes simple again. This is how you know you picked the right first action. Your mind becomes clear and you naturally focus on that one result.

Vision of the Action: Try to envision taking the first action. Ask: Where and when will you do this? What do you see? How long will it take? What will it look like when you finish this? This vision will make the first action "pop" out and seem real and doable. This is your planning brain at work.[18-1]

- Implementation

Humans are great at planning and terrible at implementation. Most people think of planning as a one-time event rather than a continuous process. Much of the early Agile movement was about pushing back on single-cycle *waterfall* planning. Implementation mastery is all about building in an iteration cycle so that there is a continuous feedback loop to realign the current state with reality.

Over Budget and Behind Schedule: Projects have a default state, which is *over budget* and *behind schedule*. If a project is ever under budget and ahead of schedule, it will naturally want to return to its default state, and the universe will enact Murphy's law to make it over budget and behind schedule again. This is a little Q Model joke that is more painful than funny because it is often true.

Success comes from Implementation, not Strategy: As we have said before, having the best strategy without effective implementation achieves nothing. Every breakthrough project will have some point of failure, which will be hidden somewhere in the implementation process. As a leader, you must face the inevitable setbacks that come with implementation.

How do you react when your plan no longer matches reality? The Q Model implementation mindset is the foundation of any powerful business leader. Again we are dealing with a paradox: we are building a vision of success and planning for smooth implementation, but at the same time we are expecting to hit unforeseen problems and complexities. On one hand, you hold the vision of success and with the other hand, you play the role of skeptic and plan for the unplanned. Mastery is the ability to hold two conflicting ideas in your mind as if both are true.

A key question is, "How soon do we want to find out that our plan is off track?" If you are operating from a single cycle waterfall mindset you probably won't find out your project is off track until it is too late for correction. A short iteration cycle has a built-in tracking function that will give you real-time feedback on everything that is going wrong.

Deadline versus Timeline: Timeline is another critical mindset shift. Often, when we are handed an issue or complex project, we experience it first in a deadline state. There is a critical date where the result must be delivered, but we have not had a chance to think through the details and make a plan. This deadline state is a dangerous place for a project. There may be pressure to produce the result quickly, which will lead to rushed decisions. If you don't have a plan or know how to start, you might freeze and be unable to make any decisions at all. If you leave the project in this state too long, you may begin to feel that you are procrastinating or that it is an impossible project, and you will lose trust in yourself and your team.

Humans Don't Plan: Of course some humans do make plans, but most do not. HBR found that 89.7% of managers have a fundamentally reactive management style. We live in the smartphone world of 24/7, always-on communication, which means constant interruptions. When you add in the pressure to deliver results, most people get pulled into the slippery slope of reactivity.

Rule 25: Planning is the force that opposes reaction

To produce high-impact results, you must carve out some empty thinking space to work through the details of the action steps, roles, and resources. Working through the complexity of these details is an ideal activity for the team. Sorry managers, but *Team* intelligence is greater than *manager* intelligence.

Clear Time Frame: Many projects or goals already have a clear time frame. Many do not. Without a time frame, it is hard to build a breakthrough. If you are dealing with an ongoing process, such as *increasing production quality*, there may not be a clear time frame, in which case you will have to make one. You can ask an open question like, "What time frame could we have for achieving a significant increase in production quality?" If your team cannot frame it, you can suggest a frame, such as 90 days. Likewise, many long-term goals are *too big* to turn into a breakthrough project. If you are working on a two-year goal, turn the first three months into a smaller project and focus on a near-term breakthrough result. Time-frame is a powerful thinking tool.

Team Planning: A team has much better thinking resources than an individual. Speaking directly with the key people who will be involved in delivering the result may seem like an obvious step. However, in the real world, many leaders want to manage everything, so they email out the action steps to the team rather than presenting them in person. Even if the relevant people read the email, they can't own the plan because they weren't involved in making it. Even if you've already made your plan, turn it into a set of questions and bring them back to your team and recreate the plan with them. It will probably end up better than before.

Implementation Engagement: Many planning meetings seem to go nowhere.

Stop having meetings like that by setting a clear conversational goal. Go back to the basics of the Q Model and discuss the current state. Ask good open-ended questions to get the team engaged in the challenge. Bring out the key issues, then build a detailed timeline and finally get everyone to commit to the first actions.

Hands-on Planning: Hands-on, literally means, that the hands of everyone on the team are touching the plan. To accomplish this, place a big flip chart paper on the table or the wall, and encourage everyone to move the Post-it notes around as they see fit, as outlined in Chapter 13. Attention leaders: if only one person is *writing* on the paper, only one person *owns* the plan, so get everyone to contribute.

Start with the End in Mind: It is always critical to focus attention on the desired state. A key metric turns a fuzzy goal into a clear one. It is easy to get lost in the details; you may have to go back to the desired end state a few times throughout the process. At some point, you may get a strong vision or an increase in energy or excitement. If you keep working through the details, eventually the results will seem doable and real. This is how you turn a vision of *success* into a vision of *implementation*.

Implementation Layers: It is essential to think about implementation in layers. People like to organize importance *hierarchically* with the most important things at the top:

> At the top level is the key goal, desired state, or vision of success.
> Below this may be key stages or milestones.
> Below this could be key results or ongoing measurements of success.
> Below this could be the teams or individual roles of people doing the work.
> Below this are the actual action steps.
> At the bottom are the details of those action steps.

You can always add more details later so don't get bogged down by trying to plan everything perfectly. It is important to scale up and down several times, so people can develop the project implementation plan from both a big picture and a detailed point of view.

Visual Timeline: The visual timeline is the ultimate planning tool. This uses the general principle we introduced in Chapter 13, but in a format specifically designed for challenging implementation management.

Most humans mentally scale importance with size, so a larger timeline workspace is better. You can use several flip chart pages laid out horizontally, but better yet, find a large whiteboard wall. The visual timeline is a standard X and Y graph. On the vertical axis, you have the implementation layers. Big picture results are at the top

and details are at the bottom. On the horizontal axis is the timeline of the project cycle. Most modern humans read left to right, so always place *now* on the left side and the *future* on the right. Map out the project start and finish dates along the top. Place the project goal or desired state in the top right.

Move the Post-it Notes: Start to fill in the timeline. Post-it notes are an ideal tool for this because you can move them. In the visual timeline process, we are holding the project implementation in a fluid state. Once you write down a key action with a pen, it is hard to move that action around in time, so get the team to physically move the Post-it notes around on the timeline. This practice of physically rearranging the Post-it notes is the most effective way for your team to get their hands on the project implementation. Remind them to ask questions and discuss the placement of each element on the timeline. Most people like to start in the present and work forward. It is also useful to jump around as you go. Ask milestone questions, like "What do we want to achieve at the end of this stage?" or "Where do we want to be at the end of month two?"

Gantt Chart: At some point, the Visual Timeline may start to turn into a *Gantt Chart*, a hallmark of traditional formal project management. Too often project management only happens at the beginning of the project and is exclusively controlled by one person. However, it does not have to be this way. Ongoing collaborative project management is all about getting everyone engaged in the implementation process in iterative cycles. There are now many effective online tools, but nothing beats a team standing around a whiteboard wall and moving Post-it notes. As they build a detailed timeline they can turn it into a Gantt Chart by estimating time blocks.

Collaborative Project Management: Ask the team to carefully position Post-it notes for all actions, resource estimates, and time blocks. Make sure your team has many small-scale interactions about what goes where and how long it will take. This is also an ideal time to kick-off the implementation planning, which can later transition to a more formal project management system if needed. Finally, make sure everyone records their actions and agrees to put them into their personal schedule. Remember to come back to the process in one to two weeks and have a current state conversation that compares the previous plan to what actually happened.

The Last Mile: Recall the last mile from Chapter 9. With project implementation, you are building the ten-lane super highway connecting two cities. We live in the city of *now*, and we want to be able to travel quickly into the city of the *successful future.* The team is investing a lot of time and energy building an implementation plan. However, it is easy to forget the most crucial part: the last mile of the highway. Specifically, all of the on and off-ramps that connect the *big highway* to the *individual* actions, time, and resources of the people who will do the work.

To create the last mile, spend some time working out individual actions, estimating resources, dealing with time issues, scheduling the details, and building time blocks. Make sure your team is thinking through the impact that all these new actions will have on their day-to-day workload. Do they actually have enough available time to produce this result, and if not, what else do they have to say "no" to? This discussion creates the foundation for a structure of accountability.

- Accountability

When people hear the word accountability, they often think of *blame*. Something has gone wrong and someone needs to be held accountable for the ensuing problem. This past-based relationship with accountability will not produce a breakthrough in your project. In the Q Model, when we use the word accountability, we are talking about a future-oriented structure of accountability that will ensure project success.

Implementation Mindset: Project managers are very good at asking, "How could you produce this result?" Unfortunately, after building a detailed plan, the ongoing implementation mindset often falls apart. The skill of managing *ongoing accountability* is lacking in the culture of many companies. Bosses accept weak promises and then complain about a lack of results. Instead, managers should put themselves in a Q Leader *support role* in which the team is ultimately accountable for the result.

Implementation is often hampered by a flood of interruptions, a weak relationship with time,[18-2] and the fragmented way people make promises. In contrast, an accountability structure can be hammered out between a manager and their team in a short conversation. Likewise, teams can build their own accountability structure independently. Whatever your role, start a discussion for a new level of accountability within your team. The first critical question is: "How will we keep our project on track?"

Shared Accountability: In the Q Model, accountability is not about the boss checking to see if the employees are doing the job. Rather, accountability needs to be framed as positive, shared, and mutually supportive. Companies have many projects and conflicting priorities, so everyone is working together to fight against distraction and the inevitable project challenges that will arise. Negotiate a frame of shared accountability in which everyone agrees that the project is important and everyone is checking in on each other to keep things on track.

> How can we make sure this project stays on track?
> How can we support each other to produce this result?
> Can I support you in producing this result?
> When we hit a challenge, how will we ask for support from the team?
> Can we set up a series of short check-in conversations?

Structure of Accountability: An accountability structure is a series of check-in conversations that support a team to stay on track and revise the plan when the project falls behind. A solid structure of accountability is the key to having confidence and certainty, even in the face of a challenging goal.

To build a strong structure of accountability, you first need some key ingredients. Above all, the plan must be realistic. Having some challenges or unresolved issues is okay; this is normal in the real world. However, overall the plan must seem achievable.

The Check-in: The check-in is simply another "How is the project coming along?" conversation that is specific to the implementation phase of the project. The check-in is another area where the Q Model is very effective. If you go back to the basics of assessing the current state outlined in Chapter 8, you will recall that it is one of the most useful tools for ongoing project management. Here some basic check-in areas:

- Check-in on the current state
- Check-in on project execution
- Check-in on implementation. Check-in on the details
- Check-in on the structure of accountability

Once a Week: Schedule a series of check-in conversations before the team makes a final commitment to the project's success. Establish a mindset of positive accountability. Whoever is managing the check-in process should frame their role as "I am here to support your success." Remember to include the team vision of success, the team identity, and a crazy project name. All these things will make the commitment stronger. If you are a manager, frame yourself in a support role and the team will happily accept your assistance to keep the process moving forward. The purpose of accountability is to support the team to ensure success in their project; they still own the result.

Tracking: Check-in conversations can be quite short. In the simplest form, you are asking one closed question, "Is the project on track?" Remember that the default answer to this question is *yes,* so you must learn to pay attention to the *quality* of the yes. If the *yes* is strong and emotionally aligned, the project is probably on track. If there is a hesitation before the *yes*, or the *yes* feels weak, you need to ask more questions and have a more detailed current state conversation.

The Promise: Don't accept weak promises. Ask the questions necessary to make the promise strong. By accepting a promise, you are likewise making a promise to support the other person to produce this result; all promises go both ways. This builds a state we call 100% committed, which permeates throughout the team.

By accepting a promise, you promise to support your team's success.

- 100% Committed

Willpower is overrated: It is easy to say *"I will"* or *"I must"* produce this result. However, over the years, we have all made promises and failed to produce results. If you are keeping all your promises, you are probably playing too small and it is time to make more *difficult* promises. Some corporate cultures say they encourage risk-taking and allow support people to have failures, but in reality business culture rewards success. It takes courage to stretch yourself and make promises you don't know how to keep. This is the nature of leadership.

In the Q Model, we live in the postmodern universe of *commitment overwhelm.* The difficult reality is that *everyone* makes promises they cannot keep and ends up dropping things when they are overwhelmed. This is not about judging yourself to be a good or bad person, but rather putting in place the systems required to manage the reality of all your commitments. This creates a paradox because you are promising to fulfill your objectives while also dealing with the reality that humans drop things. On one hand, you must be *compassionate* to the reality of the current state. On the other hand, you are getting into the details of the plan and the *structure of accountability* to make the implementation as strong as possible.

Commitment Lives in Details: You have to know what you are promising before you can actually commit. It is easy to say *yes* when you don't know what you are saying *yes* to. Before you can make a strong commitment, you need to get the work out in front of you so you can see what you are committing to. If you wish to be strong you must grind through the details before you say yes.

Conflicting Priorities: You may need to address issues of time and resources. Do you and the people on the team have enough available time? Are there conflicting priorities or other projects and deadlines that might interfere? To free up time and focus, you may have to say *no* to something else. Address these issues before you commit to the implementation plan. Finally, schedule a series of check-ins or tracking conversations for the project life cycle. These tracking conversations are the foundation for the structure of accountability.

100% Committed: We have all had this experience at least once in our life: you had a goal and you made an *absolute* promise to fulfill it. Somehow, you knew with 100% certainty that you would make it happen. Then you did what you needed to do to achieve the result. What was it that made you 100% certain that you would make it happen? Have a short discussion with your team to explore this idea. The more you work with the idea of 100% commitment, the more they will begin to express 100% commitment as a state of being.

Team Promise: A team promise is much stronger than an individual promise. When you make a promise to yourself, you have to deal with all the times in the past that you didn't keep your promises. We all know that we can be distracted or unfocused at times. With a team promise, each person is holding every other person accountable for the results. No single person can always be strong in the face of every challenge. That is why it is important to have your team to support you when you cannot see a path forward.

Unstoppable: The real promise is a promise to be unstoppable. It is impossible to predict what will happen in the future with absolute certainty. However, you can always maintain your promise to be unstoppable. This means that when you hit a big challenge, you keep looking for a solution and keep pushing hard to get the project back on track.

Commit to Commitment: Commit 100% with a strong *yes*. Commitment lives in the structure of implementation. Commitment lives in the structure of accountability. Commitment is *who we will become* in the face of the challenge.

- Reality

No plan ever survives its first encounter with the enemy. **- Douglas MacArthur**

Or better yet,
Everyone has a plan until they get punched in the face. **- Mike Tyson**

Test Reality: As you move into the ongoing implementation process, you need to test what is actually happening in the world. Remember, projects have a default state: over budget and behind schedule. The project will be out of harmony with nature until it gets back to this default state. This is how the skeptic sees project management.

The Skeptic: If you are testing the reality of what is happening *on the ground* during project implementation, it is useful to assume the role of the *positive skeptic*. Most people approach the role of the skeptic in a *negative* way that is ultimately disruptive to the team, but the positive skeptic knows that every project will hit unforeseen challenges and fall behind schedule — they are *expecting* it. If you are operating within a positive frame of shared accountability, the role of the skeptic can be welcomed by the team. With a little humor, the skeptic can assume the role of a critic and ask the necessary tough questions.

The Wise Elder: When managers and team members excel in their positive skeptic role we call them a *Wise Elder*, and inhabiting this role can be a great channel for senior leaders to make use of their business acumen. This is a careful balance between being positive and supportive and using critical thinking to challenge assumptions. This work will then be integrated into a check-in conversation.

Postmodern Productivity: In the Q Model we take a very pessimistic and postmodern view of project management and commitment. We assume teams are *bad* at delivering results on time and on budget, and that project predictable results are based on the self-referenced subjective experience of the team.[2-2] The starting point of productivity is a relative unknown, but teams can iterate and benchmark over time to move toward establishing predictability, but absolute predictability cannot be achieved. Moving toward predictability means tracking *estimated to actual* results over time and having a series of debrief conversations to establish that the team owns the process of generating predictability. However, we must recognize that as soon as we start dealing with complexity and non-linear results absolute predictability cannot be achieved. We do not state this as a truth. Instead, it is a pessimistic view that forces teams to engage in open dialogue.

- 1*hour*CEO

The History of 1*hour*CEO: In his 2001 book *Getting Things Done,*[18-2] David Allen approached time management through the metaphor of martial arts, proposing that you should approach planning your day the way a *samurai warrior* approaches battle.

Around the time I read the book in 2002, I was lucky enough to be working with a training company called Mission Control. As presented in an intensive conceptual workshop created by Brian Regnier and Brian Stuhlmuller, Mission Control was a framework for staying present, even in the face of everything that might come at you in life. Unfortunately, as I worked with the philosophy I discovered that this rigorous mindset was difficult to understand and implement for most people.

In my many years as a professional CEO Coach, I would work one-on-one with top leaders and executives. Their relationship with *time, focus,* and *stress* was always a challenge. However, on those rare occasions when they were able to focus on the most important issues, their power to produce results would dramatically increase. Through these CEO discussions, the 1*hour*CEO system emerged and has since been delivered to more than 5,000 people around the world.

The 1*hour*CEO Thought Experiment: While working with busy and overwhelmed CEOs, I would ask them to imagine how they would manage their time and energy if they could only work *one hour per day*? Rather than producing *less*, could they imagine producing *even more* results in this thumbnail-sized amount of time?

Try this on Yourself: This exercise works best if you are part of a team or have some staff reporting directly to you. However, even if you work by yourself, you can still benefit from this mindset.

- If you really only had one hour a day to work, how would you use that time?
- How would you prepare for that one hour? What would you do in advance?
- What would you do differently? How would your habits change?
- What would you say no to, or stop doing?
- How would your interactions with other people change?

More Results in 1 Hour: What if you could generate the same results as a top CEO with just one hour of work each day? The 1hourCEO is a mindset shift that will give you the power to increase accountability in your team, generate peace of mind, and produce high-performance results.

Time Scarcity: Remember, most humans habitually operate within an agreement that time is scarce. Introducing the idea of "only one hour per day" makes this much worse. This is an immediate pattern interrupt, shaking up our habitual thinking habits.

How does the 1hourCEO Work?

Time: Although you may not be aware of it, your time-thinking habits profoundly affect every element of your day. What is your relationship with time? Do you have a *reactive* or *proactive* relationship with it?

<blockquote>You can use time, or you can be used by time – it is your choice.</blockquote>

The Law of Busy: Everyone agrees that there is not enough time. We call this the *Law of Busy*, and it eats away at your ability to focus and think clearly. The Law of Busy destroys your planning and spins you into reaction mode.

Distraction: The forces of distraction are calling you every day and want nothing less than your complete lack of focus. The forces of distraction will not give up. You must face them and overcome them with a higher level of thinking.

2617: We live in the age of Attention Deficit Disorder.[18-4] How many times do you look at your smartphone every day? The average modern human touches their smartphone 2,617 times per day.[3-1] What is the cost of this smartphone addiction?

Drinking from a Firehose: All modern working-age humans are subject to an on-slaught of distractions and interruptions. This onslaught is the new normal of internet-based work and life.

Focus: What if you were 100% clear in your focus? What would your work be like? Imagine leaving work knowing that you will not think about your job again until you return. What if you could build a system that could give you clear focus and peace of mind. What if you could trust that system so much that you could *relax* and enjoy a state of *extreme focus?* Blaming their job or their circumstances in general, people believe that they can never achieve this. They never realize that the source of most distractions is *themselves.*

Mastery: What would a breakthrough in your ability to produce results look like? We have all had the experience of being able to produce a high volume of work in a short time. Think of your last big deadline. What if you could recreate that level of productivity at any time without all the last-minute stress and panic? Stepping into mastery means delivering *more* result with *less* energy. Consider that the first step in this *journey to mastery* is your peace of mind.

Peace of Mind: Here is the fundamental question that defines your ability to produce results:

Is your peace of mind more important than producing results?

Of course, the default answer is no. When you hit an emergency, you leap into action to fix it, never considering your piece of mind as even slightly important. This is the default response for most people.

What if you transformed your mindset so that you knew with 100% certainty that your peace of mind was more important than producing the result? How would you approach your work? Ultimately, you cannot have peace of mind without having a clear plan for dealing with whatever is causing you stress. Starting from peace of mind forces you to prioritize *planning* over *reacting*. It also gives you the ability to focus your thinking and produce more results in less time. But to organize your life this way, you would have to invest time and energy into maintaining your peace of mind, and you would need a system to regain your peace of mind when you start to get overwhelmed. So how can we accomplish these things?

Peaceful in the Face of Challenge: It is not difficult to feel at peace when you are walking in a beautiful forest. After 5–10 minutes you naturally experience a sense of calm and begin to relax. The real challenge is to generate peace of mind and produce breakthrough results in the face of chaos.

Peaceful Warrior: Imagine you are a Samurai warrior in 16th Century Japan, and you are in the midst of a great battle: arrows are flying, horses are charging, chaos is all around you. Despite all this, you are completely at peace. You have faced your fear and have accepted that you could die at any moment. Because you are at peace with the possibility of your own death, fear does not control you. Alongside your fellow warriors, you are aligned in mind and body as you confront your enemies in a graceful dance. This dance is a natural outcome of the years you have spent training your mind to look anarchy in the face and smile serenely back at it. Now take this mindset to work.

Trying to do Everything: Can you do everything? Yes or no? At a basic level, you know that it is impossible to do everything. However, consider that you are actually operating in default *yes mode* of trying to do everything. Something pops into your mind and without thinking you internally respond with, "Yes, I will do that". As humans, we habitually do this throughout the day. Consider that you are a "Yes, I can do everything" machine. Notice how you automatically say yes to things even when, at a deeper level, you know you won't have the time or energy to do them.

Doing Everything Robot: Think of all the things you have to do throughout each day. Think of all the little things, like buying food on your way home from work. Without realizing it, you have hardwired yourself to be a *'doing everything robot.'* You think you *can* do everything, even though at a deeper level you know that you can't. This is a small paradoxical *thought exercise*, so don't resist or try to get out of this box. A little humor helps, so we are introducing a small joke here, and the joke is on you. The only way out of the box is to laugh at how crazy you can get at times.

State of Overwhelm: Usually we can keep the whims of the *doing everything robot* in our minds reasonably at bay, so we don't notice the crazy machine that runs us. However, there are times when the system gets out of control: just before the big deadline, on the last day before you leave for a trip, the week before Christmas, or sometimes all it takes is a run-of-the-mill Monday morning. If you can somehow laugh at how crazy you and your life can become, you're well on your way to discovering the immense freedom and power that lingers once the laughter subsides.

Say No to Your Yes Machine: If you can keep this idea that you are a doing everything robot *clear in your mind* for a few days, life will start to look very different. It takes a great force of will to push back against your ingrained habits. However, by using the 1hourCEO system, you can shift your habits via a systematic, step-by-step approach.

Empty Mind: The goal of this mastery practice is to have an empty mind. The majority of people approach their work in a fragmented way, haphazardly filling their brain with all the things they need to do as if it were a junk drawer. How can you accomplish one task when there's a seemingly endless amount of other tasks popping into your mind and disturbing your thinking? If you have not captured your ideas on paper, your brain will randomly manifest them over and over again until you acknowledge them, and thus we need to create a system to organize the junk drawer of your mind.

Capture: A shift occurs the moment you commit your "to-do" ideas to paper. Now your mind can relax because the idea has been captured externally, liberating your mind from the stress of having to *think about it* over and over again. However, this liberation will only stick if you deal with the to-do item within 24 hours. You deal with it by putting it into one of the three buckets below.

One System: What are some of the most useless ways you try to keep track of what you need to do? Do you keep lists scattered throughout dozens of locations? Are they on scraps of paper or Post-it notes you can never find, or buried inside multiple daily or weekly planners? Do you find yourself asking people to remind you of the things you have to do? If so, you are using their brain as a storage container because yours is overflowing with unorganized information. It is time to move towards a single unified system of organization, which we will outline below.

Planning: You know that you need to plan and that you should plan more. But most of us *react* more than we *plan,* so we keep coming back to the question, "How important is my peace of mind?" Remember, you can't really have peace of mind unless you have a plan for dealing with the distractions that are causing you stress. If you decide your peace of mind is truly important to you, then you *must* invest time in planning. Think of *distraction* and *planning* as two opposing forces, and life can become simple again. Remember, planning is an ongoing iterative process because the plan will always get out of sync with the current state as *stuff* happens.

3 Buckets: Let's put everything in your life into three designated buckets.

1 - The first bucket is everything that has a *solid plan* or is in existence in a schedule and that you know you can realistically do.

2 - The second bucket is everything you *think* you can do, but can truthfully admit that you haven't thought through or planned.

3 - The third bucket is everything you know you will not even get a chance to look at in the next month.

Putting everything into these three buckets can be an *annoying* process because it forces you to tell the truth and make a bunch of decisions you have been avoiding. Forcing yourself to close all the open loops in your mind will clear the fog from your brain. This is where peace of mind comes from.

Schedule: Do you have a strong or weak relationship with your schedule? Do you schedule meetings and leave lots of empty space for whatever comes up? A schedule is another tool for getting things out of your mind and into a system. It forces you to have a visual-spatial relationship with time. Finally, the schedule is the missing *last mile* of any implementation process.

Push-Back: The point of having a strong relationship with your schedule and an iterative plan for your key projects is that they both give you something to *push back* against. If you aren't acutely aware of your time limitations, you default to open time, where what inevitably fills your open time are interruptions and time-wasting activities.

Saying No: The ability to effectively say *no* is what separates a junior manager from a senior executive. The ability to say *no* without *literally* saying *no* is the secret skill of a strong leader. You can steal some great strategies to do this from senior executives. Most senior executives are very good and tactfully pushing back on things they don't have time for, that's how they got to be senior executives. Remember, at a deeper level you are practicing saying *no* to your 'doing everything robot.' Anyone can fill their time with useless busyness, whereas it takes focus and discipline to truly get things done.

Never Delegate: Based on the HBR study, 89.7% of managers have a hard time delegating. On some level, they don't trust anyone enough to provide the quality they need and end up doing it all the work themselves. This may sound bleak, but here's the good news: the entire concept of delegation is out of date, so you can forget the whole idea. Instead, go back to the basics of the Q Model and strike up a conversation, using the Q Model to empower your team to produce results independently. Find out "What is in it for them?" This approach forces you into a support and accountability role, where you use other people's time to produce your results. Just remember to do this within a win-win context, where your team members have some sort of incentive at stake. Otherwise, you will eventually go back to the dysfunctional world of delegation.

Leverage Time: How do you leverage your team to produce more results? Remember, the Q Model is about supporting people and teams to take ownership of their results and move (your) projects forward. Like a lever that uses a rod and fulcrum to amplify a force, the Q Model is a device that leverages time. It can give you the time you need to produce 100x more results, as we learned in Chapter 3.

Focus: Delivering a breakthrough result requires focus. What would life be like if you could generate 100% focus on demand? The purpose of building your 1hourCEO *system* is to carve out a thinking space where you can achieve 100% focus. You can start with some basics: block out your time and schedule your conversations. Setting up an "interruption-free" time block is a good start, but if you wish to have true focus you must first deal with the ultimate source of your distractions; *yourself*.

Distraction: Most people think distractions come from the external world. Like a torrent from a firehose, the things we need to do seem to come at us in a deluge of disruption. We respond automatically by fighting for our life, doing everything we can to keep our head above water and survive. If you wish to have more power in your life, you need to recognize *your role* in this story. You have 100% control over your *response* to any distraction.

Core Values: If you want to have power over your response to distraction, you must build a strong relationship with your core values. Most people have *unexpressed* core values that get them into trouble. For example, you value being *relaxed*, so you put off your big project to kick back and watch an episode of your favorite Netflix show. Later, you remember that you should be working on the project, which causes you stress. You start to work on it but soon need to take a break so you can relax again. If you cannot see how your unexpressed core values play out, you will keep going through the loop ad infinitum. As discussed in Chapter 16, building a stable structure of motivation requires linking the long-term results you seek, to a set of aligned core values. This gives you the power to break out of your comfortable habits and form more productive and impactful ones.

Structure of Motivation: You have to keep asking the fundamental question, "Why is this important to me?" If you keep asking this question, you will discover a set of core values that link to the success of your project. Get this on paper as a *value map* and put it somewhere where you'll see it every day. Recognizing your core values is an essential step on your journey towards alignment. Begin this process with yourself, and as you build internal alignment you can share the knowledge and skills you obtain from this process with your team.

Chapter 19 - Enterprise Transformation

Introduction: Enterprise Transformation is the pinnacle of the Q Model. As you scale up from questions to people to projects to teams, the complexity and challenges will increase. The Q Model is a *Do it Yourself* system, so we encourage you to jump in and get going. However, not every Q Model leader will be able to orchestrate a company-wide project immediately. Here is a basic guide to the process of scaling a Q Model project up to the organizational level. We will review some of the basic Q Model and universal agility ideas in the context of an enterprise-wide program.

- Change is Broken

Command and Control: In the Q Model, we believe that the *top-down* cascade system of structured change is weak and inefficient. Unless you fully address the *command and control* culture and habits in an organization, transformation can only take place in isolated pockets. *Command and control* and *open and empower*ed management cannot peacefully coexist in an organization. Even if everyone says they are aligned with an open and empowered culture, the habits of command and control are deeply rooted. The question is always, "What set of habits will you use when faced with a crisis or difficult decision?" This junction is where most leaders revert back to their command and control habits.

People Die on Burning Platforms: In 2010, Nokia CEO Stephen Elop told a story about an oil rig on fire. You had to make a decision:

Option 1 - Fight the fire

Option 2 - Jump in the water and die

This story was supposed to motivate people to change. However, the CEO forgot that people always have another choice.

Option 3 - Find a new company that *isn't on fire*

Somehow the *burning platform* has become the flawed pinnacle of corporate change motivation. Fear is the least efficient motivator. When faced with a company on fire, most humans will either switch to low-performance mode or look for a job in a company that isn't combusting. As a result of the CEO's story, Nokia's employees and stakeholders took Option 3 and began to leave. The company went into its well-documented death spiral.

Motivating Organizational Change: Before we can get to the *How* of change, we must address the *Why* of change since fear is a poor motivator.[19-1] If there is no strong *positive* motivation to change, most people will stay in their comfort zone and we will get no change.

We R Stuck: Most people perceive the large organization they work for as an immovable monolith that will never change. Up to 70% of attempts to initiate change fail because *people resist change*.[19-2] The scale of the task often freezes those responsible for shaping the culture of a large organization. Unless they can demonstrate traction and momentum, change advocates will get sidelined and often end up focused on short-term matters.

TEST: Which change mindset governs your thinking?

Company change is *hard* and *slow*
Company transformation is *fast* and *easy*

You have to challenge your mindset. You must perceive that it only seems *as if* people resist change. What if you could flip your mindset and assume that *everyone* wants change?

People Want Change: Imagine that everyone in your organization wants change. [19-3] However, this is impeded because the company-level strategies needed to initiate change seem to be immovable or beyond control. However, underneath all of this, we must presume that:

> **Rule 26:** People are already 100% committed to the transformation of the company, *but they might not know it yet*

If you approach the transformation process from this point of view, you will see things very differently and change will begin to seem possible.

Fear no change: Q leaders understand that change is *natural* and *inevitable.* The world is in a constant state of change, and therefore every element of an organization is also naturally evolving. Transformation is an inherent force of nature.

The Future is Agile: Universal Agility Transformation envisions a future where the primary organizational structure of a company is the multidisciplinary team. Highly trusted and constantly engaged in breakthrough projects, these teams are given the freedom to produce outstanding results. At the top of the organization, the executive's role is to empower a *portfolio* of breakthrough project teams. Agile Leadership is about providing resources and managing risk so that the teams have a protected space for creating breakthrough results. However, unless you are part of a small start-up company, it is almost impossible to switch a company directly to this organizational model.

From Coaching Culture to Agile Transformation: Around 2005, everyone in the HR community was buzzing about coaching culture. Coaching evangelists, myself included, envisioned a perfect company architecture where everyone reported to a "Leader as Coach" and every conversation was a coaching-style dialogue. Many years later, coaching culture ideas are getting traction but most organizations remain fundamentally directive. Agile has superseded coaching as the *brave new world* of transformation. However, we must address the reality that the basic Agile process mindset does not function well once scaled up beyond a single Agile team. The Q Model offers a comprehensive system that facilitates the transformation of people, strategy, process, and leadership. Still, no organization can instantaneously switch to a new operational model. Transformation must be an iterative process that takes place in carefully structured stages. The first step is always building the structure of motivation by asking, "Why is this change important?"

You can't Manage Change: Change management and organizational development usually take place within a top-down and *tell-based* hierarchical framework. There are instances where this really is the best approach. However, a *tell-based*-approach will always have drawbacks in terms of engagement and implementation. Alternatively, an *ask-based* approach harnesses team passion and intelligence, but it can also introduce a greater risk of internal disruption.

Release Thing 1 and Thing 2: *The Cat in the Hat* by Dr. Seuss is an epic story of company transformation. Thing 1 and Thing 2 are forces of disruption that get released from their box and create chaos in the business landscape. The big deadline approaches and somehow everyone works as a team to find a solution and clean everything up just in time. By story's end, Thing 1 and Thing 2 end up back in their box and the transformation has stabilized.

Disruption – in a box: In the accelerating world of business competition, you must deal with disruption. You can pretend that the inevitable disruption of your industry will not affect you, but it is immeasurably wiser to get ahead of the curve and drive the change.

Rule 21: You can either *react* to disruption or *drive* disruption

Controlled Detonation: On one hand you must give people the freedom to take advantage of their inherent capacity for innovation. On the other hand, you must keep the disruption under control so that the business remains functional. The ideal *container* for this disruption is a breakthrough project. Placing a strategic change project into a breakthrough project puts a barrier around it so it can be nurtured, while also separating it from more static areas of the company that fear disruption.

- Enterprise Roll-out

Accelerated Enterprise Transformation: Business transformation is more than technology. It must encompass a rapid shift in the nature of a company that improves employee performance and increases the quality and quantity of results. The shift in employee mindset facilitates all other technological, performance, and strategic results. To make a lasting transformation, the process of change must integrate with strategic goals. A core team must bring the strategic plan to life by developing and implementing it until measurable results are achieved.

Enterprise Transformation Must:

- Engage executives, managers, and business leaders to accelerate growth
- Increase the speed of results as speed is a main predictor of success.
- Align all business stakeholders in a single strategic aim that touches every business level
- Don't follow; lead. Disrupt your industry and own the next high-margin blue ocean business opportunity
- Accelerate key projects. Develop an unstoppable champion team to drive results
- Drive innovation. Measure and track results that correlate directly to the company's transformation
- Drive talent, engagement, and employee retention. Keep your best people and attract more talent

They do the work: Every Enterprise Transformation program aims to provide a short and focused breakthrough program that leaves the project team with a continuous transformation capability that they will maintain independently.

Powered by Q: The Q Model questions are *sticky*. The Q Model contains many high-impact ideas and practical tools that interlink to self-reinforce sticky learning. It also creates an internal development cycle that combines feedback, success stories, and real business results. This integrated approach keeps the change process focused and constantly moving forward.

Now we will introduce some basics of the enterprise transformation process:

Team Engagement: Getting the right people on the right team is always tricky. But once the team forms, engages in the challenge, and sees some results its momentum will keep building. The more the team values curiosity, exploration, and learning, the more trust and engagement they will have in the project.

Viral Transmission: When you ask good questions, other people will start asking them too. In this way, the Q Model questions are self-replicating. Once a minimum threshold is reached, the Q Model system naturally spreads as people use the tools. The process automatically creates more internal champions and high-potential leaders. These people are the spark that drives the engine of organizational transformation.

Real Transformation: Eager for results, most business leaders rush through or skip the current state, strategic alignment, and implementation steps. In their haste, they ignore a truth sitting in plain sight: that fundamental transformation always occurs at the identity level. This is the individual, team, and company perception of "who we are." This core identity transformation must align with strategic goals, rapid implementation, and quantifiable business results to be sustainable.

10x More Results: Imagine transformation as an exponential curve. At the beginning of a curve you don't see any tangible results. You invest time and energy but you get little back. Eventually, you start getting traction and begin to see leading indicators that you are heading in the right direction. However, you are still at the beginning of the curve and there is a steep hill to climb.

We can quantify this idea using the following formula:

10 Units of energy   =   1 Unit of result

Everyone wants to be at the top of the exponential curve. This is expressed by the next formula:

1 Unit of energy   =   10 Units of results

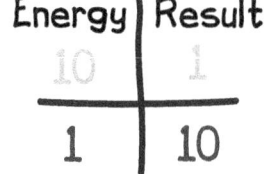

Energy	Result
10	1
1	10

Can you see that this second formula produces 100x more results? We all want transformational results. However, we cannot know how or when those results will arrive. You plant the seed, design the environment, and wait patiently. The Q Model organically drives transformation, but it is also an incremental process.

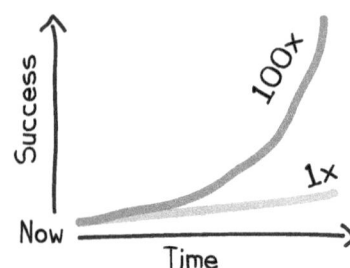

Small Shift: When you hear stories of how other companies achieved a big transformation, it all seems so simple and logical. However, it is useful to push back against the idea of the *big* transformation. There is no such thing. Instead, there are a series of *tiny shifts*. These incremental developments and changes in action and perspective compound upon each other and begin to build momentum. When combined, all these small shifts *are* the big transformation. However, in the beginning, all you see is incremental progress.

Layers of Business Strategy Implementation: Business leaders and executives can *tell* everyone the strategy, but this will rarely generate accelerated strategic results. To get things moving, you must find a way to express the general company strategy in lower-level projects. Because different departments have complex dependencies, each relevant business area will have to integrate the strategy in their own way to successfully develop and own their projects. Addressing all layers is how you achieve accelerated strategic execution.

SAP is not Simple: A good example of the difficulty of organizational change comes from my experience with SAP in 2015. At that time, the company executives had rallied around the word *simple* as a key goal and company-wide value word. This was expressed in a slick marketing campaign titled "SAP Run Simple" that was accompanied by a simplified version of HANA, their ERP customization system. However, the reality on the ground was anything but simple.

Almost every large organization that implements SAP's ERP system has their own set of horror stories to tell about the complexity of customized integration. SAP had spent years building layers of systems, features, updates, and patches on top of patches. The announcement that everything must become *simple* created corresponding layers of confusion in the company.

At the local level, we were working with teams of confused software engineers in SAP Labs in Shanghai, who themselves worked on large customization projects for enterprise customers. It took a year for them to begin to integrate the new mindset and tools into client simplification projects, and they soon discovered that the new coding environment was still not properly integrated with their legacy products. Four years later, the company and its customers were finally starting to sort out the mess.

The SAP example is important because it demonstrates what happens when a company jumps into a change process with lots of *strategy* and not much *implementation*. It also illustrates how people will quickly lose faith if the reality on the ground is too far removed from the corporate message. To mitigate these risks, big organizations must develop people and teams who can actively get ahead of the implementation barriers.

A strategy without implementation = zero: Success lives in the tiny details of implementation. In the traditional model, the executives set the strategy and the middle managers implement it. This approach is too slow. To achieve speed, the entire team must own the strategy and implementation process in each business area.

- The Company as a System

It is easier to ride a horse in the direction it is going: A horse is not a car. Unlike your car, a horse has a mind of its own and will go *where it wants to*. Even if you are skillful, riding a horse involves negotiation. You get to your destination and the horse gets to feed and rest. In the context of enterprise transformation, you can translate this as; align your change program with where the company is already going. If you are pushing against the prevailing force in an organization, you cannot win. As stock market investors say, *don't fight the market.*

Understanding this comes back to the ancient law of *Tao*. Two forces may seem to be locked in opposition, but there is always movement between them. Find the area that is moving and give it a nudge in the direction it is already going. The whole discussion of breakthrough project selection is really about finding that right place to tap.

Use the Force: An organization is made of forces. The Q Model questions are designed to gently *shape* and *focus* the forces of commitment and passion that already exist in a team or company.

You can look at any organization as a system. In any system, there will always be parts that make up the whole. There will be a transfer of energy, ideas, or resources moving between those parts. The goal is to create a high-impact shift with a small amount of energy. If you can find the part of the system that is blocked and ask the right question, you will almost always generate an organizational shift.

How do you make the transformation process automatic?
How do you energize the people in the organization so that they can sort out the barriers that are stopping change?

Organizational Design: Another way to view the *company as a system* is through the discipline of Organizational Design.[19-4] Most companies are organized hierarchically with departments and reporting lines, but this formal 'org chart' structure is a poor illustration of all the day-to-day communication and activities that actually happen. This distinction becomes critical when a change or transformation process is introduced.

In Organizational Design we say, "The org chart is not the company." If you have ever gotten lost in the woods, you may have discovered that *the map is not the territory*. A map is a depiction of your terrain from 10km *in the air,* which is very different than what your eyes convey to you from six feet off the ground. In other words, the direct reporting lines of authority are only one way to look at a company's structure. The org chart will never reflect the network of relationships and discussions that take place throughout the company.

When a complex organizational change is introduced, people and teams will need to step outside the formal structure to get *new* and *difficult* projects to work. At this point, the hierarchical structure of the company can either *block* or *enable* the organizational shift. Different parts of the company often fight against each other, which blocks the change. This is why it is critical to develop teams that can think beyond their local department's point of view and holistically strategize about the success of the entire company.

A company is part of a larger external system. It is critical to look at the broader ecosystem, which can include investors, suppliers, customers, and other stakeholders. How a project or product *creates value* can be mapped into a model or flowchart that includes all the internal and external elements. Giving your team a glimpse of this broad system allows them to think strategically about your entire industry, market, or sector. This *global view* is also a key element of Missioning, which we explored in Chapter 17.

Multi-Silo Teams: Company departments, business units, and divisions tend to increase their *frame of agreement* over time. Naturally, the people in *marketing* will look at the world very differently than the people in *engineering*. As they work together, the people in those teams will continue to agree that their way of looking at the world is the *right* way. They will naturally advocate for their internal point of view, and this leads to department silos and *groupthink*. In the Q Model, we advocate *multi-silo* teams and projects as the ideal vehicle for facilitating dialogue between the key people in different groups. As these groups develop a shared team vision and team identity, company silos break apart and once-divided teams become a united force.

Formal versus Open: A we approach a company transformation, some parts of a company will naturally argue for *stability*, while others will advocate for *growth*. Some people will see a vision for success while others will see a big risk. Some parts of the company will want to manage and control the risk with formal structures. However, as the transformation hits challenges, change advocates will need an open system that can bypass the barriers of the formal system. There is a tension between formal and the open, and these forces can work in opposition or alignment.

Manage Stability: Because stability is important in any organization, don't abandon the formal structures altogether — never change for the sake of change. There will always be a COO or CFO who sees risk at every turn, so you must demonstrate that this risk is well managed and worthwhile. You can do this by focusing on a narrow strategic result and using the transformation process to achieve that specific goal. This confines the change to a breakthrough project and insulates the rest of the organization from too much of it. Always be upfront about the risks; most new business models and breakthrough ideas don't work in the beginning. People know that projects can fail because they have seen all the initiatives that failed in the past.

- Flipped Leadership:

The Q Model approach flips the change process upside down. Instead of managing a top-down change process or looking for an outside consultant or an external strategy, the Q Model empowers the core executive team to energize their internal strategic capacity to deliver business results. Because this transformation is internally generated across many levels in the organization, employees cannot resist it. The flipped leadership approach quickly generates the momentum needed to produce a breakthrough in results.

The Flipped Matrix:

Approach	Traditional Business Change	Q Model Enterprise Transformation
Start	Problem focus. Trigger the reactive brain with danger.	Solution focus. Orient toward future success.
Process	Need many problems to get people moving. Tell them to change.	Ask Questions. Use the tools in real projects. People inspire themselves. Naturally drive change.
Outcomes	Introduce a new organization structure or business process.	Transformation of mindset, habits, strategy, and culture.
Main Theme	Need to change. Change or die.	Change is natural and automatic. Change is easy.
Mindset	We must resist the change. We must survive the change.	We enjoy creating the future. We want achievement. We want to help others.

- Breakthrough Project Design

Knowing Where to Tap: The big problem with most organizational change initiatives is that they tend to run out of energy before they can achieve liftoff. If you are taking people away from their core responsibility for training or some side project, it will seem like a distraction. Knowing where to tap is about finding a key point of leverage, and the phrase usually refers to some smart external experts who can introduce the perfect solution. However, in the Q Model view of the world, there are no smart external experts. At the very least, we could presuppose that no external expert knows your business as well as your team of internal experts. In the Q Model, knowing where to tap means finding the ideal point of internal leverage. This comes down to finding the right breakthrough project.

Project Driven Transformation: A breakthrough project is an ideal container to explore and develop one segment of a company's transformation. It is essential to place a project breakthrough within the context of a company breakthrough. The initial design of a small breakthrough project must align with the overall company goals and strategy.

Design Breakthrough Projects: The word breakthrough has been repeated so many times that it has become almost meaningless. However, in the Q Model, we use the term *breakthrough project* in a very specific way so it is worth explaining. A breakthrough project can be sourced from anywhere. Any existing project or goal can be converted into a breakthrough project. It is an ideal container to develop and kick-off a company-wide transformation.

Projects are Everywhere: A breakthrough project can come from anywhere. It can be an existing project or a goal that gets turned into a project. Breakthrough projects can come from:

> Existing projects initiatives or goals
> New high-potential products or services
> Fresh *out of the box* ideas of *skunkworks* projects
> Mission-critical internal process improvements
> Outward-facing projects that enhance customer experience or value

Project Selection Process: The first stage of designing an *ideal* breakthrough project is the project selection process. Project selection can include existing organizational initiatives or new projects that can be created to fit your organizational breakthrough needs.

How do you select the right projects? There is no absolute rule, but here are some guidelines that form a hierarchy of priorities for project selection. The best projects tend to include:

- Revenue growth or market expansion
- General company strategy or achievement of strategic goals
- Goals aimed externally at the market or customers
- Adding more value to customers or clients
- Adding value in your industry's ecosystem
- Developing or launching a key product or service

External Facing: Notice that all these areas are externally facing. Too much internal focus can become a barrier to change. Many large companies focus blindly on internal issues, but by addressing external priorities first you naturally create a hierarchy of importance. Internal processes should serve the creation of external value, and large companies often fail because they get this backward.

Refining the Project: In refining the project, you should work with the key stakeholders and analyze each project.

- Look for critical organizational breakthroughs and enterprise transformation opportunities.
- Look at the business as a system and analyze where processes or communication may be blocked or constrained.
- Address the most challenging operational issues.
- Include effective collaboration between multiple stakeholders from different areas of the organization.

KPI versus Breakthrough: A good question to ask is "What is the difference between a breakthrough project and a regular project?" We can answer this question using your existing relationship with KPIs. KPIs are not fun. If you don't deliver them, something bad happens. Delivery of your KPI is a "regular" project — it is your job. Conversely, a breakthrough project includes a stretch for an exciting future result. Since we don't know how we will arrive at that future, we need to give the key people room to be curious, explore, and even fail. A great breakthrough project will often trigger a mix of fear and excitement. Notice the very different set of emotions in a *breakthrough mindset.*

Leverage Vision: A breakthrough is a shift in strategy or implementation that results in a sudden increase in results. It is essential to presuppose that a breakthrough is possible even if you don't know how it will happen. The shift from *business as usual* to a breakthrough mindset is all about gently stretching the goal or results. When I analyze a potential breakthrough project, a key question I ask myself is, "Where's the breakthrough?" At a basic level, we are asking people to step out of the box and scale up their vision.

Add More Breakthrough: The most important part is the breakthrough. The critical step is to add a *stretch* or *vision of success* into the project. If there is no larger vision of success you end up with a regular project and business-as-usual performance. The reason most company projects are *not* breakthrough projects is that managers kill the vision by demanding short-term results.

To shift from a regular project to a breakthrough project, a core team of committed people must be given the time and space to explore the strategy, processes, and systems required to produce the big result. This requires patience and nurturing from the senior leaders who provide a protected space for the team.

Where are the key barriers? With each project, you must analyze the main challenges or barriers to project success. Most busy and overwhelmed managers avoid considering potential problems, but this is a key step in refining the project focus. Ask, "What is the most challenging part of this project?" and use this question to bring out the barriers.

4-6 Breakthrough Projects: The goal is to establish and accelerate three to 4-6 high-potential growth initiatives in the company, and this includes overcoming the barriers associated with each project. It is critical to associate each project with existing internal company measurements or KPIs. These numeric goals should link to a topline financial metric, such as revenue growth or profit margin.

Multi-Layer Teams: The Q Model process is about getting the key people from different layers of the organization into open discussion, so they can sort out whatever is slowing down the transformation projects. Supporting leaders to achieve this can begin at the *top* of an organization or in the *middle*. At the top, the Q process begins with executive team conversations that align key goals with execution to trigger the next level of strategic thinking. In the middle of an organization, selected project leaders and teams can begin to deliver innovative solutions and robust implementation. A key goal is developing a core team of internal champions that can keep the process moving independently.

You should avoid separating strategic transformation from day-to-day business results. For the most part, the entire profession of organizational development takes place *in isolation* from the everyday concerns of senior executives. Unless the process is linked directly to specific business deliverables, programs become *yet another* time-wasting leadership program.

Transformation Layers: In the Q Model process we recommend a multi-layered approach to quickly influence people across an organization. This process can scale across the entire enterprise, from individual managers and executives up to management, executive, and functional teams. Each layer of the organization has different needs and requires different resources. By default, most selected project teams will want to work within their existing functional teams, but this will limit the impact.

External Dependencies: Remember that the biggest challenges in implementing a complex change project are external dependencies from *other parts* of the organization. The number-one delay in project implementation is *waiting for something* from some other group that doesn't care about your project. To deal with this you must try to anticipate those dependencies in advance, and get key people from potentially dependent parts of the organization to join your team. In general, at least 30% of your team should be composed of people from outside any functional group. Recall from the Missioning Team Identity section at the end of Chapter 14 that "outsiders" on the team must take ownership of the project result so they can go back to their department and resolve whatever is blocking progress.

> "The problem wasn't collaboration *within* the teams themselves,
> but rather collaboration *between* the teams."
> **- Stephen Dunning, The Age of Agile** (Quoting General Stanley McChrystal)

Secret Project: Until you have solid executive support, start with a secret company transformation project. This will create the same protected space of a start-up team working in a garage. As you build momentum, turn your project into an open secret. But keep a little mystery to maintain the "top-secret" high-alignment state. It takes time to nurture a team, and in the interim, they must be protected from deadline and KPI-oriented leaders. As they achieve initial results, use those results to begin building a broader buy-in.

- Project Buy-in:

Building *project buy-in* is all about developing strong internal support and a broad agreement about *why* a goal is important. To develop a project buy-in an enterprise program must align with business goals and growth initiatives while also linking directly to key business results. The latter in particular is a critical step for ensuring success.

The most common reason programs fail is a lack of executive support. If you are starting from the top, conduct one-on-one or executive team strategic sessions that establish a strategic vision and align key goals with execution. If you are working from the middle of an organization, select project leaders and teams and support them to deliver and implement solutions. Either of these approaches can be used to develop a group of executive sponsors or champions who will drive organizational buy-in.

More Breakthrough Projects: The trick to getting strong executive buy-in is to identify the three to five near-term projects that will add the most value to an organization. Run a few initial Q Model sessions with the teams to provide a direct experience of exactly how the Q Model process will support them to get those projects moving. Likewise, as the executive leaders collaborate on these three to five critical projects, they will begin to engage in the process fully. The critical question for getting a broad project buy-in is, "What do we want to achieve?" Ask the leaders to give you three critical projects, goals, or metrics.

More Buy-in: Getting a buy-in from your key leaders is always tricky. Obliging leaders to attend a series of team discussions is one way. Another is having leaders participate in a pilot project. If these leaders see the transformation project as a distraction, they will always push back, as it will seem like the program is taking them away from their deadlines, KPIs, and business goals.

But the point of a breakthrough project is to deliver a strong result using a current project — a breakthrough solution that can be immediately applied to a project deadline. However, most busy managers won't believe this is possible because they are already pushing their team to work hard. Every transformation project needs a program supporter or executive sponsor who will convince skeptical leaders that their investment of time and energy is worth the trouble.

Long-Term Results: To build this support, the leadership team must ultimately consider how committed they are to the long-term goal of transforming the company. You can always focus the transformation program on two goals: meeting short-term goals and designing a long-term transformation in the company. It may be important to balance these two things to create harmony in the leadership team.

You must also get leaders and managers to start thinking about long-term strategy. Moving from short-term deadlines to long-term strategic company transformation is a big shift. You can kick off a small pilot to begin this shift, but at some point, the leaders will have to agree and rally around the idea that company transformation is critical for long-term success.

- Universal Roll-Out Process:

Content versus Process Transformation: You can use the Q Model rollout process to introduce the Q Model, but you can also use it to introduce many other kinds of organizational transformation approaches. By separating the Q Model rollout process from the Q Model content, we can use the former to rollout many other kinds of company change initiatives.

Content Rollout: From a content point of view, we are asking "What is the new thing we want to roll out?" This content could be a new strategy or technology. It could also be a new methodology, such as Lean Startup, Agile, the Q Model, or something else.

Rollout Process: Below we will demonstrate how to use the Q Model as a universal roll-out process that encourages the adoption of any new strategy or methodology. At the process level, we are asking "How?" and "Why?" *How* do we get people to adopt these new skills, and *why* do they want to do this?

For example, many organizations will want to introduce something like Agile, but they often approach it the wrong way. They'll do some Agile training, but fail to realize that you cannot *tell* someone how to *become* Agile. Agile is something a team learns by doing. Agile projects may be introduced, but low-level teams and unsupported projects will be selected to reduce the risk. This creates a conflict because managers see their people being taken away from important things to work on some *fake* project so they fight against the change. By stark contrast, everything in the Q Model has been carefully designed to avoid fake projects and failed roll-outs.

Here is a general outline of this universal rollout process approach:

- Turn the most important company goals into breakthrough projects
- Develop multi-silo teams for each project
- Turn the content or model into questions and a process
- Run a series of strategic brainstorming and whiteboarding sessions
- Use the content or model to develop effective solutions
- Develop an implementation plan to roll-out the solutions
- Give each team member enough time and space to work on the project
- Assign champions to energize your team
- Collect success stories and track results
- Iterate through a series of cycles to build momentum.

We have used this universal rollout process dozens of times with different kinds of strategic change initiatives or roll-outs of new methodologies. It must be adjusted based on the current state of an organization, so the above is just a basic roadmap. As you review the Q Model ideas, tools, and mindset, there are many more elements you can apply to this universal rollout process.

- Project Phases:

How Q Model Enterprise Transformation Works: The following are some general stages for any company-wide program.

Current State: Meet with teams and begin to understand the current strategy, company goals, and business challenges. Discuss the current state and start to turn the current strategy into a big picture company breakthrough plan.

Corporate Analysis Process: Begin with the analysis of the current state. Remember the basic current state questions and use them to identify the challenges or barriers that are blocking progress. Make sure to talk with people at many levels in the project, as frontline workers will have a different viewpoint on the challenges than the senior managers.

Warm-up: Skeptical leaders and technical experts won't believe that the Q Model works until they see results. It is useful to send a *guinea pig* team through the process first, using them to develop a few internal champions or an executive sponsor.

Intensive: An intensive Q Model program usually means setting aside one or two days for a strategic project retreat. It is always difficult to pull people away from their work for two days, so it is important to frame this as two days of highly focused work on the *most critical result* for the company.

If you can block out this kind of time for an intensive offsite event, it is one of the most effective ways to accelerate breakthrough projects. Gather the key executives, managers, and strategic project leaders for each project. Introduce the Q Model and get the teams engaged in developing breakthrough solutions and a model for success. Focus the teams on the key steps for strategic implementation and set up tracking metrics. The real breakthrough is always the ownership and engagement of the teams that will tackle the ongoing implementation.

Ongoing: Build a weekly program to keep the breakthrough projects moving. You can think of this in Agile terms as an iteration cycle. Often this is a series of check-in meetings every 7 or 14 days. As a general rule, as long as the projects keep moving forward, the overall company transformation process will build momentum. However, there will always be unseen forces that will seek to derail the company transformation project.

The ongoing program is critical to maintaining the high-alignment state and delivery of business results. Normally we plan for success, but Murphy Law often intrudes. Navigating the first 21 days is a critical milestone, so schedule a *planned program breakdown* for this date and, if nothing is going terribly wrong, celebrate the achievement. Planning for a *scheduled malfunction* is part of the *skeptic mindset*, where you *expect* the team to get distracted by all the business-as-usual interruptions and lose focus around this time. To avoid this, keep reiterating the case for *why* the breakthrough project is critical and continue to build buy-in from the executive supporters. Once you get to the 45-day mark, the program will tend to stabilize and become "the way we work every day."

Program Adoption: Target 80% adoption. This goal requires a strong commitment to follow-up implementation from the entire team. We will address this more in the next chapter in the section on Implementation Program Design.

Tracking Results: Tracking success measurements and KPIs are critical. Everyone invests time and energy in a project, so it is essential to demonstrate success with real numbers. It is suggested that both parties collaborate on picking the final tracking metrics. Some potential tracking metrics that range from leading to lagging could include:

- Program participation, feedback, surveys
- Skill adoption, follow-up skill tracking, follow-up participation
- Follow-up success stories
- Feedback from teams and managers
- Existing business metrics, achievement of targets

Project Completion: It is important to set an end date and end state for each project, even if the project will immediately turn into an ongoing business process once it is finished. Most people in companies experience day-to-day work as an endless series of problems and few feel appreciated for the hard work they do. Building some kind of ceremony to mark the end of the project and showing your appreciation to the team creates a state of completion. This leaves people energized and ready for the next challenge, instead of burned out and thinking of leaving.

Assessment of Results: It is essential to have a process to debrief and assess program performance and results. Look at the actual results, what the team achieved and what they did not. Ask what worked well and what could have been improved. This is another current state conversation, so assess these things through a non-judgmental frame.

Internal Business Case Study: Ask your teams to integrate the tracking data and summarize all results into a simple case study. Use this to demonstrate your success internally and get more buy-in for more transformation projects.

- Implementation Map:

Here is a general map of a broad enterprise program that might typically go through the following stages over a 12-24 month roll-out process. Depending on organization readiness, leadership buy-in, and program scale, some stages might be combined or skipped.

Step   1   Initial Warm-up   Months 1-2

Conduct a needs analysis and run assessment
Establish the challenges and current state
Build trust and relationships with the core team
Develop a comprehensive program plan
Enroll several supporters into a secret team with a code name

Step   2   Initial Projects   Months 2-4

Identify key high-impact projects, business goals, and growth initiatives
Conduct strategic Q Model sessions for carefully selected project teams
Conduct small pilots to demonstrate results and generate buzz
Generate some strong initial traction to demonstrate effectiveness
Generate a team of internal champions

Step   3   Executive Breakthrough   Months 3-6

Warm-up several potential executive champions
Target several active projects linked to revenue and strategy
Run several one-on-one or team executive sessions to gather alignment
Agree upon measurements of a successful strategic transformation
Amplify a clear vision and value of this successful strategic transformation
Present a strategic transformation pitch and proposal

Step   4   Larger Pilot   Months 4-8

Propose a big test to demonstrate results
Pick a critical project with specific strategic deliverables
Design a measurement system with leading and lagging indicators
Run a pilot program with coaching, consulting, and training elements
Conduct a fully supported follow-up program to integrate results
Document an internal mini-case study to pinpoint results

Step   5   Roll-Out Phase 1   Months 6-12

Continue high-level strategic transformation conversations
Internally message a strategic challenge as a series of open questions
Conduct roundtable events to establish alignment and buy-in
Roll out breakthrough project programs to 10–20% of selected staff
Establish ongoing strategic breakthrough projects lead by champions
Run peer-to-peer programs to lock in skill development
Continue tracking and reporting metrics for the strategic transformation
Run bottom-up strategic sessions. Harvest success stories

Step   6   Roll-Out Phase 2   Months 12-24

Continue high-level strategic transformation conversations
Message strategic transformation champion success stories
Roll out programs for more staff, including previous champions
Continue tracking and reporting metrics for the strategic transformation
Run a larger strategic breakthrough program for 20–40% of selected staff
Find any areas of misalignment and address them privately
Continue to align the strategic transformation with company goals
Establish a fully aligned mission, vision, and value structure

Post-program: Continue tracking and reporting metrics

Chapter 20 - Transformational Learning

GSK: Transformation Adoption

In 2011 GlaxoSmithKline (GSK) Canada ran a Q Model program for all their leaders and mid-level managers. Everyone engaged during the intensive phase of the program, and many delivered breakthrough results. The completion of the two-day intensive marked the start of a 90-day ongoing program, where we asked each of the senior leaders to support their direct reports in the adoption of the skills and mindset. It was here where the real challenge began.

During the ongoing phase, one *supportive* regional leader in particular, demanded that all his key managers attend every follow-up session and use the Q Model tools every day for the first three weeks. In this supportive leader's team, *everyone* became a program champion at the end of the 90 days. Every member of his team could tell captivating success stories about how they used the Q Model to solve business challenges in their operations. These champions went back to their teams and repeated the process. Based on our work with many companies, the average benchmark rate of 90-day champion development is 79%. The supportive leader in this program was the first executive champion in *any* company to achieve a 100% rate. Right after the implementation phase, he was promoted to a VP role.

This first story illustrates what we call *people transformation*, a fundamental shift in the actions and mindsets of a large group of managers and employees.

Another *unsupportive* regional leader in the same program had just been promoted and was anxious about his security in his new role. Worried in particular about his end of quarter numbers, he only wanted his managers to focus on "work", and was so dismissive of the Q Model program that he avoided scheduling any follow-up sessions. After two months of this, his frustrated team bypassed him and arranged their follow-up sessions directly. At the *end* of 90 days, his team achieved a 22% champion development rate, just above the 16% company average at the *start* of the 90-day program.

80/20 Transformation: This example illustrates the critical nature of executive support for an ongoing follow-up program. Any *transformation* will rapidly revert back to *business as usual* if it is not supported through a critical gestation period. Over and over we have found that people transformation results follow a kind of 80/20 rule. Around 20% of managers will fundamentally shift their mindset and actions at the end of an intensive. With strong follow up and the support of a senior leader, this number will climb to 80% at the end of 90-days.

Transformational Learning: While most of the Q Model focuses on business strategy, solutions, and results, at a lower level we are always dealing with people who are adopting the skills and mindset required for *conducting* Q Model conversations. In this chapter, we will focus on how to achieve a breakthrough in transformational learning and skill adoption that can rapidly spread throughout an organization.

What is Transformational Learning? Think of a peak learning moment in your life. Everyone has had many moments where they reconnected with their love of learning. These moments always link to some kind of insight or transformation that expands your thinking and mindset. How do we build a system to consistently deliver this kind of peak moment that rekindles a lifelong love of learning? To answer this question, let's take a close look at the core elements of this system.

Facilitated Learning: Even if you don't do any formal training, learning is always happening around you. Asking good questions and conducting Q Model conversations will naturally accelerate this process. As you conduct Q Model conversations, you are developing a *facilitative leadership* style, which is in turn developing into a transformational *training* skill. A good experiential trainer is always facilitating team learning. We encourage you to integrate all three of these approaches into all the conversations, presentations, and training you conduct. Asking good questions and encouraging team dialogue is a universal skill, and by using the Q Model you are also teaching the Q Model to your team.

Engage: We designed the Q Model to embed a transformational learning approach into every conversation. We have consistently found that learning engagement translates into a higher level of on-the-job engagement and passion in both work and life in general. With the Q Model, we introduce or reacquaint managers and executives with the magic of accelerated learning. This yields a high ROI on the investment of time and energy.

Hands-On Learning Experience: The Q Model transformation system embeds real projects into a leadership transformation process. This makes projects relevant to everyday work. Because the Q Model uses a hands-on experiential style of learning, leaders find their ideas quickly turning into new habits as they implement them using the Q Model tools. We have documented below that a well-delivered Q Model program consistently delivers a transformation in mindset and behavior for up to 80% of program participants. This is what we call *people transformation*.

Information versus Transformation: Most traditional training is based on an academic model of knowledge transfer, which typically has a low level of effectiveness. The problem with this model is that the instruction does not link to real day-to-day work, so the training process is abstract and theoretical, meaning that ideas don't stick in the mind. Leaders also have to leave their job to attend this kind of training, and the time spent away from work is too costly to be recouped by the knowledge that is gained. The most significant risk is that managers and executives will reject the entire idea of training and development. Do you want employees complaining about "another useless leadership training seminar" to be your net result?

Sticky: Most lecture-based training has a 5% rate of information retention. By contrast, transformation-based training can yield up to 79% fundamental habit and mindset change. This makes the Q Model approach 15 times more effective than traditional training.

Here is Edgar Dale's pyramid of learning, which we mentioned in Chapter 3.[1-5] His data shows the level of information retention based on different kinds of learning activities.

Lecture	5%
Reading	10%
Audio Visual / Video	20%
Demonstration	30%
Discussion Group	50%
Practice by Doing	75%
Teaching Others	90%
Application in a real situation	90%

Most leaders and educators know about these principles, but they rarely do the work to design a learning experience that provides an immediate application of ideas into a real situational context. This is exactly what makes learning sticky instead of forgettable.

Sticky Learning:

Sticky is the simple idea that new information needs to be linked to other ideas to stick in your mind. The brain is being overrun with information every moment of your waking day, 99.9% of which must be thrown away because your brain deems it irrelevant. However, this is not just about retaining information. When learning becomes *hyper-sticky* it can fundamentally transform the mindset and behavior of everyone on a team. At one level you could approach this discussion by asking:

How can we make our *training* programs sticky?

But at a deeper level you could ask:

How can we make *every discussion* in our
company into a hyper-sticky learning experience?"

You don't need to understand all this to get going — just use the Q Model and all the sticky learning will happen automatically. However, to give you some more insight into how the Q Model works *under the hood,* we will now explore the three required elements for sticky learning:

1 – Experiential   **2 – Intuitive**   **3 – Visual**

1 - Experiential Learning:

Experiential learning has become quite popular in the past few years, but most of it just scratches the surface. The Q Model offers mastery of an experiential learning legacy that first took shape in 1981. The process starts with hands-on exercises with real projects that drive engagement and sticky learning. Powerful learning exercises are the key to high-impact training, and a deep understanding of how to convert concepts and ideas into learning exercises is the foundation.

Transformation only happens when participants build a conscious awareness of their new mindset and can declare their insights to the group. This is accomplished with 1-on-1 debriefs, table dialogues, group whiteboarding, and team presentations. All of this builds a strong team identity that links to project success.

One of the most overlooked elements of sticky learning is *relevance*. The more that a topic is relevant or important to the learner, the stronger any associated experiential learning will become. Rather than discuss abstract management ideas, use those concepts to build a breakthrough in a current project or goal. Based on this approach, can you see that all the parts of the Q Model that you have been studying in this book were formulated in advance for sticky experiential learning? Notice how asking questions, addressing project challenges, building a vision of project success, whiteboarding solutions, linking value words, and committing to take the first action in seven days are all hyper-sticky activities.

Project Embedded Learning: The Q Model Project Breakthrough system uses a *project embedded* learning approach. Always work with real projects to automatically create situational learning. The process must be hands-on and experiential, so select meaningful and challenging projects that deal with real issues. This will automatically create a situational learning environment that is down to earth, tangible, and quick to produce results.

2 - Intuitive Learning:

The logical mind has a narrow focus, limited learning capacity, and is resistant to ideas that challenge the status quo. Real learning happens organically, as insights "pop" into your mind and are welcomed to stay. This is called *intuitive learning,* and it creates an accelerated learning state whereby you trigger a mindset shift by embracing confusion rather than running away from it. It forces you to confront challenging ideas and integrate them into your broader understanding of the world.

For example, on the first day of an intensive, we always set out to overwhelm the logic system by introducing *too many* challenging ideas for the average person to assimilate. We ask everyone to be OK with their confusion and frame this as a part of the breakthrough experience. Much of the best work happens during the "sleep break" between day one and day two. On day two, we support people to integrate the ideas by having them present their own holistic overview of everything they learned on day one. We conduct an in-depth table debrief with the teams, making sure that every table builds a visual model of the complete system and declares their insights. With this approach, 80% of the participants will step into a complete *holographic* understanding of the system. The 90-day implementation program will make the shift permanent by anchoring the learning and high-alignment state into normal day-to-day activities.

3 - Visual Learning:

Recent research indicates that visual-spatial learning is the key to dealing with complex problem-solving.[13-1] The essence of accelerated learning is to fully engage the visual-spatial thinking system and create a vivid learning experience via visual tools and whiteboarding.

The first rule is "no PPTs" — all content and ideas are best delivered with co-created flip charts and a whiteboarding process because visual exercises drive engagement. The visual brain is best energized with intensive color usage, brainstorming with Post-it notes, and integration of visual models.

If you go back to Chapter 13, you can review the section on whiteboarding and visual modeling from a visual learning context. Just remember, any time you engage in whiteboarding, visual modeling, or value mapping you are also engaged in visual learning.

- Q Model Adoption Process:

Often people approach the Q Model as a conversational method. In this context, the Q Model is an iterative tool for increasing the quality of conversations in a team, project, or company. You can introduce the Q Model ideas and practice having Q Model conversations with your team. However, you can also use the Q Model *universal rollout process* to introduce other breakthrough strategies or methods. In either case, the most important question is "how many people are adopting the new mindset?"

Adoption Model: The Q Model is also a *process model* for effectively introducing and energizing the adoption of *any* new strategy or process methodology. It is important to note that we are presenting a universal process for enabling the adoption of new systems, strategies, and ideas. You can use the Q Model rollout process to introduce the Q Model, but you can also use it to introduce many other kinds of organizational transformation strategies or approaches.

For example, when we were working with Hoerbiger China, several of the breakthrough project teams were focused on dealing with a stalled Lean Manufacturing initiative in the company. Using Q Model tools and principles to energize the project, we were able to get the Lean Manufacturing initiative back on track by dividing it into several separate breakthrough projects. The teams asked questions, had conversations, used the whiteboarding tools, and all of the Q Model project implementations tools. At a *content* level, they were focused on Lean Manufacturing but at the *process* level, they were using the Q Model to energize their rate of adoption to Lean. You can break this approach into the following implementation layers:

Business Result   **Project**   **Content or Process**   **Adoption Model**

Separating the adoption model from the learning content is a critical distinction because everyone tends to *fall in love* with their preferred approach or method. We all have a bias for the tools or approaches most familiar to us. When you break apart the content from the adoption model it is easier to be objective in selecting the best tool or approach to fit situational needs.

You can see how we mapped out these implementation layers for the Hoerbiger project here:

Result: 18% increase in manufacturing efficiency in one year
Project: 8% reduction in operational waste in 90 days
Content: Reenergize Lean Manufacturing
Adoption Model: Q Model teams, projects, daily questions, weekly conversations

Implementation Program Design:

The 90-Day Implementation Program: Besting the aforementioned 5% rate of retention for lecture-based training, an intensive and transformational two or three-day training period usually delivers a fundamental habit shift and mindset change for up to 20% of the participants. However, the addition of a well-structured 90-day implementation program will provide a transformational shift for up to 80% of the participants. We have included post-program survey results of some of our large corporate programs near the end of this chapter.

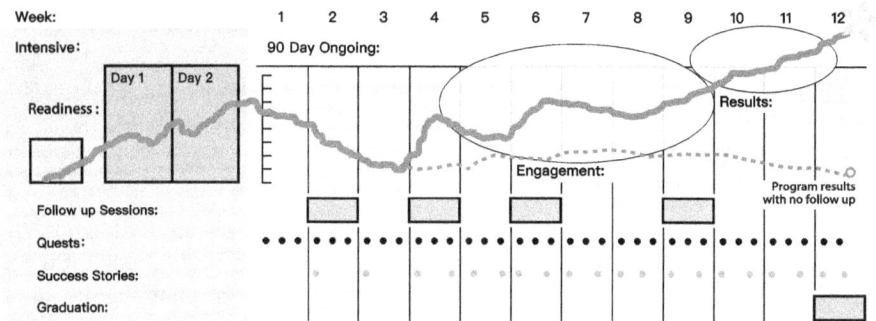

Leadership Support: A well-managed implementation program requires support from many leadership levels. This requires a strong overall commitment to the success of the implementation process. The training program's goals must align with the general business goals. It is important to have strong support from a principal executive sponsor who fully participates. As external consultants, we design many follow-up components to *push* the program adoption, but it is critical to have senior leaders and direct managers who *pull* for program adoption.

It is also critical to identify key risk areas, such as end-of-quarter deadlines or holidays. Assign a dedicated internal coordinator who *chases* the participants to engage and report and who can identify breakdowns in participation early. As mentioned earlier in the chapter, schedule *in advance* a program breakdown on day 21 and plan accordingly.

What is a Champion? Over the years we kept searching for a clear measurement of *who is a champion* until we stumbled upon an ideal gauge. Simply ask the participants to give an example of how they used a Q Model tool to solve a business issue. Champions usually have many interesting stories to tell and love to share.

We have defined a champion as anyone who has strongly internalized the key Q Model ideas and used them to deliver business results. We expanded this to include anyone who has demonstrated a fundamental shift in their mindset and maintained this upon returning to their regular work environment? As you develop a group, champions will naturally emerge. They are easy to spot by their passion for the new ideas and commitment to the success of their leaders and teammates?

Tracking: The internal coordinator works to track the participation, skill development, and project implementation of the teams. Tracking leading metrics that gauge participation is critical, and can include program participation, feedback, surveys, skill adoption, skill tracking, follow up participation, success stories, and program feedback from the team and managers. However, always remember the real goal is tangible business results, not numbers on a tracking document.

Implementation Elements:

Team Identity: The participants become a team and build a strong success-based team identity.

Commit: The team authentically commits 100% to action every day and program success.

Champions: Natural program champions emerge and drive team progress. Champions are the ultimate high-potential pipeline in an organization. Don't hire talent — make talent.

Follow-up Meetings: Onsite or online meetings that present new tools and re-engage activity.

First 21 days: Engagement in the first three weeks is a crucial predictor of success.

qTeam Sessions: Arrange ongoing qTeam sessions to address project implementation challenges and drive the new mindset with the core champion group.

Success Stories: Authentic success is the fuel that drives team transformation. Harvest, message, and rebroadcast these stories.

Messaging: Internal messaging of success stories back to the group builds momentum.

Celebration: Strongly praise and reward small initial successes and big wins.

Completion: Create a meaningful completion process. Support people to be proud of their achievements.

The rate of Champion Development: The most useful leading indicator of the success of a program is the rate of *champion development*.

Typically, we track champion development at the *beginning* and *end* of the 90-day implementation program. We ask participants a series of skill adoption questions that track their daily usage of the Q Model tools. The ultimate measurement of a champion is their ability to tell an inspiring success story about how they used the tools to deliver some small breakthrough business result.

The rate of Champion Development: Survey results

Company	90 day start	90 day end
Golder	19%	78%
Amex	21%	81%
GSK	16%	68%
SAP	27%	89%
Average	**20%**	**79%**

Why Programs Fail: It is also very useful to put on your skeptic hat and consider the *worst-case* scenario so that you can plan for the *best case*. Most transformation implementation programs *fail* for the same set of reasons:

• Leaders fail to understand the importance of the follow-up implementation program.

• Internal leaders try to make the participants "happy" and do not push for program adoption.

• Senior leaders think the lower-level staff need to be "fixed" and do not engage in the practice and mindset themselves.

• Senior leaders or direct managers not aligned in advance with the mindset shift undermine the implementation program, either directly or indirectly.

• Program implementation is viewed as *in competition* with other priorities, deadlines, KPIs, or critical projects.

Chapter 21 - MetaQ

Thinking Agility

MetaQ: How to think outside the box. What is human intelligence? In the first half of the 20th century, psychologists attempted to represent a human being's level of intelligence by a single Intelligence Quotient number, or IQ score. They did this by conducting problem-solving tests and grading people on a bell curve. Certainly, within the *narrow scope* of solving the limited types of problems represented in these tests, the results are quite accurate. However, knowledge of your high or low score will usually *hurt* you more than it *helps* you. In the modern world, the idea of a single IQ score seems misguided. People express intelligence in many unique ways, and in recent years the concept of Emotional Intelligence or EQ has become very popular. While EQ provides a critical counterbalance to the cold, logical measurements of an IQ test, we must go beyond both to reach the next level of high-alignment leadership.

> Be careful what you measure: Whatever is measured becomes *stronger*

Thinking Agility: Human thinking potential is about much more than logic or emotion. Remember, we live in an age of accelerating complexity and change. Dealing with change requires flexibility. Dealing with the accelerating *speed of change* requires you to develop unique skills and new ways of thinking. Great business leaders think beyond short term solutions, seeing past the data to get fresh insights. In the modern world of continuous transformation, how can we measure this kind of *out of the box* thinking?

Meta:	Above, beyond, outside, a Greek prefix
Quotient:	The result of dividing one number into another
MetaQ:	A transformational measurement of the ability to think outside the current mindset

What is MetaQ?

- MetaQ is a model of common business thinking habits
- MetaQ is based on 40 years of observational research
- MetaQ is a business leadership assessment process
- MetaQ embeds high-performance transformation into a simple assessment system
- MetaQ is fully integrated into the Q Model enterprise transformation system

The Problem of Assessment:

Assessment is a vital tool for understanding the current state of an organization. Traditional assessment systems, such as MBTI and DISC focus on individual personality types. Although they can provide organizational insights, they can also compound problems:

- People who take the assessment view the results as an external judgment
- Their reaction to external judgment makes them resist change
- There is no clear path to behavioral change

- They don't know what to do with the results
- The assessment creates a label: "you are an *orange* person,"
                                                 "he is an *agreeable* person,"
- Personality "type" labels can push people into a corner

Labels are Great, Everyone Should Have One: Traditional assessment models attempt to categorize people into existing personality types based on a scientific model. It is assumed this will lead to greater reflection and growth. In practice, these labels can be as distracting as they are fascinating. The real danger of personality assessments is that once we categorize people they tend to *stay in* their categories. The moment people internalize a label as part of their identity, their attachment to it becomes a *self-fulfilling* prophecy. As well, some top performers can be very self-critical of themselves. These kinds of assessments can reduce performance unless the process provides a positive developmental growth path. If you put people *in a box*, you must show them how to get *out of the box* or they will be stuck there. MetaQ is a system for out-of-the-box thinking.

Thinking Habits: The MetaQ assessment takes a very different approach that provides individuals and teams with insights into their thinking habits. These thinking habits link to small actions that support breakthrough project success. Focusing their attention on a small group of actions and behaviors, managers and leaders can use MetaQ to drive project results and reach a more advanced level of collaboration. This includes tiny action steps that make the MetaQ shift easy to implement in day-to-day activities.

The Law of Attention: According to the Law of Attention, whatever you pay attention to gets stronger.[11-1] People like their old habits so you tend to get *more of the same.* This is why so many innovative new initiatives often end up back in *business as usual.*

To transform the results of the business we need people to focus their attention on solutions that are *outside of the box* of their normal thinking habits. However, it's tough to break old habits because people and teams tend to stick to the approaches they are most comfortable with. For example, the stock thinking habits of engineers, accountants, and marketing people are deeply ingrained and often the root cause of the barriers that block a company transformation. MetaQ brings these thinking habits into the light where people can see them. By focusing the attention on the habits that block effective communication and solutions, people can *get out of the way* so that projects keep moving.

Questions are Transformational: Since the development of coaching in the mid-nineties, it has been demonstrated that asking questions is fundamentally transformational. The transformational nature of questions means that the act of conducting an assessment will change the individual.[10-2] This observer effect is well documented, but most traditional assessments miss this critical point. The MetaQ assessment model uses carefully designed questions that focus attention on the desired state of the individual and team. The process naturally triggers dialogue that propels the team toward a higher state of alignment and performance.

The MetaQ Assessment Model

MetaQ: Assessment Drives Performance: MetaQ is a model of the common thinking patterns and work habits that are common to every manager or business leader as they go through their day. The powerful insights you receive from this model link to tiny action steps you can take to increase your team's performance and directly produce results.

The MetaQ model arranges six common thinking habits into a scale of opposing extremes. For example, some people are very good at getting into the *details,* while others are very good at looking at the *big picture*. Here is how such a scale appears:

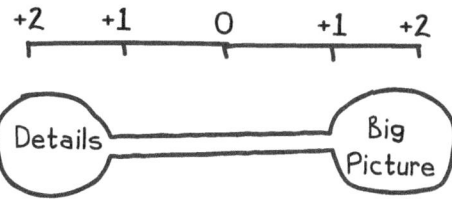

People tend to immediately place themselves at one end of this scale or the other. What seems most comfortable to you, detail or big picture thinking?

We like our habits: Habits are contextual. You may need to be very *detail-oriented* to fill in your expense report, but you might need to *think big* when you are planning something a month away. We change our habits as we move from task to task, but we also develop a core set of *preferred* habits that we default to on a daily basis. This core set of patterns will become evident when people are under stress or excited by a big project. Over time people get so locked into these patterns that they become second nature.

Core Versus Learned: Can you be good at both ends of the scale? Yes — some business leaders are as good at getting into the details as they are at seeing the big picture. While being able to strike this balance is a sign of a great leader, even for them there is usually a *core habit* at one end of the scale and a *learned behavior* at the other.

Think of a CEO who loves looking at the big picture when it comes to success. Over time they learn they have to get into forecasting details, so they develop a skill for detailed thinking in this area. Despite now being capable of employing both extremes, whenever the CEO gets excited about a new project they will default to their big-picture thinking mode and ignore the planning details.

Know yourself and you will win all battles **- Sun Tzu, The Art of War**

Recall that the core MetaQ thinking patterns tend to show up most strongly when we are under stress, and that stress can be either negative and positive. We all understand negative stress but we rarely think about positive stress. We can define positive stress as excitement: the excitement for new ideas, projects, or opportunities will often bring out the default thinking habits in a person or team.

The 6 Scales:

The Quick Assessment: The MetaQ assessment below has six scales that each reflect two opposite thinking habits. This will help you identify *where you land* regarding your specific problem-solving habits and more general thinking styles.

The simplest way to do the assessment is to simply look at this list and find the pattern that seems strongest. Often we know ourselves well enough to find the strongest patterns intuitively. However, there is a more formal version of the assessment that uses 24 questions to deliver a score for each scale, which is not presented in this book. Look through the following six MetaQ scales. Find one or two that seem to show up everywhere in your life.

The Six Scales:

Detail: We like to get into the details of our work. Managing the small things in a project is critical.	vs.	**Big Picture:** We like to look at the big picture and think through large abstract ideas.
Reflection: We like to think carefully before making a decision. We must take care of relationships.	vs.	**Action:** We need to get into action right away. Getting project results is essential.
Now: We need to respond right away. I am available all the time. Call or text me if there is a problem.	vs.	**Planning:** We need a well-managed and long-term plan. We need to think through all the steps in advance.
Possibility: This project could be very successful. We need to ask questions to find solutions.	vs.	**Process:** We must direct people to follow the process and procedure. We need to measure and track results.
Individual: I need to achieve my KPIs and targets. I mostly work one-on-one with my top performers.	vs.	**Team:** We need to work together as a team and support everyone. Our project will help our customers.
Open: I like to explore new ideas. I enjoy starting new projects. I love to ask great questions.	vs.	**Close:** It is essential to make decisions and resolve issues. I like finishing things and scratching them off my to-do list. I enjoy completing projects.

Can you change your MetaQ Thinking Habits? Yes...! (and No.) Remember, we are talking about thinking habits, not personality types. Habits can change. However, over time most people tend to settle into one set of thinking patterns instead of another. The good news is that a *thinking pattern* is very different from a *learned behavior*. Simply maintaining an awareness of your MetaQ pattern will create a shift in your thinking patterns. To shift a learned behavior, we simply focus on the tiny actions that correspond to the opposite end of the MetaQ scale. By taking these actions every day, any team that endeavors to maintain MetaQ awareness and shift their thinking patterns can quickly make progress and achieve lasting positive change.

The MetaQ Visual Model:

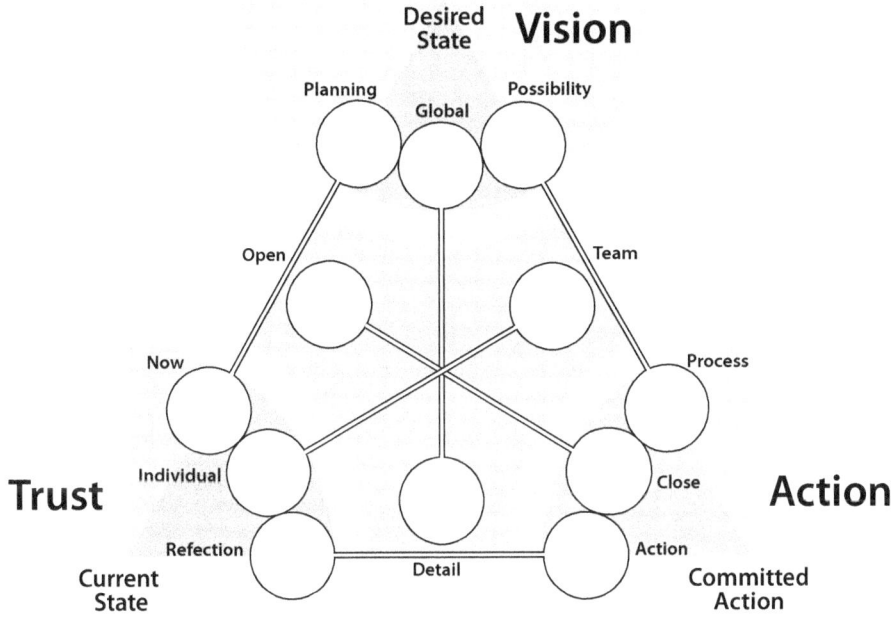

Focus on the Weak Area:

Teams will tend to dislike or feel uncomfortable with other teams that have opposite MetaQ patterns. For example, engineering teams must focus on product details, while marketing teams must focus on the big picture of how a product fits into the market. Someone needs to be able to translate between these alternative and often opposing points of view, or you will end up with a failed product. Unfortunately, few people are good at both ends of the MetaQ patterns.

Core habits make people strong: People are proud of their strengths, and MetaQ habits define what is most important to individual human beings. Be careful: when you ask people about their weak MetaQ area, they can take it as an insult or personal attack because people resist change. This resistance is why most change management programs fail.

The good news is that you don't need to change your MetaQ habits. Once you know where you are strong, all you need to do is practice the tiny actions that produce success at the opposite end of the scale. Most people usually report that this feels a little uncomfortable at first. However, once you try it for a few days and see that the actions are straightforward, you get immediate and momentum-building results.

CEO Appreciation Day: In 2017, the Q Model team worked with a top-performing CEO in a tech company, who we have agreed not to name. He was very concerned about his performance. He focused on the individual results of a few of his senior leaders, who were also his buddies. He scored at the top of the *individual* MetaQ scale, which automatically placed him at the bottom of the *team* scale. Once he learned this he became curious and promised to take one *team-related* MetaQ action every day. Among the first moves he made was to publicly appreciate one person from the company for their work. Another action was to include the opinions of more people when making key decisions. He stated that these things felt very *alien* and *fake* at first, but he persisted, and at the end of each week he updated one of our coaches on all the tiny actions he had completed. This action had a dramatic effect. Within 30 days, the engagement of the entire team has shifted positively. He didn't think he had done much, but it was evident to everyone else that he had changed a lot, and that his level of performance had dramatically increased.

MetaQ Team Project Habits: Projects are the key to success, but every project has different stages and unique challenges that require individuals and teams to adopt different MetaQ habits depending on their needs. Since almost no one is well-balanced across all six MetaQ patterns, people who produce quality insights and results in one stage may not fare as well in other stages. With the MetaQ assessment data in hand, people and teams will become aware of who is strong and who is weak in a given area. Remember, you don't need to redesign the entire team — simply get everyone to practice one of the tiny actions listed below every day. This will maintain team member awareness of weak areas, and many issues will naturally self-correct.

Every Enterprise Transformation program begins with three to five collaborative breakthrough projects. Think of each project cycle like a flow chart or system: it only takes one blockage in the system to slow everything down. But if we can find that block and get things moving again, the performance of the entire system will dramatically increase. The key to success is to use those breakthrough projects as a learning environment to practice the new MetaQ actions.

6 Thinking Hats: In this illustration, the six MetaQ scales are mapped onto the three corners of the Q Model. For example, working with the current state of a project requires listening and building trust, while working with the desired state requires more big-picture thinking.

Current State: Where is the project at right now?

Detail	Get into the details
Reflection	Think carefully about what is needed
Now	Focus on the most pressing issue now
Individual	Focus on how are people doing

Desired State: What do we want to achieve?

Big Picture	What does success look like?
Possibility	Imagine the possibility of success
Planning	What are the steps, stages, and resources?
Team	Support the team, link contribution and customers

Committed Action: How can we stay motivated and on track?

Process	How can we systematize our process?
Action	What is the critical action in the next seven days?

The Formal Assessment Process: In the formal MetaQ assessment process we ask people a series of questions, then ask them to scale themselves based on the answer that seems most true. Individuals score themselves and the scores can be combined into a team score. This produces a visual cluster effect that offers a treasure chest of insights into your team member's strengths and weaknesses; aggregating this data across groups shows equally insightful organizational clusters. MetaQ is an effective way to create a profound awareness of individual and team habits.

We ask questions that link to all twelve ends of the six scales. If you *strongly* agree with one statement, circle +2 for that end of the scale. If you *generally* agree with one statement, circle +1. If you agree with both statements in a balanced way, circle the zero. We add the numbers from each scale, and the results allow us to make a detailed assessment. Finally, we add the numbers that link to Trust, Vision, and Action and get the final set of numbers, which we call the MetaQ Score. A team can do the assessment on paper in about 15 minutes, but ideally, they do the assessment in advance on the MetaQ Website.

Below is the final MetaQ score for all the leaders and managers from a mid-sized tech company. When the leaders and managers saw these numbers they got very curious and immediately began discussing how they could apply this insight to their current breakthrough projects.

Trust: 93
Vision: 156
Action: 114

Take Action: Once you find your strongest MetaQ areas, look for the opposite weak areas — where you are strong determines where you are weak. Find your three weakest areas, then look for the tiny action steps that go with each of them. You will be able to put these to work right away and increase your team performance and business results.

The 3 Corners of the Triangle: You can also view the results based on the three corners of the Q Model triangle. As a general rule, focus on the corner with the lowest score.

If you are Strong in Trust and Current State:

Focus on Committed Action
Take action in an area you have been avoiding
Just do it on one task today
Make a decision that you have been avoiding
Focus on the one key action you need to take
Ask "What are the next steps?" once today
Map out the next steps for a task
Draw a flow chart of a business process

If you are Strong in Vision and Desired State:

Focus on trust and the current state
Ask for feedback from one person

Ask "How are you doing?" once today
Ask "What do *I* want?" once today
Write down one career goal today
Once a day, take three deep and relaxing breaths
Post one value word in your workspace and look at it
Appreciate one person you work with
Write down three things that make you proud of yourself

If you are Strong in Committed Action:

Focus on vision and the desired state
Ask one strong open-ended question
Ask "What are some ways to begin?" in a conversation today
Come up with three ways to resolve an issue
Have a mini-brainstorm with one person
Ask "What would success look like?" once today
Imagine achieving a small goal
Make a clear picture in your mind of success

Next Level: Compare and discuss your MetaQ results with your team. You can integrate the MetaQ results into the complete Q Model system. This will allow you to use the MetaQ insights to accelerate a larger breakthrough project.

MetaQ is deeply integrated with the Q Model, it can link internal awareness to specific external behaviors and business results. Most important of all, MetaQ supports leaders to stop and reflect on their habits, making it an ideal tool to kick off a Q Model based Enterprise Transformation program.

Completion: Q Model Mastery

The Q Model is a *mastery system* with many layers:

Skill: Asking good questions and conducting breakthrough conversations are skills that anyone can develop. Set your sights on mastery of the Q Model skills.

Mindset: The mindset of the Q Model is expansive. Catching yourself when you get stuck and using the tools to get unstuck is the essence of the Q Model mindset. The more you operate within this mindset, the stronger you will become.

Visioning: Your visioning system will generate a tangible image of any future you are brave enough to imagine. As you build commitment, strategies and solutions will appear that open new doorways of opportunity. Keep building your vision for Q Model mastery by asking, "Who will I become as I master the Q Model?"

Value Transformation: Building internal alignment is not a one-off event. If you dare to ask for more from life, you must be ready to endure what it throws at you in response. Generate the energy you need to face these challenges by discovering and aligning yourself with your core values.

The Path: A tall mountain to climb, the journey to mastery starts with a single step. Instead of stopping yourself by visualizing all the hardships you will endure, put one foot on the path and begin. Don't worry about the end result — just stay on the path and keep moving. At some point, you might discover that you enjoy climbing mountains.

The path is the end, the end Is the path

The Game: Foremost, remember that mastery is a game. The word 'challenge' is magical: solving even the most insurmountable problem becomes *possible* the moment you declare it to be a challenge. As you get stronger, facing the challenge will become a game. Sometimes you will win or lose a round, but you will keep playing because you enjoy the game.

Seek, above all, for a game worth playing. - **Robert S. de Ropp**

Beginner's Mind: The paradox of mastery is that it is grounded in the unstoppable force of *beginner's mind.* Just as the ideogram for the Chinese word *Zhu* means both master and child the Q Model process moves back and forth between simplicity and mastery. Accordingly, the true sage is the one who can approach even the most complex of problems with the curiosity, innocence, and excitement of a child.

Mastery is Calling: Listen carefully and in the distance you will hear the most beautiful music. Once you knew this *sweetest melody* well, but somehow you forgot. Now you can hear it again, clearly. Uniting a child's sense of curiosity and wonder with the courage and determination of an adult, this is the song of mastery and it is calling to you.

Completion: Q Model Mastery

The Q Model is a *mastery system* with many layers:

Skill: Asking good questions and conducting breakthrough conversations are skills that anyone can develop. Set your sights on mastery of the Q Model skills.

Mindset: Catching yourself when you get stuck and using the tools to get unstuck is the essence of the Q Model mindset. The more you operate within this mindset, the stronger you will become.

Visioning: Your visioning system will generate a tangible image of any future you are brave enough to imagine. As you build commitment, strategies and solutions will present themselves that open new doors of opportunity. Keep building your vision for Q Model mastery by asking, "Who will I become as I master the Q Model?"

Value Transformation: Building internal alignment is not a one-off event. If you dare to ask for more from life, you must be ready to endure what it throws at you in response. Generate the energy you need to face these challenges by discovering and aligning yourself with your core values.

The Path: A tall mountain to climb, the journey to mastery starts with a single step. Instead of visualizing all the hardships you will endure, simply put one foot on the path and begin. Don't worry about the end result — just stay on the path and keep moving. At some point, you might discover that you enjoy climbing mountains.

The path is the end, the end is the path

The Game: Foremost, remember that mastery is a game. The word 'challenge' is magical: solving even the most insurmountable problem becomes *possible* the moment you declare it to be a challenge. As you get stronger, facing the challenge will become a highly enjoyable game. Sometimes you will win or lose a round, but you will keep playing because you enjoy it so much.

Seek, above all, for a game worth playing. - Robert S. de Ropp

Beginner's Mind: The paradox of mastery is that it is grounded in the unstoppable force of *beginner's mind*. Just as the ideogram for the Chinese word *zhu* means both master and child, the Q Model moves back and forth between simplicity and mastery. Accordingly, the true sage is the one who can approach even the most complex of problems with the curiosity, innocence, and excitement of a child.

Mastery is Calling: Listen carefully. In the distance, you will hear the most beautiful music. Once you knew this *sweetest melody* well, but somehow you forgot. Now you can hear it again, clearly. Uniting a child's sense of curiosity and wonder with the courage and determination of an adult, this is the *song of mastery* and it is calling to you.

History of Q

The history of the Q Model begins with Milton Erickson in the 1950s. The Q Model includes elements of sports psychology, Neuro-Linguistic Programming (NLP), positive psychology, and coaching that were developed during the 1980s and '90s and continue to be used today.

The Q Model is a solution-focused cognitive process for breakthrough business results. Using tools and principles developed from more than 35 years of neuroscientific research, it has evolved naturally through observational feedback of thousands of conversations and experiential modeling of what fails and what works.

The 1950s: Our unique lineage starts with Milton Erickson, an American psychiatrist and psychologist who used an unconventional approach to assist his clients in creating a shift or transformation in their lives. Codifying many conversational principles for transformation, he helped his clients design their own tools for achieving high-alignment states.

The 1970s: In the 1970s, a group of students led by John Bandler and Richard Grinder started researching Milton Erickson and several other transformational practitioners, in an attempt to model and systematize the extraordinary results Erickson and his peers were consistently achieving. They eventually developed many models, which they collectively called NLP or Neuro-Linguistic Programming.[22-1]

The 1980s: At the time NLP was coming into the public consciousness in 1981, I was fortunate enough to be exposed to something called *EST Training*. EST was always controversial, but its core philosophy — a mixture of existential emptiness, declarative ontology, and Zen-like transformation — was simple enough. EST introduced millions of people to the idea that anyone can generate a breakthrough in their life, which is of course, a fundamental tenet of the Q Model.

Coming back to NLP, by the mid-80s NLP had become a pop psychology movement, and I was lucky enough to find myself working with Marilyn Atkinson as she opened five NLP Institutes across Canada. Still a young adult, I ran the marketing for these organizations and spent years trying to refine complex ideas into simple messages. I also spent hundreds of hours working with several of the founders of NLP, including Robert Dilts and Connie Rae Andreas. Many of the tools and ideas I was exposed to in these years are profoundly interwoven into the Q Model.

I often joke that I was raised by wolves in a forest. In this case, it was a forest of NLP and transformation, the latter of which became my *way of looking* at the world. Once I counted all the hours I spent studying personal growth systems and realized the number had exceeded 10,000 before I reached the age of 21. It was evident to me that transformation was the key to success in everything, from business to life.

In the early days, NLP was not well integrated with academia. Suffering from claims of outrageous results and a lack of scientifically validated research, later many of the ideas in NLP were replicated and substantiated in sports psychology, and this provided the in-depth research results needed to substantiate the early *bleeding-edge* ideas. Many of these early NLP ideas and tools are now so normalized and accepted that they have been seamlessly integrated into the general field of positive psychology.

The 1990s: A core idea in NLP is called the Logical Levels. Introduced by Gregory Bateson as a linguistic model for the evolution of human language, later Robert Dilts presented it as a structure for how people organize their *model of the world* hierarchically. However, as the Logical levels was adapted into NLP, most people focused on using it to address limiting beliefs.[22-2] In the 90's Marilyn Atkinson took this work and re-focused the top layers on value and identity, and presented it as the core of human transformation.[22-3] Fundamentally, the Q Model Triangle is a reflection of the Logical Levels and models the triangle shape.

NLP had one big problem. It was a great core technology that was missing an application. Coaching was that missing application, but the coaching movement didn't pick up momentum until the early 1990s. Around this time, Marilyn Atkinson began integrating Milton Erickson's technologies, the most effective NLP tools, and other integrated and focused methods into a unified technology she called *Ericksonian Solution-Focused Coaching*.[22-4] Soon after Marilyn launched *Erickson Coaching International* and presented the first 16-day *Art and Science of Coaching* program, which quickly spread around the globe.

The 2000s: Again, I was very lucky to be exposed to this early work in 1999, and began a personal quest to reduce this technology into its core elements. I was working as an executive coach, so this gave me an ideal setting to test and refine tools and ideas quickly. My specific goal was to simplify *Solution-Focused* into streamlined ideas, messages, and tools that anyone could quickly understand and practice immediately.

By 2004, I was determined to bring the fruits of my labor to the world of business. With Marilyn's preliminary work, I developed a series of *Manager as Coach* programs that have now been presented in dozens of countries around the world. I also published the book *Business Transformed: Master the 17 Questions that Transform Business*.[22-5] Building a network, my growing team and I continued to refine our system for turning the elements of coaching and coaching culture into an operational management and leadership system.

During the late 2000s, working with Erickson Coaching International, I would travel almost 200 days per year. I spent thousands of hours running coach training programs across China, Russia, India, and Europe. Independently, I would also work directly with large companies worldwide to deliver corporate programs, facilitate strategy sessions, and directly coach executives. As more leaders and managers used the Q Model tools and systems, we gathered feedback and tracked results. All of this allowed us to accelerate the process of refining the Q Model.

The Q Model began in 2005 as a coaching culture program. We were on a quest for a simple conversational road map for busy managers who needed fast results. Starting with the Logical Levels model and its triangle shape, we envisioned a journey from *current state* to *desired state* to *committed action*. We kept coming back to the triangular visual model, as this shape seemed to stick with the students.

The Q Model, as presented herein, was not finalized until 2009. Foremost, the Q Model evolved because our managers kept telling us they liked it and used it every day.

In 2013, we began to codify the many large organizational breakthrough programs we had run into an *Enterprise Transformation* system. Working in China during the economic boom from 2010 to 2016 provided an ideal country-wide testing facility. Managers were eager for fresh western leadership ideas and companies were desperate for a competitive edge.

Back to Agile: As a teenager, I led a small team of friends in the development of five computer games using an *Agile-like* method, complete with sprint cycles and weekly debriefs. Of course, this was years before the invention of Agile; we had simply stumbled upon a similar process because it was a pragmatic way to keep our project moving forward. Years later, in the 1990s, I watched as Scrum emerged and was struck by how deeply familiar its methods and mindset seemed.

Around 2010, Agile methods began to evolve into Agile leadership and Agile transformation, which correlated with the beginning of the digital transformation movement. I noticed that there were many parallels between the Q Model and the world of Agile transformation, and this began our process of fusing it all into a unified theory of Agility.

MetaQ History: MetaQ began with a large body of observational research into the collective thinking patterns demonstrated by humans. The MetaQ assessment model integrates selected elements of the *NLP Metaprograms* developed from research in the late 1970s by Bandler and Grinder. [22-1]

The Metaprograms emerged from observational research data that was modeled to find common patterns. Marilyn Atkinson worked in this community of researchers and later presented the Metaprogram data to me. More than 60 possible Metaprograms were identified and tested, but this number was later reduced to about 15. With MetaQ we focus on the six patterns that are most relevant in a business context.

In developing the MetaQ system, we interlinked Metaprograms with the idea of a scale or state-line moving between opposites. The early developmental work by Marilyn Atkinson on state-lines influenced this approach. We also took inspiration from the 4-D Assessment System developed by Charlie Pellerin for NASA, [6-6] from which we observed that any assessment process can be fundamentally transformative. We noticed that the 4D system could also be adjusted into two sets of opposing forces, which linked back to the structure of Metaprograms. The MetaQ system adapted this early research to fit the needs of a modern business context.

About the Author:

Paul Gossen: An Enterprise Transformation Evangelist as well as the founder and CEO of the qDrive Institute, Paul Gossen brings a high-energy and irreverent style to the world of business that triggers fresh leadership thinking and drives results.

Working with executives and business leaders to engineer enterprise transformation, he is a master transformational trainer who travels 200+ days per year to deliver breakthrough results for people and companies around the world. He is deeply committed to advancing coaching, Agile, and transformation methodologies.

Before this, he was an entrepreneur and technology executive. He started his first company, Paradigm Creators, at the age of 13, and published a hit computer game called *Gemstone Warrior*. Later, his Vertegri *imediaEngine* was a key factor in the return of Steve Jobs to Apple and the company's subsequent transformation. He grew up in a milieu of human-potential learning and studied NLP, EST, Buddhist philosophy, human transformation, art, and design.

He has been a coach, trainer, and enterprise transformation specialist since 1999. The author of three books and a keynote speaker, Paul has conducted more than 3600 hours of coaching and more than 300 corporate training programs. He also conducts high-level coach training with Erickson Coaching International. He has delivered international projects across Europe, China, Russia, India, and the Americas, and conducted dozens of enterprise-scale programs with companies such as SAP, Alibaba, GSK, and American Express.

Paul has a creative and unique way of making complex ideas come alive in visual models. He lives in Vancouver, Canada and tries to avoid the temptation of endless international travel.

Glossary:

Endnotes:

[1-1] Low Performance: Heike Bruch and Sumantra Ghoshal, *Beware the Busy Manager*, HBR Press, 2002. HBR's 10-year study of 10,000 managers found that 89.7% of managers squander their time in ineffective activities. 10.3% of managers spend their time in a committed, purposeful, and reflective manner.

[1-2] Blue Ocean: W. Chan Kim and Renée A. Mauborgne, *Blue Ocean Strategy*, Harvard Business Review Press, 2015.

[1-3] Strategic Leadership: A 2015 PwC study of 6,000 senior executives conducted using a research methodology developed by David Rooke of Harthill Consulting and William Torbert of Boston University. Only 8% of the respondents turned out to be strategic leaders, or those effective at leading transformations.

[1-4] VUCA Leadership: *What VUCA Really Means for You*, HBR, 2014.

[1-5] Albert Einstein: "If you can't explain it to a 6-year-old, you don't really understand it yourself." Although regularly attributed to Einstein in internet memes, the original quote, which translated to English goes something like "If you can't say it simply, then you don't yet understand it well enough," is believed to originate from French philosopher Michele de Montaigne.

[1-6] Leonardo da Vinci: "Simplicity is the ultimate sophistication." This is another apocryphal internet meme, the quote apparently originating from the 1931 book *Stuffed Shirts* by Clare Boothe Luce.

> While endnotes are *usually* serious, please respect that we have added a little humour, especially regarding the many internet memes which proliferate.

[1-5] Learn by Doing: Edgar Dale, *The Cone of Experience*, 1946. Also known as the pyramid of learning. Additional studies in the 1960s were performed by the National Training Laboratory Institute for Applied Behavioral Science and many other university researchers.

[2-1] Visual Rehearsal: Martha Epstein, *The Relationship of Mental Imagery and Mental Rehearsal to Performance of a Motor Task*, Human Kinetics Journals, 1980. Elite athletes can improve their performance up to 30% by repeatedly visualizing each step of their performance.

[2-2] Postmodern Productivity: Collaboration with Marilyn Atkinson and Peter Stephanyi. Additional note: We suggest that team productivity is a relative unknown and teams can be benchmarked over time to move toward established predictability, but *absolute* predictability cannot be achieved.

[3-1] Distraction: *Putting a Finger on Our Phone Obsession*, Dscout, 2016. "The top 10% of smartphone users click, tap or swipe on their phone 5,427 times a day. That's the top 10 percent of phone users, so one would expect it to be excessive. The average is 2,617 times a day."

[3-2] Wikipedia - Mutually Assured Distraction: This is *not* an actual Wikipedia entry, unless perhaps some aspiring Wikipedia contributor has added it on my behalf.

[3-3] Change or Die: A. Deutschman, *Change or Die*, Fast Company, 2005. This study revealed that when heart disease patients who had undergone traumatic bypass surgery were told if they did not adjust their lifestyle they would die, or at best undergo the life-saving procedure again, only 9% modified their behaviour.

[3-4] Risk needs Tell: Adam Galinsky Maurice and Schweitzer, *Friend & Foe*, Crown Business, 2015. This study revealed that collectively led teams of Mount Everest climbers are up to 50% more likely to suffer deaths than those with a single leader.

[3-5] Trust Predicts Loyalty: *Trust Predicts Employee Loyalty*, Leadership IQ, survey, 2007. From a survey of 7209 company staff, approximately 32% of a worker's desire to stay or go is the result of a lack of trust towards their boss.

[4-1] The Traveling Salesman: This math problem, first developed by Irish mathematician Sir William Rowan Hamilton in 1843, demonstrates the limits of computation to solve exponentially difficult problems.

[4-2] Hats versus Roles: Edward de Bono, *Six Thinking Hats,* 1985. Moving from fixed roles to a metaphorical way of thinking, the use of hats is a simple way to increase the thinking flexibility of a team.

[6-1] 50% Trust: EY survey, 2015. A survey of 9,800 adults found that less than half of global professionals trust their employer, boss, or team.

[6-2] Trust is face to face: *Egocentrism over email,* Nicholas Epley and Justin Kruger, Journal of Personality and Social Psychology, 2006. In research conducted comparing email communication to voice communication, they found that people overestimate their ability to convey their intended tone when they communicate via text. Trust is almost four times more difficult to build via email or text.

[6-3] Communication Tone: Albert Mehrabian, *Non-verbal Communication*, 1967. He found that 7% of a message was derived from the words, 38% from the intonation, and 55% from facial expression or body language. In other words, the vast majority of communication is not carried by our words alone.

[6-4] Rapport is Mirroring: Greg Stephens, *Neural Coupling*, PNAS, 2010. fMRI brain scans demonstrate that in both the communicator and listener, similar regions of the brain fired when engaged in unrehearsed, real-life story telling, leading the team to conclude that our *mirror neuron* brain cells synchronize during successful communication.

[6-5] Human Tone: *The Neuroscience of Human Vocal Pitch*, Dichter, Breshears, Leonard, Chang, Weill Institute for Neurosciences, Cell Experimental Biology, 2008. "Among primates, humans are uniquely able to consciously control the pitch of their voices, making it possible to stress a word in a sentence to convey meaning. Chang and his colleagues examined a region of the brain called the bilateral dorsal laryngeal motor cortex (dLMC) and demonstrated that this directly controls voice tone and emphasis on keywords in a sentence."

[6-6] A $4b Deadline: Charlie Pellerin, *How NASA Builds Teams*, Wiley, 2009. The 4-D Assessment System.

[8-1] Coach Position: Marilyn Atkinson, *Flow The Core of Coaching*, Published 2011. Coach Position refers to listening from a neutral observer position. Coach Position ranges through time, and includes wisdom from the past and an imagined future success. Coach Position integrates many principles from Milton Erickson.

[9-1] Strategic Vision: John H. Zengerand Joseph Folkman, *The Extraordinary Lead-*

er, McGraw Hill Professional, 2009. Study of 47,000 global leaders. The single biggest differentiator between top management and middle managers was their capability for strategic vision.

[9-2] The First Company Backlog: I have heard several undocumented stories about the *Brain Room* developed in 1986 by Werner Erhart, the founder of EST. Supposedly, this was a room in which the walls were covered in index cards each representing a different company project, strategy or development idea. Cards at the top had the highest priority, with lowering importance as the cards descended. Apparently the room had thousands of cards, so this could not be a very *streamlined* company backlog.

[10-1] Questions and Insight: Robert Lee Hotz, *A Wandering Mind Heads Towards Insight*, Wall Street Journal, 2009. "Sudden insights are the culmination of an intense and complex series of brain states that require more neural resources than methodical reasoning. People who solve problems through insight generate different patterns of brain waves than those who solve problems analytically." Adds University of Pittsburgh psychologist Mark Wheeler in the same article, "Your brain is really working quite hard before this moment of insight."

[10-2] Questions Focus Attention: Vicki Morwitz, Eric Johnson, and David Schmittlein, *Does Measuring Intent Change Behavior?*, Journal of Consumer Research, 1993. A study with 40,000 participants revealed that simply asking someone if they were going to purchase a new car within six months increased their purchase rates by 35%.

[10-3] Questions Focus Attention: *Do You Have a Voting Plan?* Anthony G. Greenwald, Journal of Applied Psychology, 1987. Asking citizens whether they're going to vote in an upcoming election increases the likelihood that they will by 25%.

[10-4] Team Intelligence: James Surowiecki, *Wisdom of Crowds*, Published by Anchor 2005. Surowiecki argues that large groups of people are smarter than an elite few, no matter how brilliant — better at solving problems, fostering innovation, coming to wise decisions, even predicting the future.

[10-5] Open-Ended Scale: Marilyn Atkinson, *Inner Dynamics of Coaching*, Exalon Press, 2007. The Open-Ended Scale was first developed in 2002.

[10-6] Question Brainstorming: Matthew May, *Winning the Brain Game*, McGraw-Hill Education. 2016. Matthew calls the team question-generation process "frame-storming," while Hal Gregersen, executive director of MIT Leadership Center, calls it "question-storming."

[11-1] Law of Attention: Reason and Mycielska, *The Psychology of Mental Lapses and Everyday Errors. Prentice-Hall; Englewood Cliffs, 1982.*

[12-1] Internal vs External Visualization: John Ratey, *A User's Guide to the Brain*, Vintage, 2002.

[12-2] Visual Neural Overlap: Dijkstra, *Vividness of Visual Imagery Depends on the Neural Overlap with Perception in Visual Areas*, The Journal of Neuroscience, 2017. "The neural substrates of visual imagery and perception overlap in areas beyond the visual cortex and the degree of this overlap in these areas correlates with the vividness of mental representations during imagery."

[12-3] Visual Thinking: *Visual Processing and Self-Awareness,* Smith, Grabowecky, Suzuki, PMC Library, 2009.

[12-4] Gretzky's Secret: Wayne Gretzky and Rick Reilly, *Gretzky: An Autobiography*, Harpercollins, 1990.

[13-1] Visual Spatial Intelligence: Howard Gardner, *Theory of Multiple Intelligences*, Basic, 2006. "Visual spatial judgment is the ability to visualize with the mind's eye. It is defined as a human computational capacity to solve spatial problems of navigation, visualization, and relationships. In this theory, creativity also arises as a response to contextual problems."

[13-2] Whiteboarding: Visual thinking tools were included in *The Art and Science of Coaching*, Module 2, 2003. The program was filled with visual models and gave instructions on how to use them in a conversation.

[13-3] 60% of people are visual learners: Walter Burk Barbe, *Modality Characteristics of Gifted Children*, G/C/T Journal, 1981. Tested individuals demonstrated approximately 30% visual strength, 30% mixed (visual) strengths, 25% auditory with 15% kinesthetic.

[13-4] 4 Quadrant Thinking: Marilyn Atkinson and Peter Stephanyi, *4 Quadrant Thinking Vol-I*, Erickson Press, 2019. The 4 Quadrant Whiteboarding process was first developed by Marilyn Atkinson in 2002.

[14-1] Shared vision: Peter Senge, *The Fifth Discipline*, Doubleday, 1994. "Shared vision plays a vital role in a learning organization, providing the focus and energy needed for learning. A consistent alignment of team member vision increases productivity."

[15-1] Team Identity: Marilyn Atkinson, *Creating Transformational Metaphors*, Erickson Press, 2012.

[15-2] Metaphoric Identity: Paul Gossen and Marilyn Atkinson, *Velocity Instant Fluency*, Velocity Learning Press, 2014.

[16-1] Addiction to Learning: Vienna's Center for Medical Physics, *fMRI Insights on Insight*, DOI, 2018. Additional note from text: "Neuroscience correlates the concept of creative problem solving with a positive healthy addiction to dopamine. Dopamine is a neurotransmitter and hormone that functions by sending signals to other nerve cells. The release of dopamine is associated with motivation, concentration and learning."

[16-2] Money Causes Stress: Glucksberg, *The influence of strength of drive on functional fixedness and perceptual recognition*, Journal of Experimental Psychology, 1962. In the candle experiment, Glucksberg found that adding a monetary reward caused stress and shut down the creative thinking and problem-solving abilities of the participants.

[16-3] Pay for Performance: *Pay for Performance*, London School of Economics Research, 2009.

[16-4] Business Value Chain: Michael Porters, *How Competitive Forces Shape Strategy*, Harvard Business Review, 1979.

[16-5] Constructivism: John Piaget, *Psychology and Epistemology: Towards a Theory of Knowledge*, Grossman, 1971.

[16-6] The Mirror Test: Gordon Gallup, *Chimpanzees: Self Recognition*, Science Magazine, 1970.

[16-7] Cultural Values: Hitlin & Piliavin, *Values*, Annual Review of Sociology, DOI Journal, 2004. Additional note from text: "Sociologists have found that values must be activated in individual and group consciousness to effect action. Sociology currently speculates that an individual's values, shaped through late adolescence, tend to be stable through life."

[16-8] Value Transformation: Connirae Andreas, *Core Transformation*, Real People Press, 1994.

[18-1] Humans Enjoy Planning: Jaak Panksepp, *Affective Neuroscience*, Oxford University Press, 2004. Additional note from text: "There are seven core instincts in the human brain: anger, fear, panic-grief, maternal care, pleasure/lust, play, and seeking. Seeking is the most important and all mammals have this seeking system, wherein dopamine, a neurotransmitter, is linked to a reward in planning activities.

[18-2] Wasting Time: Paychex.com, 2016 of 2,000 employees. More than 15% of telecom and utility workers reported wasting 3 hours or more per day.

[18-3] Getting Things Done: David Allen, *Getting Things Done*, Penguin Books, 2001.

[18-4] Workplace Distraction: *Udemy Workplace Distraction Report*, 2018. 54% of employees report that workplace distractions lower their performance.

[19-1] Move Away from Risk: Evian Gordon, *Influence*, Pearson UK, 2000. "The motivation behind much of our behaviour is driven by the desire to minimise *threat* and maximise *reward*. Neuroscientists call this fundamental principle the '*walk towards, run away*' theory."

[19-2] People Resist Change: Mount Eliza Business School found that over 70% of change initiatives fail because of *people resistance* — not because they weren't good business ideas driven by sound analysis, systems, and facts.

[19-3] People Want to Change: *Designing the organization for the future,* Deloitte survey of 10,400 business and HR leaders across 140 countries, 2017. They found that 88% of respondents selected designing the organization for the future as the most important human capital issue.

[19-4] Organisational Design: Naomi Stanford, *Guide to Organizational Design*, Economist Press, 2007.

[22-1] NLP: John Grinder, Judith DeLozier, and Richard Bandler, *Patterns of the Hypnotic Techniques of Milton H Erickson Volume II*, Meta Publications, 1975.

[22-2] Logical Levels: Robert Dilts, *Changing Belief Systems With NLP Neuro Logical Levels*, Meta Publications, 1981.

[22-3] Inner Alignment with Logical Levels: Marilyn Atkinson, *Step-by-Step Coaching*, Exalon Press, 2007.

[22-4] Solution-Focused Coaching: Marilyn Atkinson, *Inner Dynamics of Coaching*, Exalon Press, 2007.

[22-5] 17 Questions: Paul Gossen, *Business Transformed*, Leadership Inc Press, 2006.

www.ingramcontent.com/pod-product-compliance
Lightning Source LLC
Chambersburg PA
CBHW060827170526
45158CB00001B/102